AKENSIDE SYNDROME

Scratching the Surface of Geordie Identity

AKENSIDE SYNDROME

SCRATCHING THE SURFACE OF GEORDIE IDENTITY

JOE SHARKEY

Jajosa
BOOKS

First published in 2014 by Jajosa Books Ltd

ISBN: 978-0-9928700-0-3

A CIP catalogue record for this book is available from the British Library

All design and typesetting by Wayne Gamble

All historic images and photographs appear by kind permission
of Newcastle Libraries © unless otherwise stated

All modern photography by Paul Stephenson © unless otherwise stated

Every effort has been made to trace and obtain permissions from copyright holders.
If there are any inadvertent omissions, copyright holders should contact the publisher

Jajosa Books Ltd
2 Dolphin Court, High Street
Petersfield, Hampshire
GU32 3JP

www.jajosabooks.co.uk

Printed and bound in the UK by Martins the Printers, Berwick-upon-Tweed

ACKNOWLEDGEMENTS

Malcolm Dix descended on this project like a benevolent Dickensian uncle and has been a constant source of support and encouragement. He is a fine citizen of Tyneside. His near neighbour, Andrew Blight, a lifelong friend, helped secure interviews and sent me many relevant articles. Gaining new friends has been a happy by-product of my research, and Keith Armstrong deserves a special mention. Many others have helped along the way and I extend my thanks to them all; Brian Aitken, Jean Brown, David Buckley, Michael Chaplin, Rob Colls, Sophie Doughty, David John Douglass, Martin Ellis, Simon Elmes, Hilary Fawcett, Laura Forker, Jonathan Freedland, John Hall (of Luckies), Judith Holder, Brent Howard, Derek Johnson, Bill Lancaster, Eamonn Maddick, Sally Magill, Yve Ngoo, Jeremy Paxman, Tony Reid, Sarah Rigby, Pete Shelley, Phil Sutcliffe, Bernard Trafford and Chuck Verrill. *The Guardian* and ncjMedia were particularly generous regarding permissions. And whole-hearted thanks to everyone who agreed to be interviewed for this project – I enjoyed speaking to every one of you. Sincere apologies to anyone I've inadvertently missed out.

ILLUSTRATION & PHOTOGRAPHY ACKNOWLEDGEMENTS

Wayne Gamble has done a fantastic job of designing and typesetting every aspect of this book and his patience, professionalism and guidance throughout, under difficult circumstances, has been much appreciated. Paul Stephenson, another lifelong friend, generously offered to do the photography gratis. Members of staff on the sixth floor of Newcastle City Library were a great help, locating many appropriate images and photographs. I would also like to thank Amber Film and Photography Collective, The Cathedral Church of St Nicholas, Newcastle upon Tyne, Dods, Gay Men Tyneside, the Laing Art Gallery, ncjMedia, the National Portrait Gallery, Newcastle Panthers, Newcastle University Library, Special Collections, Northern Pride, the Royal College of Physicians, Show Racism the Red Card, Swan Hunter, West Newcastle Picture History Collection, and the following individuals; Peter Basham, Sheena Butler, Sue Clayton, Ann Dixon, Mrs Rosalind Dobson, Chris Donald, Simon Donald, Graham Dury, Roger Fern, Malcolm Maybury, Fred Millican, Sarah Mulligan, Mark Nichols, Sarah Richardson, Graeme Rigby, Ellie Robertson, Pete Robinson, Angela Stanger-Leathes, Simon Thorp, George Todd, Iain Watson, the Rt Rvd Martin Wharton, Melanie Wood and Tony Whittle.

Author's Note

There are thousands of words to follow but I cannot compose a single sentence that could even begin to express the sadness in my heart, knowing that my dear wife Jane and our beautiful son Sam are not here with me to see *Akenside Syndrome* published. This book belongs to them, as I do.

**The book to read is not the one that thinks
for you but the one which makes you think**
Harper Lee

Wake the people and make them think big
Henrik Ibsen

For Jane & Sam

Eternal Love Prevails

CONTENTS

PREFACE

ORD GLENAMARA LOOKED AT ME AS IF I WAS SOME SORT OF NUTTER. He hadn't heard what I'd said the first time so I repeated it slowly and clearly: "This one's for the Geordies." His speech earlier had been impressive. Eloquently lauding Northumbria University's burgeoning reputation, he reeled off a list of countries from where students had been enticed. But no mention was made of the many state-educated local students afforded the opportunity to pursue an academic route at the former poly-technic – an aspiration often denied them by more elitist institutions. Perhaps this was an act of modesty on his part, considering the integral role he played in implementing greater access to education when better known as Ted Short, Labour MP for Newcastle Central from 1951 to 1976.

This omission bolstered my determination to regale him with the regional-identity-affirming one-liner (though the follow-up of an Alan Shearer-like salute to the punters in the audience was reluctantly dropped). My reiteration elicited a somewhat bemused and slightly unnerved look from our esteemed Chancellor, and – deciding that this was probably a good time to release my grip on his hand – I strode off and exited stage left, allowing the graduation ceremony production line to resume its orderly pace. As I reoccupied my seat in Newcastle City Hall I awarded myself a figurative pat on the back; I'd said it, I hadn't bottled out, and I'd kept the promise I made to my best mate at Northumbria, a fellow Geordie from Northumberland who was unable to attend what should have been his graduation also.

It was during a conversation with this friend a year or two earlier that I had jokingly christened myself with the well-known moniker of Geordie Warrior. Discussing those 'introduce yourself to the seminar group' monologues that undergraduates are obliged to perform, as well as the fact that I'd been randomly placed in a sub-group of students with distinctly 'un-Geordie-like' names such as Camilla, Arabella, Annabella and Rupert, he asked me what I usually said in such situations. Quite simple, I assured him: "Hello, my name's Joe Sharkey and I'm a Geordie Warrior." Anything to add to that? No. That pretty much sums it up. Later my mam took the tongue-in-cheek repartee further by placing the soubriquet alongside a congratulatory graduation photograph she had put in the *Evening Chronicle*.

What had begun as a throw-away remark to a fellow Northumbrian, intended to raise a smile whilst reinforcing a shared sense of loyalty to our region (and infused with a dash of class tribalism for good measure), was now in the public domain and taking on a life of its own. Conscious of the fact that I would soon be embarking on a two-year tour of duty in the land of the chirpy and the pukka (Jamie Oliver was just getting into his stride in those days), I decided to further display my allegiance to city and region by having *Geordie Warrior* engraved on the inside of a recently purchased ring. A secreted assurance of fidelity and faithfulness, it would serve to remind me of where I came from. While all around ate jellied eels or sushi, and drank lager-tops or spritzers, I would never forget that I was from the land of stotties and Newcastle Brown Ale. At the slightest sign of pretension or affectation the ring would unleash preternatural powers and smite me for not remaining true to the values enshrined by the Fellowship: *The Geord of the Rings*, if you like. Emboldened by my adopted pseudonym, adorned with the monitorial ring, and with the treasured memory of Lord Glenamara's perplexed face fresh in my mind, I would leave Newcastle with a strong, secure sense of identity and of who I was. A Geordie. And a proud one at that.

So why, amidst all this bolstering banter and bravado, was I simultaneously telling the counsellor I'd recently started seeing that at times I really questioned whether or not I 'belonged' in the North-East? Although two years later in October 2002 I would write from Guildford to a friend and say: 'despite my deep love of Newcastle I will not be returning to live there permanently for a very long time, if at all', it seems clear that ambivalent feelings toward the North-East had taken root long before I actually left. As part of a Master of Arts (MA) course undertook in London and Surrey, I wrote a screenplay prosaically entitled *Adrian's Wall*. Ostensibly a Japanese/Geordie cross-cultural comedy drama, it was subtextually laden with ambivalent feelings toward my much-loved home town and region. The eponymous protagonist, Adrian Bigge, was immersed in North-East history and culture to the point where he led guided tours along Hadrian's Wall dressed as a Roman Centurion. But the wall part of the title was intended to work metaphorically as well as literally. On a metaphorical level I wanted the wall to symbolise entrapment, claustrophobia and restriction.

Fast-forward a few years to the spring of 2004 and I found myself witnessing a humorous and slightly bizarre situation on a flight back to London from Newcastle. Sitting at the very back of the plane (a general preference for not having people sitting behind me having been intensified by an incident on the X87 bus a few years earlier, when a group of kids from Blakelaw attempted to set fire to the pony-tail I was then sporting), it became apparent that the famous person who the WHSmith assistants in the departure lounge had been gossiping about was sitting directly in front of me. Some confusion ensued as the cabin crew attempted to get to grips with the fact that their celebrity passenger – a well-known Geordie in the public eye – had been allocated a seat right next to another passenger with exactly the same name. Apparently only one of them was registered as being booked on that particular flight and credit card details needed to be re-checked.

Despite the unwanted extra attention this episode brought the famous passenger, he handled it with a good deal of grace and patience. As the drama was playing itself out, the two namesakes began chatting and engaged in a conversation that was to last virtually unbroken throughout the whole flight. Covering a variety of topics the two chatted readily and without embarrassment or inhibition, displaying (or so it seemed to me) several cherished Geordie traits. Both were friendly and down to earth; both spoke with Geordie accents – the famous one being slightly broader despite no longer living in the area; and despite his fame, there were absolutely no signs of pretension or celebrity preciousness. From my back-seat vantage point I mentally congratulated him for staying true to his roots and remaining, unlike some other famous Geordies I could think of, a *proper* Geordie. It was all good. And then he said it: "I hate Newcastle. I think it's one of the ugliest cities in the world."

Now I've watched crime documentaries where experts claim that witnesses can rarely, if ever, remember verbatim what was said in any given situation, but that phrase seared into my consciousness. It was the emphasis given to the word *hate*, coupled with an underlying sourness with which the sentiment was spat out, that jarred me out of what had hitherto been a rather perfunctory and unavoidable eavesdrop (given that two people sitting directly in front of me in a confined space were talking in tones that were hardly hushed). The non-famous Geordie reacted diplomatically by politely disagreeing and mentioning some of the fantastic architecture and on-going regeneration work in Newcastle. The moment passed and their conversation moved on to the next topic. But I was left agitated and uncomfortable. And it wasn't just the fact that this famous son of the North-East had aligned himself with J. B. Priestley in *English Journey* by denouncing the supposed aesthetic deficiencies of Newcastle that made me feel uneasy.

In fact the implied architectural context of his comment was almost irrelevant – it was too ill-informed to be taken seriously. And perhaps he was specifically referring to some of the uninspiring, utilitarian suburbs and estates beyond the city centre, of which all major British cities have their share. Perhaps the one he was brought up in, the Tyneside of his childhood, was etched in his mind when he uttered the denunciation. In which case some might think he was making a reasonable if somewhat exaggerated observation. But it wasn't *what* he said, it was the *tone* in which he said it that did for me. For it was enunciated with a depth of feeling symptomatic of an ailment hitherto unacknowledged; an ailment that particularly afflicts Geordies who have left the region, and that by that time I was already calling Akenside Syndrome.

Named after Mark Akenside, the 18th century son of a Newcastle butcher who achieved a modicum of success as a poet, became physician to Queen Charlotte in 1761, and was famously touchy and sensitive about his humble origins, Akenside Syndrome is a condition of feeling ambivalent towards Newcastle or Tyneside despite often retaining a strong emotional bond with and/or sincere affection for the area. A vague sense of unease and feeling of not quite belonging or fitting in is also a common characteristic of the condition. The information plaque next to All Saints' Church, near Akenside Hill on Newcastle's Quayside, says of Akenside: *He is said to have been ashamed of his native place, so that "he would sneak through Newcastle when occasion called him thither".* While acknowledging that naming it after Akenside is, to a certain extent, a conceit (being ashamed of your native place is not necessarily the same as having feelings of ambivalence towards it), it should also be observed that the condition can range from the relatively mild and harmless to the profound and detrimental to a person's sense of well-being; a kind of neurosis even.

Famous Geordies whom I suspect of having experienced Akenside Syndrome include Lee Hall, Paul Gascoigne, Brian Johnson of AC/DC, Robson Green, the late novelists Gordon Burn and Catherine Cookson, Jimmy Nail and Sting. Indeed, being of a generation who remember the man formerly known as Gordon Sumner berating his hometown after The Police came to prominence in the late 1970s, I feel that Sting is the quintessential modern-day personification of Akenside Syndrome. But having lived away from the North-East for almost four years when the incident on the plane occurred, I knew for sure that it was folly to think of this condition as afflicting only Geordies who were famous celebrities or in the public eye. I had experienced it myself and talked to and observed many exiled Geordies who, if not always admitting to or understanding it, undoubtedly betrayed symptoms of Akenside Syndrome. Those comfortable being open and honest about it knew exactly what I was talking about, felt that it resonated with them, and volunteered examples from their own experience.

And so as the plane touched down in London and the namesakes parted company, having pointlessly swapped ticket stubs at the request of the non-famous one (can you imagine the difficulty in persuading your mates down the pub that a ticket stub with your exact name on it belonged to your famous namesake who you just so happened to be sat next to on a plane?), I disembarked with a steadfast resolution to write this book. Partly for my own psychological well-being, and partly with a vague desire to help any fellow Geordies who might happen to read it achieve 'that greater freedom and understanding which comes from self-knowledge', I determined to investigate, analyse and understand better what it means to be a Geordie, what the modern-day staples of 'the most pungent regional identity in Britain' are, and, more specifically, exactly what it is about Geordie identity and culture that causes Akenside Syndrome.[1]

For regions, no less than nations, are imagined communities. Who the Geordies are depends upon who they imagine themselves to be. The 'North-East' is essentially a state of mind to do with histories and feelings about itself.

Geordies: Roots of Regionalism, co-edited by Rob Colls and Bill Lancaster

Regional identity and culture are elusive entities, and both are ideological categories which are hard to break down and deconstruct, and difficult to analyse.

Keith Gregson and Mike Huggins, *The Media, Regional Culture and the Great North Run: 'Big Bren's Human Race'* in *Culture, Sport, Society Vol. 4, No 1*

We would not judge a city like Newcastle on the basis of MTV's *Geordie Shore*; we do not think all of that city's inhabitants are rude, gym-addicted and sociopathic.

Nicholas Lombardo, communications director of Napoli football club in Italy, May 2014

It's the most American place I've seen in the U.K. ... I came in without the misplaced pre-conceptions that Britons can have about Newcastle and loved it.

Herb Kim, creator of renowned Tyneside tech conference *Think Digital,* who is originally from New Jersey and moved to Newcastle in 2002 (later moving to Liverpool), talking to Chris Stokel-Walker for BuzzFeed in 2014

After all, people who have never been to the north-east *do* often have rather distorted ideas about the region.

Louise Taylor blogging at www.guardian.co.uk, 21st November 2013

INTRODUCTION

BORROWING FROM BENEDICT ANDERSON'S CONCEPT THAT NATIONS are all to some extent 'imagined communities', the co-editors of *Geordies: Roots of Regionalism*, a collection of polemical essays first published in 1992, make an important point. Regional identity is not about incontrovertibly concrete concepts, rigidly prescribed dogma or innate biological traits. More accurately it is a fluid, abstract and malleable notion that has more to do with representation, interpretation and perception – specifically how we perceive ourselves and how we are perceived by others. Therefore Keith Gregson and Mike Huggins make an equally valid point. Whereas Colls and Lancaster present the backdrop for North-East identity as a kind of blank canvas, Gregson and Huggins seem to imply that what is drawn on said canvas will very much depend on who is holding the paint brush.

Academics tend to tussle over what words such as 'identity' mean; what constitutes it, to whom it can be applied, where it resides and at what period of time it came into being etc. etc. Quite understandably they often plump for a definition which complements their own ideological, political and cultural outlook on life. I'll politely decline getting involved in such debates and simply try to clarify one or two things in this introduction before we head off on our journey. Firstly, and obviously, this is a book about those who identify themselves as Geordies and who would be identified as Geordies by others. It examines the potential benefits of being identified as a Geordie by looking at four staples of the culture in modern times (Class, Accent, Drink and Football), one or more of which many Geordies would identify with.

But it also delves into the darker side of this version of Geordie identity, examining contentious issues that don't get much of an airing in more syrupy, sepia-tinted books on the subject. It is maverick not mainstream, merrily mixing methodologies and switching styles; blending academic with impressionistic and anecdotal, analysis with opinion, sociology with social commentary, and personal biography with the thoughts and experiences of others. Petty parochialism about who can rightly consider themselves Geordies in geographical terms is not on the radar here. Newcastle, Tyneside and the North-East will be used interchangeably at times in a way that might infuriate the isolationist and the insular. Unless you are writing a particularly dry or formal piece of work, I would suggest that this is inevitable.

If a better understanding of the version of Geordie identity that we are examining is to be attained then, we must first acknowledge the powerful and pervasive nationwide resonance of the Geordie *brand*. In *The Likes of Us: A Biography of the White Working Class*, Michael Collins talked about how the caricatured image of the cockney became a 'recognisable brand' in the twentieth century.[1] Germaine Greer adopted a defiant tone when championing what she perceives as the positive traits of the Essex Girl brand, and Stuart Maconie has reflected on how the 'brand of regional daftness' exported by some northern comedians and entertainers of years gone by may well have been 'injurious to the north's health, contributing to a view of northerners as good-hearted simpletons'.[2]

Greer also maintained that the terms *brand* and *stereotype* can be interchangeable, and when we consider that one of the concerns of Colls and Lancaster was how the concept of Geordies 'could further degenerate into stereotyped joke figures, usually daft males,' the pertinence of Maconie's lament becomes apparent.[3] It should therefore be acknowledged from the outset that at times it will be the Geordie brand/stereotype upon which an attempt at dissection and deconstruction is made. Sometimes it will be this superficial veneer – a fragile yet durable gloss which can tarnish and add lustre with the same stroke – that is examined. From one perspective at least, this is the surface that needs to be scratched.

Critics of MTV programme *Geordie Shore* could be heard denouncing the 'outdated' and 'cartoonish stereotypes' portrayed in the show, whilst Tom Gutteridge complained in *The Journal* that the producers had employed 'what they consider the ultimate dumb, drunk stereotype: the Geordie.'[4] And although this illustrates how more often than not the word *stereotype* carries a negative connotation (for instance, in *The English* Jeremy Paxman claims 'Stereotypes are comforting, save us the trouble of fresh thought'), they can be employed in a positive sense also.[5] If we were to talk about Geordies being friendly then it could reasonably be argued that we were perpetuating positive stereotypes.

When I walked into a kebab shop in Newcastle late on a Sunday night in 1996 and unthinkingly exhibited this cherished stereotypical Geordie trait, by initiating a drunken conversation with a heavily tattooed muncher with a Newcastle top on, he and his mate duly set about me, kicking me in the head until my left ear was almost completely black, and thus reciprocating my friendliness by way of another, somewhat less positive stereotypical Geordie trait: that of violence and aggression.

The autobiographies of Sting, Jimmy Nail and *Viz* founder Chris Donald (creator of quintessentially uber-aggressive Geordie family, the Bacons: Mutha, Fatha and Biffa) all make reference to experiences of raw Geordie aggression in their formative years. From an outsider's perspective, in his travelogue *Up North* Charles Jennings referred to Newcastle's 'reputation as a great place to get your head filled with a mixture of broken glass and someone else's teeth.'[6] Furthermore, in a statement that although a generalisation does not seem entirely unreasonable, a British Council guide produced in Poland declared: 'Given their history, it is no surprise that Geordies are fiercely proud of their heritage, to the extent that they may be construed as aggressive.' The guide went on to say that Geordies are 'generally happy-go-lucky, humorous, hard-drinking, friendly and generous', and looking at the whole we can see how popular perceptions of Geordies paradoxically incorporate both friendliness and aggression.[7]

Stereotypes can obviously work both ways, and in attempting to understand Geordie identity better we have to accept that the Geordie brand – the Geordie stereotype – will never be far away from the core of the analysis. When discussing stereotypes about English national character in *Watching the English: The Hidden Rules of English Behaviour*, Kate Fox stated that although they are, 'not necessarily 'the truth, the whole truth and nothing but' ... [they] probably contain at least a grain or two of truth. They do not, after all, just come out of thin air, but must have germinated and grown from *something*.'[8] As it is for the English so it is for the Geordies and indeed almost any stereotype, be it cultural, regional or national. Therefore it should be made clear that when 'Geordie' traits, qualities, conventions, attitudes and the suchlike are discussed within these pages, it is not done with the implication that all or even a majority of Geordies share these attributes.

This book does not simply seek to regurgitate popular, positive perceptions of Geordies in an uncritical parrot-like fashion, and is no more inclined to label a wide and diverse population as monkeys and morons. Anyone seeking a hatchet job or a hagiography will be disappointed – it is conceived of as neither. And while an exploration of the heterogeneous reality that lies behind the homogenising stereotypes is one of the aims, when seemingly generalising observations are made, they are done so in the same spirit with which Fox observes the 'hidden rules' of English behaviour:

> we do not mean – and this is important – that all English people [in this case, Geordies] always or invariably exhibit the characteristic in question, only that it is a quality or behaviour pattern which is common enough, or marked enough, to be noticeable and significant.[9]

Relating all of this back to the issue of the Geordie brand, two definitions of the word *stereotype* are of interest to us. For discovering the extent to which **Definition A**: 'a standardized image or conception of a type of person etc.', morphs into **Definition B**: 'an idea, convention, etc., that has grown stale through fixed usage' seems particularly apposite.[10]

As a respected social anthropologist, Kate Fox has spent much of her professional life observing and recording the behaviour, conventions and 'collective understandings' of groups of people from different cultures across the world. It is a contention of this book that a strong sense of collective identity can influence behaviour and thinking, thus behaviourism is embraced along with other critical practices, and it is to Fox's incisive survey of English behaviour that I again turn in order to make a further clarification. One of the principal effects of globalisation, she argues, has been 'a resurgence of concern about ethnicity and cultural identity in almost all parts of the world'. She also claims that regionalism is endemic in England, but produces a pre-emptive parry against 'fervent regionalists' who might think that their own 'separate' regional identity ought not to be lumped in with a generic impression of Englishness:

> The trouble is that virtually all nations have a number of regions, each of which invariably regards itself as different from, and superior to, all the others.[11]

Bearing this in mind it should be noted that having spent over twelve years living in Surrey and Hampshire, I will be speaking from empirical experience when discussing some of the marked cultural differences I perceive between certain areas in those parts of the country and Tyneside.

Nonetheless, it is difficult to disagree with Fox when she says that although towns, cities and regions can be highly individual, they will often have enough shared commonalities with the dominant culture to make them recognisably English. The authors of *Tyneside: A History of Newcastle and Gateshead from Earliest Times*, for example, suggested that the 2004 vote of 'No' to a regional assembly in the North-East indicated: 'Local patriotism … was not the same as nationalism' and that Tyneside still remains 'English to the very bone.'[12] Mindful of this, recent commentary on notions of both regional and national identity will be closely engaged with here. And while an exploration of Geordie identity is pursued, it is with keen awareness that Geordie culture and identity is inevitably a sub-culture of the English whole. And from another perspective part of a conceptual North, for which the act of travelling back to from the South is, according to Stuart Maconie, tantamount to 'crossing time zones, political borders and linguistic and cultural frontiers'.[13]

Although accepting that any exploration of Geordie identity has to consider the broader national context, there can be no doubt that a historic sense of separateness and isolation from the rest of the country has existed in the North-East, trenchantly observed by Harry Pearson:

> In the North-East, England, or rather the notion of England, seems a long way off. The North-East is at the far corner of the country but it is separated by more than just miles. There is the wilderness of the Pennines to the west, the emptiness of the North Yorkshire moors to the south and to the north, the Scottish Border. The nearest major city to Newcastle is Edinburgh, and that is in another country. Sometimes the North-East seemed more like an island than a region.[14]

This island-within-an-island mentality was appealed to by Sir John Hall when he evoked comparisons between Geordies and the Basques in Spain, coining the phrase 'Geordie Nation' whilst attempting to replicate Barcelona's sporting club on Tyneside in the 1990s.

Also in the early 1990s, the co-editors of *Geordies* maintained that the North-East found itself as 'the forgotten corner of a British nation-state', and quoted from an article by Peter J. Taylor in which he asserted that Tynesiders were 'outside our own national identity'.[15] In the same collection Barry Carr discussed how the 'Englishness of the North-East has long been ambivalent', and suggested the region is 'different and apart' from dominant perceptions of English national identity which reside in the South.[16]

A chapter by Charles Phythian-Adams in *Northumbria: History and Identity 547-2000*, published in 2007 and edited by Rob Colls, is entitled *The Northumbrian Island*, but such sentiments are by no means the preserve of academics. Entertainers including *Auf Wiedersehen, Pet* actor Tim Healy have also evoked this sense of apartness. Speaking before the 2004 regional assembly referendum, Healy insisted: 'It's always been a bit like England, Ireland, Scotland, Wales, and then the Geordies', whilst singer Brian Johnson's recollection of an altercation with Chuck Berry had a similar theme.[17] Apparently Berry told somebody Johnson was Scottish and that was the final straw, prompting the AC/DC frontman to reflect that as a Geordie he's kind of English but not fully English.

Some say this persistent sense of detachment can be traced back to Northumberland and Durham's exclusion from the Domesday Book in 1086, or further to the ancient kingdom of Northumbria. Later the Tudors embedded an inexorable trend towards metropolitan centralisation, and it has been suggested that at that time: 'the North was seen as a place apart, different, potentially hostile, in need of a specific instrument of suppression' – an observation that will be imbued with a Thatcherite resonance for many modern-day Tynesiders of a certain age.[18]

History has its part to play in this book, of course, but often it will be latent and implied, playing a supporting role rather than the romantic or romanticised lead. That is not to repudiate Tyneside's rich history in any way, or denigrate the importance of it in people's sense of themselves. The local history shelves of North-East bookshops groan under the weight of books that expertly detail and delineate this history. I readily recommend them to you. But keep your wits about you. Napoleon once said *What is history but a fable agreed upon?* and as Bill Lancaster has cannily observed, historians can be both 'makers and breakers of "myths"'.[19]

Reinforcing the historic sense of isolation and separateness from within the region, and complementing the notion of the North-East as a place apart from without, there exists a prevalent perception of Newcastle as a quasi-colonial outpost to which fictional characters can be exiled. In Jane Austen's *Pride and Prejudice* the disgraced Wickham and Lydia Bennet are expelled to Newcastle after their scandalous elopement, prompting Mrs Bennet to observe: 'They are gone down to Newcastle, a place quite northward, it seems, and there they are to stay, I do not know how long.'[20] Considering the transport and travel implications, exiling characters to Newcastle from further south in Regency England is at least understandable as a plot device. However, in the modern age of planes, trains and automobiles we have also seen Todd Carty returning to *Eastenders* as Mark Fowler having been banished to Newcastle as his back story, and Curly Watts being excommunicated from Weatherfield to Tyneside when Kevin Kennedy decided to leave *Coronation Street*.

Added to these, the latest example of expelling a TV character to Newcastle was Detective Nicky Cole (presumably a pun on Cole to Newcastle), played by Don Gilet in *55° North*. Although the positive aspects of basing the short-lived series in Newcastle around the exile's exploits should be embraced, we can ascertain two things from these televisual deportations. On the one hand it would appear that there are some lazy, unimaginative scriptwriters and story developers out there. Of more immediate concern, it would also appear that Tyneside's place in the English popular imagination is roughly equivalent to that of Siberia for the Russians and Alaska for the Americans.

Despite being only four or five hours from London in a car, less than three hours on the train and a mere forty-five minutes (with a tail-wind) when taking a flight, Stuart Maconie's perception that the North-East is 'a long way away … and it's not on the way to anywhere except Berwick or Oslo via slow boat' is endemic throughout the country.[21] A.A. Gill used very similar words but went a little further by declaring: 'The north-east isn't on the way to anywhere anymore … the sense of place is anything but romantic. For a thousand years, this must have been the most unpleasant and frightening corner of the British Isles.'[22] And raising the bar a notch further still, in *It's Not Grim Up North* Brian Sewell avowed that he 'can't think of any reason for going to Newcastle unless you have to. I think that has been the situation for donkey's years.'[23]

Similarly, while the August 2009 edition of *Waitrose Food Illustrated* magazine referred to Northumberland as 'an undiscovered jewel', the recommendation came a little too late for former *Sunday Times* journalist, Judith O'Reilly.[24] A year earlier in 2008 she enjoyed a publishing success with *Wife in the North* (based on her blog whose subtitle used to read: *Just how grim can it get up North? Very, one woman's lonely journey into the Northern heartlands*, referred to in the first page of the book as the *northern wastelands*). It was based on her reflections and feelings following a move to Northumberland from London advocated by her husband, and although it must be emphasised that O'Reilly's website now has a more conciliatory subtitle, and that there is an element of tongue-in-cheek commentary to it all, the tedious banality of the original highlights what former Conservative MP Derek Conway, raised on a Gateshead council estate, has said about how the North-East is perceived: 'It's a two-hour and 50 minute journey, it's not the Outer Hebrides. Newcastle isn't a distant frozen village away from anywhere, a perverse perception of the Oxbridge elite.'[25]

Also apparently dismayed by the perceived distance from Newcastle to the capital was another journalist, Tim Adams from *The Observer*, who joined protestors on a coach from Tyneside for the march against government cuts on 26th March 2011. His subsequent article began like this:

> The first thing to note about getting from Newcastle to London is the obvious one: it's a long way. No wonder it took the Jarrow marchers 22 days. Fortunately, the Coalition of Resistance (Tyne and Wear section) has arranged coaches … But still.[26]

Unlike O'Reilly, Adams did indeed attend Oxbridge but Conway makes a mistake in ascribing such perceptions to so small a group. In my experience it is far more widespread and mainstream, and not confined to the metropolis or particular social groups. Taken altogether it reeks of the small-minded, small-scale thinking of a psychologically and economically fragmented yet geographically small island. And it is against this historic backdrop of defensive dislocation from within, and misplaced misapprehension from without, that an examination of Akenside Syndrome must necessarily be conducted.

THE FOUR PILLARS OF
GEORDIE IDENTITY

You see, in this school, as on Tyneside generally, almost everyone was working-class. Our fathers worked on the railway, in the factory, in the shipyard, most of them, and you get the scale of it for this area if you reflect that a factory or shipyard employing five thousand men would be unlikely to count more than two hundred and fifty middle-class folk among them.

The reflections of Willie Kiddar in Jack Common's
Kiddar's Luck, first published in 1951

Newcastle remains a beguiling, 'walking city' of 'rough spontaneity', where 'the dominant ethos, the "establishment" if you like, is – rarity! – working-class'.

Bill Lancaster quoting acclaimed travel writer John Ardagh in *Sociability and the City (Newcastle upon Tyne: A Modern History)*, published in 2001

The north is a metaphor for class, I still feel the working class is the majority class; full of resilience, stamina and wit, but it also has to recover from horrible macho politics.

Beatrix Campbell discussing regional identity prior to the referendum on a North-East Regional Assembly, *The Guardian* 27th October 2004

It's a fiction. We are not all middle-class now, and we wouldn't want to be … This is a massive scam, this horrible mutation of all into some homogenised vision of middle-classness.

Suzanne Moore, *The Guardian* 26th March 2011

I was simultaneously wracked by, and revelling in, the realisation that I belonged nowhere; that culturally, and in class terms, I was a displaced person.

Gordon Burn, the late Newcastle-born novelist, comparing himself to Lawrentian characters when recalling his adolescence on Tyneside in *Living Memories, Guardian Review* 11th June 2005

PILLAR ONE

Class

THERE CAN BE LITTLE DOUBT THAT FOR MUCH OF THE TWENTIETH century a strong majority of Tyneside's inhabitants thought of their conurbation as being a working-class area, and that when those from outside the region think of Geordies it is invariably working-class people and characters that instantly spring to mind. By employing the observation about Newcastle being a city where the working class remain the establishment at the end of *Sociability and the City*, historian Bill Lancaster seemed to imply that the sentiment retained a powerful resonance at the turn of the century.

Previously, in his personal contribution to *Geordies*, Lancaster claimed that Tyneside had 'perhaps the oldest working-class culture' in the country and that Newcastle's 'value system, politics, myths and symbols are essentially working-class.'[1] When rebutting the notion that 'most people these days regard themselves as middle class', Steve Gibson, chairman of Middlesbrough Football Club, insisted 90% of people in that town 'would say they were working-class', and it would come as no surprise if a correspondingly hypothetical survey on Tyneside at the turn of the twentieth century yielded a similarly high percentage, if not quite the 19 out of 20 ratio estimated by Kiddar in the early 1900s.[2]

Seen in this context we can see how Rod Liddle's infamous 'monkeys and morons' jibe against the alleged eating habits of Geordies (derided by Stuart Maconie as 'a sneering bit of fluff attacking north-easterners' that exemplified 'the metropolitan Uncle Tom ... frightened, insecure, a snob') can be interpreted as a sneer against a particular class, rather than a specific city.[3] Liddle would have chosen Newcastle's citizens to be the target of his playground name-calling, and to localise his broader criticisms of working-class diets, in the sure knowledge that his largely right-wing, Tory-voting readership in *The Spectator* (then edited by Boris Johnson who has of course made, or overseen, similar denunciations about 'working-class' conurbations such as Liverpool and Portsmouth) would make an instinctive, conditioned equation: Newcastle/Geordies = working class.

Having shaken up the combustible kaleidoscope of class in identifying the first pillar of Geordie identity, an acknowledgement is required. When discussing class it is certainly true that the 'words we have to choose from can sound patronising, crass or unkind', with even the term 'middle class' 'these days often used as a venomous synonym for smug, unadventurous or selfish.'[4] This seems a fair appraisal of how the middle classes are sometimes labelled, but as Owen Jones has shown in *Chavs: The Demonization of the Working Class*, it is those at the lower end of the social scale who are the most common target for this pernicious English tendency to thoughtlessly employ class as a crude indicator of character. Certainly there is no anti-middle-class term of popular abuse comparable to the word *chav* (a word that according to the Fabian Society 'betrays a deep and revealing level of class hatred ... This is middle class hatred of the white working class, pure and simple'), and no website dedicated to deriding and pouring vulgar abuse on the middle classes comparable to *ChavTowns* (formerly *ChavScum*).[5]

It's therefore essential when discussing class to acknowledge David Cannadine's broadly accurate assertion: 'Classes, like nations, are sometimes more, and sometimes less, than imagined communities.'[6] Collective behavioural stereotyping is to be avoided wherever possible, and when class *culture* – rituals, norms, customs, beliefs etc. – is discussed here it is with full awareness of reasonable observations that have been made on the subject including, '"Working classes" is a descriptive term, which evades as much as it defines', and the 'definition of middle class has become so blandly all-encompassing that it is almost meaningless.'[7] Nonetheless, working and middle class have been and still are commonly used terms of reference. Inadequate, elusive and crassly oversimplified for sure, but their historic and continued prevalence in public discourse and personal consciousness means it is necessary to both utilise and explore them in relation to Geordie identity.

Before going on to discuss Newcastle's middle classes, it may also prove useful to examine the limitations of an irritatingly pervasive myth about class in this country. There is a commonly held perception that people from poor, low income or traditionally working-class backgrounds who do well for themselves financially but do not consider themselves to be middle class, are either being disingenuous or are in some form of denial about their true social standing. It is a confused, contradictory and ill-thought-out argument often propounded by commentators from further up the social scale, or by observers from working-class backgrounds who have slavishly embraced the convoluted and snobbish nature of conventional class norms. The type of commentator who would no doubt deride FA Cup-winning manager Lawrie McMenemy, born and raised in Gateshead, for claiming (when I asked him which class he considered himself to belong to): "I would still always say I was working class. To say any other when you've been born that way would be wrong. It's giving the impression that you want to leave that behind. I don't want to leave that behind."

Barbara Ellen summed this phenomenon up in *The Observer* when accusing Melvyn Bragg of being a 'class Uncle Tom' after watching the first episode of his 2012 BBC television series *Melvyn Bragg on Class and Culture.* 'Have you ever noticed how successful people aren't permitted to remain working class; that there is no such thing as a visible high-achieving working-class?' she enquired. She went on to suggest that 'people are always depicted as trying to "escape" the working class, when really they are just trying to escape poverty and lack of opportunity. It's as though as soon as a working-class person becomes successful, the middle classes swoop down to claim them as their own ("Great news – you're one of us now!"). If the seduction doesn't work, then the mockery begins.'[8] Owen Jones would no doubt concur having insisted that, advocated by both Thatcherism and New Labour, the 'glorification of the middle class – by making it the standard everyone should aspire for, however unrealistically – is a useful ideological prop for the class system.'[9]

A system which Jonathan Freedland claims 'is defined by a whole battery of traits which have nothing to do with raw cash' – a claim reinforced by Kate Fox: 'class in England has nothing to do with money … in no other country is social class so completely independent of material wealth.'[10] Clearly we need to be careful about advocating an absolute separation of 'class' and 'money'; for instance, in their influential book *The Spirit Level: Why Equality is Better for Everyone*, Richard Wilkinson and Kate Pickett encourage us to:

> regard the scale of material inequalities in a society as providing the skeleton, or framework, round which class and cultural differences are formed. Over time, crude differences in wealth gradually become overlaid by differences in clothing, aesthetic taste, education, sense of self and all the other markers of class identity.[11]

But there is undoubtedly scope for a differentiation between simply wanting to improve your lot in life and self-conscious social class aspiration, striving to be 'middle class'. Therefore when *GQ* editor Dylan Jones talks in woefully cliché-ridden terms about class, claiming that people with a bit of money are newly-minted middle-class but regard themselves as well-off working class, and even well-intended observers such as Ferdinand Mount reflect on the 'downward mobility of the mind … [and of] belonging in [their] mind to the working class' of people from working-class backgrounds who rise the economic scale, they seem to miss the broader point.[12]

It may be less surprising to hear self-described class traitor and Tory philosopher Roger Scruton, who has talked of discarding his 'proletarian coarseness', refer to his father remaining working class 'in spirit … long after he had left it' and retaining 'towards his social origins an intense nostalgia', but he, like Jones, Mount and others, appears to endorse and perpetuate the misguided belief that simply earning a certain amount of money or having a certain job makes you 'middle class' rather than 'middle income'.[13] The latter group is what Tony Blair seemed to be describing when discussing his old Sedgefield constituency in his autobiography: 'The new estates were private estates of three- and four-bedroomed houses, and while the people who lived there couldn't be described as 'middle class', neither were they 'working class' in the sense of Andy Capp. They drank beer; they also drank wine.'[14]

Tellingly, although what materially constitutes this imagined transition from working to middle class is often put forward (home/car ownership, a certain type of job, earning X amount of money etc.), we rarely hear exactly what it is that constitutes a similar transition from middle to upper class. We could ask Bryan Ferry, except he skipped the middle bit out. Do the vast fortunes of people like Sting, former Newcastle United chairman Freddy Shepherd, Brian Johnson and Alan Shearer mean they have joined the ranks of the upper classes? Of course it doesn't, at least not in itself. In 2013 Cheryl Cole was said to be worth £14million, so does that mean she's accepted as middle or upper class? Far from it. Instead she endures jealous jibes and insecure invective from the condescending commentariat, who gleefully label her a chav.

The misleading, mendacious conflation of an economic system of class stratification with the traditional system of social class in England, with its 'elaborate nuances of social status and social identity', is a persistent modern-day myth about class.[15] With regard to issues of class relating to Geordie identity and Akenside Syndrome it is important to understand this, because as Scruton himself has noted: 'myths that are accepted become as influential as truths'.[16]

So what of middle-class Geordies? Do they think of themselves as Geordies? Are they accepted as such by their working-class counterparts whose ethos, it is claimed, permeated the regional capital for much of the last century? Jesmond and Gosforth are the two suburbs that inevitably spring to mind when thinking of Newcastle's middle classes. In March 2006 I was working in a bookshop in Guildford when a man I took to be in his fifties, who hailed from Jesmond, bought a bio-chemistry book for the wallet-lightening price of £83.50p. Having picked up on my accent and volunteered the information that he was from Jesmond in what seemed like a spirit of kinship, I briefly mentioned that I was doing research for a project on Geordie identity. Without hesitation or affectation, he replied: "We certainly have a strong one." Clearly an intelligent, articulate man and coming from the suburb of Tyneside most commonly associated with the middle classes, I found his sincere use of the collective pronoun *we* interesting. It seemed to be anecdotal affirmation of a claim made by Bill Lancaster; namely that Newcastle's middle classes share a high degree of cultural identity with the working classes in a city where there is a 'dominance of regional over class identity'.[17]

Having spent the first twenty-seven years of my life living in Newcastle that was certainly the over-riding impression I always had. That on the whole a tangible spirit of egalitarianism and empathy existed between Newcastle's different social groups, and that class division, enmity and pretension – '[historically] used, quite fiercely, to maintain barriers, to inflict pain and to identify kindred spirits' – simply hasn't prevailed in Newcastle or on Tyneside in the same way that it has in other parts of the country.[18] That the majority of Geordies, regardless of their background or which social category they fit in to, reject the artifice, affectation and underlying animosity of the traditional class system. Talking of regional press coverage of the Great North Run since its inception, Gregson and Huggins identified 'the conscious rejection of social class elitism in terms of the Run', and such a narrative thread has also been observable in wider Tyneside society.[19]

If this is the case, then to what extent can Newcastle claim to be a *classless society*? The term is fraught with difficulty and to declare a place a modern-day example of this utopian ideal can invite ridicule, with a few carefully chosen statistics or examples of inequality revealing the claim to be starred with lacunae. In *A History of Modern Britain* Andrew Marr declared a pretence of classlessness to be part of the essence of early 21st century British culture, whereas Owen Jones adopted a more scathing tone in *CHAVS*, lambasting 'the ludicrous mainstream political view that Britain is now a classless society'.[20] Looking further afield, it is a term employed by David Cannadine when describing the United States of America as 'the pioneering and prototypical classless society', yet a chapter-heading in Jonathan Freedland's largely pro-American polemic *Bring Home the Revolution: The Case for a British Republic*, is entitled *Dream On: Searching for the Classless Society*.

Both Freedland and Cannadine, however, acknowledge that a certain spirit of classlessness exists in America despite the existence of huge inequalities of wealth and power, with Cannadine claiming: 'these do not translate into corresponding inequalities of social prestige or social perceptions.'[21] The disparity in wealth may not be quite so dramatic on Tyneside but the sentiment can be seen as historically applicable, and perhaps informs Bill Lancaster's assertion that one of Newcastle's most important modern characteristics is 'a strong sense of classlessness', and that the city itself is in 'a curious sense … a classless city'. He also maintains that a 'cultural convergence of class' has prevailed in Newcastle, which 'has resulted in other social groups being more sympathetic to working-class needs and interests.'[22]

The idea of cultural or social convergence is something that Ferdinand Mount also considers when contemplating 'quiet republics' including Switzerland, the Scandinavian countries, the USA, Australia and New Zealand, where top earners' 'pleasures, habits of speech, opinions and allegiances do not seem sharply removed from the common run.'[23] Having systematically dismantled any claims that Britain can consider itself a classless society on the grounds of economic equality or equality of opportunity, he correctly contends that a high level of social convergence is what the majority of people are referring to when they talk about classlessness, yet doubts the extent to which this country has achieved levels comparable with the quiet republics. Looking at the country as a whole he is undoubtedly right, but Newcastle's claim to be an enclave of relative classlessness within the fragmented whole is not without some credibility.

It would be going too far to echo renowned twentieth century historian A.J.P. Taylor's assertion, that the radical hotbed of Manchester was 'the only place in England which escapes our characteristic vice of snobbery', and claim that Newcastle is immune to the English Disease.[24] But before moving away from the city in 2000 it never seemed prevalent to me, residing only in peripheral pockets far removed from the dominant ethos. Indeed compared to the levels of undignified striving, tacit yearning for, and hypocritical engagement with the old class system that I've encountered whilst living in Surrey and Hampshire (the dynamics of which are a fertile breeding ground for snobs when defined as 'a person who strives to associate with those of higher social status and who behaves condescendingly to others'), on Tyneside it seemed negligible.[25] Though there is an urban versus rural dimension to that comparison, like Pennsylvania in the 1750s, when it comes to Newcastle's inhabitants: 'the meanest among them thinks he has a right to civility from the greatest.'[26]

Assertions such as these can lead to accusations of mawkish sentimentality, regional bias and a tendency to view Newcastle specifically, and Tyneside generally, through rose– or perhaps black and white–tinted spectacles. That is not the case. Compiling a list of cross-cultural universals, Robin Fox observed that 'a system of social status and methods of indicating it' is common across all human cultures, and to suggest that Newcastle is somehow exempt from this would clearly be ridiculous.[27] Nonetheless, to say that Newcastle exudes an aura of classlessness which in some ways reflects the American-style money system, but is perhaps more culturally comparable to the Scandinavian countries, and arguably Australia and New Zealand, does not seem unreasonable. As various commentators have observed, the fact that the lyrics of Geordie anthem *The Blaydon Races* celebrate Tyneside's ordinary citizens seems to reinforce the idea that it is a place of the people. Especially when compared to the cringe-worthy forelock-tugging of the British national anthem, *God Save the Queen*, which glorifies and vindicates deference, social class hierarchy and elitism.

A lot of Geordies from working-class backgrounds who rise through the economic scale seem to reject many of the non-economic aspects of *embourgeoisement*, and 'the truly mind-boggling silliness of the English class system', in the full knowledge that the 'absurdity of people who have 'made it' financially being foolish enough to believe they have risen up the social scale is a source of huge amusement in Britain, and a staple of our popular culture.'[28] Hence the vindictive vitriol poured on Cheryl Cole. All things considered, the assertion that despite increased economic prosperity in the second half of the twentieth century, 'there was very little evidence that prosperous members of the working class crossed a great social (and political) divide and became middle-class Tories', seems particularly applicable to Newcastle, Gateshead and South Tyneside.[29]

Therefore when the frankly laudable act of financially successful people from poor or working-class backgrounds retaining a sense of solidarity and allegiance with people from similar origins, and still considering themselves to be working class, is portrayed as inconsistent, nostalgic or fanciful, it seems slightly odd. Owen Jones is right to say that when it comes to identifying which class we belong to, 'self-identification is an ambiguous, subjective business and people of all classes might, for various reasons, mischaracterize their place in the social pecking order', but when Ferdinand Mount suggests that a perceived 'downward mobility of the mind may be seen as an endearing moral gesture, or by the less forgiving as humbug. But it remains only a gesture', he misses an important factor.[30]

Remaining emotionally and politically aligned with the working classes, if not materially 'belonging' to that group any longer, as many financially comfortable Geordies appear to do, is not only admirably demotic but also *entirely consistent* with the 'rules' of the traditional class system which have, superficially at least, nothing to do with money. And besides, while not as important as actual political action, in creating an atmosphere of classlessness gestures are of crucial symbolic importance.

If Tyneside really is such a harmonious oasis of social cohesion and amiable citizenship, the question might reasonably be asked how a condition such as Akenside Syndrome can possibly take root. In order to unearth the answer a nod must be made to postmodernism, with its multiple meanings, perspectives and insistence on the primacy of interpretations over facts. An understanding of what the area has become, or is becoming, must naturally be complemented by an appreciation of what has went before. For if we accept that 'shared class characteristics and clear-cut class boundaries … rarely if ever existed in fact' on Tyneside as in the country as a whole, then we must also acknowledge that if a working-class *culture* has been domi-nant throughout the area in recent times, this may be a potential source of ambivalent feelings within individuals.[31] The 'overwhelmingly collectivist and socialist objectives of the people of the Northern region' in recent history is hard to dispute, and it is to the day-to-day reality of living within what may be called a collectivist environment (as opposed to an exploration of the actual political philosophy) that we must turn, in order to examine the possibility of this being fruitful ground for Akenside Syndrome to ferment.[32]

Kate Fox maintains that the English 'are a nation of curtain-twitchers, endlessly fascinated by the tabooed private lives of the 'members of our social setting'', and while this may be a national cross-class malaise, there can be little doubt that the tightly compacted, insular world of a traditional working-class environment provides a particularly rarefied example.[33] There will always be a certain amount of conformity pressed upon the individual in any human society, but in a strongly collectivist environment the employment of community disapproval as social control, added to the tacitly intrusive and vaguely menacing communal belief in the *right* to know the business of others, has the potential to create an especially constrained, clammy and claustrophobic atmosphere.

Michael Collins captured the essence of this when recalling his childhood in Southwark, then a predominantly white working-class area of London:

> that ubiquitous eye of the neighbours that helped cocoon us as kids, trans-lated into nosiness and interference when we were adolescents, and how it seemed to be checking for a code to which we were expected to conform, and which appeared to threaten any ambitions beyond the familiar and the well-trodden, when we were heading for adulthood.[34]

The image of being cocooned is apt, conveying feelings of warmth and pro-tection while simultaneously suggesting an envelope of restraint and control from which the individual must strive to escape if he or she is to flourish. A literary Tyneside example of what Collins describes can be found in *Kiddar's Luck*, in which Kiddar is talking about his father:

> And there by the slight fold of a lifted curtain, he encountered an Eye. Now I appreciated this story because I, too, was encountering that Eye, frequently. It was Mrs Rowley's, and there was no doubt about it, the woman was a natural overlooker.[35]

Robson Green also illustrated the point when, prior to a split from his wife Vanya in 2011, he talked about living with his family in Surrey and consid-ered the pros and cons of his upbringing in the North-East: 'The plus side of being brought up in a mining village is the strong sense of community. The downside is that everybody knows your business.'[36]

Comments about being brought up in a rural Northumberland mining village, although relevant, clearly cannot be held up as representative of the area as a whole. A certain deprivation of privacy and insularity are surely universal facts of life in small rural villages, rather than a phenomenon particular to the North-East. Yet while the alleged comments of departing footballers likening Newcastle to a 'goldfish bowl' and a 'big football village' can be interpreted as containing at least an element of sour grapes, the observation by Harry Pearson that the 'North-East remains something of a village, and like all villages it is rife with gossip', should perhaps afford us greater pause for thought.[37] As should the conurbation upgrade suggested by journalist Danuta Kean in an interview with Geordie author Martyn Waites: 'Newcastle ... though a city, it feels like a market town ... there is always "somebody who knows somebody".'[38]

Certainly when I first moved away from Newcastle there was a sense of liberation on some levels. From people in some respects but more generally from a vague, uneasy sense of being *known* and unable, in the environment that I inhabited, to satisfactorily progress through the subtle phases of reinvention that some psychologists insist we must continuously navigate throughout our lives in order to stay healthy. Of course, this kernel of personal biography can be framed within an infinitely wider context of universal human experience concerning rites of passage, the reconfiguration of familial bonds forged in childhood, establishing your 'self' as an autonomous entity and taking your own path in life. Nonetheless, as holocaust survivor and eminent psychiatric professor Viktor E. Frankl has talked of it being 'well known that an enforced community life, in which attention is paid to everything one does at all times, may result in an irresistible urge to get away, at least for a short while', it does not require too great a leap of imagination to speculate on the possibility of life in a strongly communal or collectivist environment, with *the ubiquitous eye of the neighbours*, creating similar desires and longings.[39]

Working-class culture is an easy and popular target for comedians, cultural commentators and 'social critics' from across the political and ideological spectrum. In *Mind the Gap: The New Class Divide in Britain*, a thoughtful examination of how the working classes have come to be deprived of respect in the modern era, Ferdinand Mount, an upper-class former Tory adviser and chief speechwriter for Mrs Thatcher, talked of 'a long and bitter campaign to deride and eclipse them', and of how they have been 'subjected to a sustained programme of social contempt and institutional erosion'.[40] For Owen Jones, Mount's late boss was largely to blame for this. Avowing 'just how mainstream middle-class hatred of working-class people is in modern Britain', he concludes: 'From salt of the earth to scum of the earth. This is the legacy of Thatcherism – the demonization of everything associated with the working class.[41]

Similar sentiments can be found in Michael Collins's examination of comparable themes, in which he claims that the white English working class were consistently portrayed as the butt of the joke in twentieth century artistic output, and remain 'the only group of people that the chattering classes are happy to hear mocked and attacked.'[42] The review of Collins's book in *The Sunday Telegraph* professed that it 'forces us to confront our "acceptable" prejudices,' and Charles Jennings, a self-described middle-class 'snotty Londoner', outlined the inherent hypocrisy of such class-based judgements when reflecting on the historic enmity of the North/South divide (which often runs, or is at least perceived to run along class lines: North = working class, South = middle/upper class). 'This isn't the same embarrassment or shame one might feel about holding some sort of vile prejudice against racial or sexual minorities,' he acknowledged, thus supporting the theory propounded by Wilkinson and Pickett in *The Spirit Level* concerning 'downward prejudice' and 'discrimination and snobbery. Although racial prejudice is widely condemned, class prejudice is, despite the similarities, rarely mentioned.'[43]

All of which is relevant when considering class and its potentially symbiotic relationship with Akenside Syndrome, because Tyneside is still widely perceived as a predominantly white English working-class area. And as Harvey Taylor has said (localising Collins's broader national observation): 'The working-class culture of the North-East has been the subject of constant parody. Stereotyping the region in terms of selected cultural idiosyncrasies is in danger of becoming a popular pastime in itself.'[44] The ill-advised 2001 WHSmith ads set in Newcastle, featuring a black and white football top-wearing Nicholas Lyndhurst as part of a family of fat, thick and generally uncouth Geordies is one obvious example of this. There are many others. And yet while it is certainly not the intention to join the condescending chorus of Pecksniffian piety aimed at working-class culture here, it would be negligent and lacking in self-awareness not to acknowledge that there are *some* aspects of traditional working-class culture that *some* people may have found alienating, and that may have provoked conflicting feelings towards Tyneside.

Existing within the framework of traditional working-class culture there has always been a robust thread of conservatism; mainly of the relatively harmless 'stick to what we know' variety but occasionally, on an individual level, spilling over into a more visceral, Alf Garnett-like bloody-minded intolerance of difference. The claim that 'an increasingly conservative working class … [has] been common-place in most post-industrial societies', may therefore chime with some brought up in Tyneside's working-class neighbourhoods during deindustrialisation, and the 'insularity and attachment to place that defines the white working class, and which is born of a lack of opportunity' can, naturally enough, be restrictive in itself.[45] Furthermore, as Bill Lancaster pointed out in *An Agenda for Regional History*: 'whether on the coalfield, or in the heavy industrial districts of the three north eastern rivers, the working-class ethos of the region is often overwhelming. Aspects of working-class life can be endearing, but for some the industrial heritage can be a curse.'[46]

Kevin Keegan's father was a miner (though brought up in Yorkshire, Keegan's grandfather was a survivor and hero of the 1909 West Stanley pit disaster) and, when Keegan was a child, would say to him: 'I don't want you to end up working down the mines like me.'[47] Similarly, when I spoke to Glenn McCrory, brought up in Stanley and still the only boxer from the North-East to achieve world champion status, he recalled: 'My grandfather made my mum *promise* that she wouldn't let any of us go down the pit.'

Robson Green, meanwhile, has talked of how looking out of the window at his school and seeing the surrounding mines gave a sense of what might be in store for pupils. And of how his father's 'greatest wish was for me to never spend so much as two minutes down a mine, let alone the 40 years he was sentenced to … When I was a kid, I used to see my dad come home dead shattered after his shift, his body so dirty and black. It was scary to see his bath water. So when I grew up and moved away, I felt as if I'd escaped.'[48] Green has mentioned this sense of escape a number of times recently and the theme of escape can feature prominently amongst those who have experienced Akenside Syndrome. The possibility of there being a generational dimension to the condition for some, linked to the North-East's industrial heritage and its subsequent decline, seems strong.

Speaking of an earlier era, Keith Armstrong maintains that despite Jack Common's 'strong sense of community and identification with the city of Newcastle upon Tyne,' he knew that 'as a rebel and a writer he was different and needed to escape and reject the values of his father and the local parochialism which they reflected.'[49] And when considering the potential effect on certain individuals of what are sometimes thought of, rightly or wrongly, as working-class prejudices such as anti-educationalism and a bias against the arts, a generational perspective must also be factored into the equation. For while it is imperative to acknowledge that a certain degree of collective behavioural stereotyping is always evident in such class-based generalisations, to deny that a strain of these prejudices has existed on Tyneside would be self-deceiving.

One of the central themes of *Billy Elliot* is the dramatic tension between the protagonist wishing to explore and fulfil his artistic potential and the confining, restrictive nature of his cultural environment. Some might argue that the anti-arts ambience depicted typifies the 'long ingrained mistrust of high culture and a natural loyalty to its own tastes' that, while by no means describing the whole, is certainly a recognisable aspect of some traditional working-class environments.[50] Greg Brenman, one of the producers of the *Billy Elliot* film, has talked of the personal resonance he felt this aspect of the story had for writer Lee Hall: 'Lee had grown up wanting to write poetry, wanting to be a playwright in rough, tough Newcastle. So there were parallels.' Hall himself has said: 'I was a young kid, growing up in the east end of Newcastle … I had no idea what a play was, or how you wrote them.'[51] Indeed, while not ignoring Hall's recurring theme of class-related access to the arts, it could be argued that the pitmen painters were closer to exceptions than the norm. Visiting the site of the group's hut in Ashington with Robson Green for a recent documentary, Jack Charlton recalled him and his mates peering in and saying they were daft.[52]

Hall might empathise with Wilkinson and Pickett's appraisal that to 'a degree, working-class people resist the imposition of education and middle-class values, because becoming educated would require them to give up ways of being that they value.'[53] Certainly some of the characters he portrays, such as Billy Elliot and Oliver Kilbourne would. From just such an education-resistant perspective, when the 'conflict of loyalty' that the late North

Shields-born playwright Tom Hadaway felt when writing his contribution
to *Geordies* for a university press is taken into account (in which he talks of
his Uncle George, 'a coble fisherman out of Cullercoats ... without benefit
from his schooldays ... [who] was given to saying disparaging things about
the nature of education'), to suggest that being brought up in a culture where
examples of such mistrust and indifference exist may provoke feelings of
ambivalence does not seem far-fetched.[54]

As Kiddar's school scholarship exams approach, he observes: 'it was rare
that any parental prod urged us to make a race of it', and with regard to
homework; 'Even our parents didn't like us doing it, and that shows you',
also relating how: 'my mates began to develop an adult scorn if I went on
too long about something I'd been reading.'[55] The comments of Gordon
Burn, born and raised in the West End of Newcastle, in which he maintained that the phrase '"He's a big reader" wasn't necessarily a compliment
where I was growing up', and that he was 'culturally, and in class terms ...
a displaced person', appear to reinforce this impression, as does Lee Hall's
similar assessment: 'Where I grew up, the notion of reading books didn't
make you a swot, but a poof.'[56]

Nor does it seem unreasonable to suggest that although a certain spirit
of classlessness – or class solidarity – can be said to have historically existed
in Newcastle and its close environs, this does not necessarily mean that the
complex ambiguities and multiple anxieties associated with class in this
country do not penetrate the consciousness of individuals. As the late multi-
award-winning North-East writer Alan Plater put it: 'scratch any critical
consensus and it will bleed contradictions and paradoxes.'[57]

So while Newcastle's claim to be a classless society may bear some casual
scrutiny, this does not mean that issues relating to class have not contributed
toward symptoms of Akenside Syndrome incubating within individuals. Or
that class cohesion on Tyneside is a hermetically sealed given. Following
renowned French anthropologist Claude Lévi-Strauss, many commentators
have noted the human tendency to think of the world in terms of binary
oppositions, and, on a social level, 'the traditional, populist way of looking
at the world, as being irrevocably divided between 'us' and 'them".[58] The
familiar English working-class perspective on this universal condition, in
which society is divided into 'us' (the working class) and the 'posh' (middle/

upper class) has surely been evident on Tyneside, and such dichotomous division can undoubtedly cause distress and disequilibrium.

Kiddar's Luck abounds with class-based collective identity phrases such as 'the likes of us', 'one of my condition' and 'one of our sort'. Although perfectly understandable given the historic dynamics of class-based identity in England (and Jack Common's leftist political outlook), when this instinctively divisive mind-set is psychologically established as a person's default position (whether from the perspective of 'us', 'them', the 'posh' or any other side of a socially conceived binary opposition), the potential for conflicting and confused feelings can be great. *Should I like people like 'them'? Am I actually more like 'them' than 'us'? 'They' have not accepted me as one of 'them'. This aspiration that I hold dear just isn't for 'the likes of us'* etc. etc. Sting, for example, has recalled feelings of inadequacy and alienation, and a fermenting sense of resentment towards Newcastle and what he felt he was being invited to aspire to, when, as a pupil at St Cuthbert's school in Newcastle, he was invited to the large detached houses of middle-class schoolmates in Darras Hall.

Chris Donald is slightly younger than Sting and in a recent BBC documentary he displayed a consciousness of dichotomous class division on Tyneside, but from a middle-class perspective. He talked of the Jesmond of his childhood being 'culturally a million miles from working-class areas like Byker and Shieldfield', and of the divide between the working-class Shieldfield end of Sandyford Road and the Jesmond end where, if you lived at that end, you were 'middle class and posh like what we were.'[59] In his autobiography *Rude Kids* he explains that he never showed the initial editions of *Viz* to his colleagues at the DHSS, as they 'were all regular, working-class sorts of people. They liked drinking in the Bigg Market and disco dancing, so I thought it might be a little left-of-field for their tastes', and recalls the 'obvious divide between the middle-class political ideologists ... and the working-class printers' at The Free Press co-operative where the magazine was first printed.[60]

Although one of the fundamental elements of the huge popularity and success of *Viz* was its brutal parodies of Newcastle's working-class culture, Donald himself appeared to display empathy with working-class Geordies in the documentary. He referred to the middle class having "won the war" in and around the Jesmond area; a *Dad's Army*-like graphic with arrows depicting invasion accompanied by his voice-over asserting:

> While the working class were getting pissed in town, the middle class were breaking out and buying up their property. One wave went through Sandyford, and another into Shieldfield.[61]

And yet there is a dissonance between Donald's observation and his own personal experience. In an essay entitled *The Reconstruction of Newcastle: Planning since 1945*, Professor David Byrne of Durham University discussed the financial problems faced by Newcastle City Council at the turn of the millennium, due in part to 'the flight of the middle classes outwith Newcastle's city boundaries.' A video promoting the council's *Going for Growth* strategy made it plain, according to Byrne, that 'the fundamental problem lies in the preference of many middle-class people who work in the city to live anywhere but Newcastle.' Byrne concluded his essay with the pessimistic diagnosis that 'Newcastle may well have gone too far to come back as the mixed class city which city officers and councillors are now pinning their hopes on.'[62]

Donald, who moved to north Northumberland in 1991, in part because he felt 'Newcastle was changing ... and I wasn't sure that I liked it any more', appears to have been an example of this alleged middle-class Diaspora.[63] We'll find out more about his relationship with Newcastle in due course, but for now must contemplate how Bill Lancaster's assertion that some people can 'find local culture embarrassingly working-class', certainly opens up a potential source of ambivalence for middle-class Geordies. Indeed before making reference to John Ardagh's 'the dominant ethos is working-class in Newcastle' observation, Lancaster made a similar point to Byrne: 'the middle classes in particular prefer the suburbs that lie outside the civic boundary ... The other side of Geordie culture is not so endearing. The mannerisms can appear aggressive to outsiders and, coupled with dialect, can seem frighteningly tribal.'[64] Tyneside's claim to be a largely classless conurbation may be tenuously verifiable in certain abstract respects, but it is certainly not without its contradictions and paradoxes.

Discussing class entails navigation of an issue laden with pitfalls and booby-traps – no doubt I have fallen into the former and detonated a few of the latter several times here – and trying to construct a coherent argument can seem as futile as Newcastle United's attempts to win a major trophy since 1969. A.A. Gill has encapsulated the problem:

> Any argument that depends on class for its structure will quickly dissolve into a Jesuitical dissection of definitions of terms. What do you mean by working class, upper class, the sub-divisions of middle class?[65]

But Gill's assertion that there is no longer a class system, and that it should be considered an ex-class system, is far more problematic. Wilkinson and Pickett's assessment, based on years of research, analysis and observation, seems far closer to the truth: 'The ways in which class and taste and snobbery work to constrain people's opportunities and wellbeing are, in reality, painful and pervasive. They are forms of discrimination and social exclusion.'[66]

The English class system is like the bad terminator in *Terminator 2* – it occasionally assumes different outward clothing but its skeletal structure remains rigidly intact. Jonathan Freedland talks of how 'Britain has teemed for centuries with an elaborate ecology of classes and sub-classes, all incubated in a climate of deference and superiority', and Ferdinand Mount maintains that 'the dismal divide continues ... we pretend that it isn't there or at least that it is not as bad as it was', when referring to the country's 'unexpiated curse ... of class division.'[67] David Cannadine finds the fact that 'many scholars have concluded that class doesn't matter anymore ... to put it mildly, rather odd. It is not a conclusion which I (or most Britons) share', while Kate Fox avers that 'class-consciousness pervades every aspect of English life and culture, but also exposes our reluctance to acknowledge this issue.'[68] Therefore when examining the conditions in which Akenside Syndrome might evolve, it is clear that class simply cannot be dismissed and will rear its ugly head wherever we turn.

I had fights [at Cambridge University] about me accent with loads of those fellers you get from third-class public schools. They used to think I was speaking German.

The late Sid Waddell, writer and legendary Geordie darts commentator

On my billing if I'm anywhere [other than the North-East], I won't let them put 'Geordie Comedian'. I don't want to deny my roots but people are stupid and if it says 'Geordie Comedian' they think 'Well, Bobby Thompson – we'll not understand him.' So I don't let them use 'Geordie Comedian' in my billing; it has to be 'from the North-East' … It's purely about other people's perceptions.

Brendan Healy, North-East actor, stand-up comedian and musician

Regional accents might have become politically correct in some circles but most of us feel that they are something of a hindrance if we want to get on in life. More than four in five admit to changing their accent to accommodate different situations.

Judith Holder, *It's Not Grim Up North*

The question [Sting is] most often asked on the streets of Newcastle after 'Can I have your autograph?' is 'Where's your Geordie accent gone?' His honest, if sardonic, response is part of what makes him hard to accept within the tenets of regional pride. "I realised very young that the guy reading the news wasn't speaking Geordie," he says. "Access to power and success had to mean changing the way I spoke."

Phil Sutcliffe, *Sting: Where the Hell Have You Been? Q magazine* February 1991

I only use the Geordie accent when I get angry, unconsciously. My kids would always know when I was serious when I started to speak in that funny voice as they called it.

Sting on *The Andrew Marr Show,* BBC1 8th December 2013

… in general, cliverness meant also softiness, hard Geordie meant hard lad, lack of accent meant softy. Geordie, a badge of hardness, taalkin' posh or properly or English meant collaborator, sneak, crawler, softy.

Miner turned author David John Douglass

PILLAR TWO

Accent

FINDING MYSELF LIVING IN A GRAND MULTI-MILLION POUND MANOR House nestling in the Surrey Hills only a couple of months after leaving Newcastle was quite surreal. The owner of the Manor, a formidable woman in her nineties and the widow of a former Tory grandee, rented out rooms in what was previously the servants' quarters to postgraduate students from the local Law College. An acquaintance from Northumbria University who was attending the college had alerted me to the possibility of a room becoming available. After an eccentric interview with the nonagenarian in which it was tacitly agreed between us that the country was going to the dogs under those awful New Labour whippersnappers ("Pretend you're a Tory" being the only pre-interview advice that my acquaintance had given me), I secured my lodgings.

Disingenuousness was something that Seb, the third student living at the Manor, presumably did not have to resort to during his own interview. Privately educated on the south coast, he was training as a lawyer, a proud Tory, and particularly keen on George W. Bush winning the 2000 US presidential election. Given our different backgrounds and contrasting political outlooks we were never likely to become bosom buddies. But he was a nice enough bloke and in those early days I felt it would be churlish not to make an effort to socialise occasionally. On one such occasion Seb, his girlfriend Melissa (who had attended Bristol University, was training as a barrister and who, despite coming from Yorkshire, spoke crystalline Received Pronunciation) and I were in the students' lounge watching television.

It was quite late and we'd had a bit to drink when I made some small-talk remark about the programme we were watching. Seb acknowledged my comment but as I began to turn my head to carry on the conversation, I noticed Melissa putting her mouth close to his left ear. Perhaps due to the amount she'd drunk, perhaps erroneously emboldened by my position several metres to Seb's right, her attempt at whispering so that I wouldn't hear failed. Pretending I was absorbed in the TV programme, I listened and watched as she mimicked what I had just said. Mocking and disdainful, she placed a particularly caricatured emphasis on one particular word. As she withdrew to her former position a complacent smirk settled on her face. Seb emitted a quick, low snort of approbation.

Almost two years later in August 2002 I was back in Newcastle for a friend's wedding. Seb and Melissa had moved on to London to complete their training by this time, whilst I remained at the Manor as my part-time MA drew to a close. Late in the evening I found myself talking to a Scotsman I'd just met that day; about what I have no idea. As our conversation continued, a very close friend of mine who I've known since I was five years old swayed over to us. He stood listening to what I was saying for a few seconds before angrily interrupting, berating me with the damning if slightly slurred words: "Here man, say it like a Geordie!"

Although taken aback and angry, I decided to simply defuse the situation and direct the conversation elsewhere. In both instances, with Melissa and my friend, I cannot recall the exact word or words that I used to elicit snobbish condescension from the former and indignant remonstrance from the latter. Not that it matters because for both *how* I said it was all-important. Taken together they perfectly illustrate the quandary that many people who leave the North-East often face: a linguistic Catch-22 in which you're damned if you do and you're damned if you don't. A verbal tightrope whose safety nets depend on the arbitrary whims and discretion of the listener; a precarious balancing act that might just be a significant contributory factor in some people's experience of Akenside Syndrome.

Let's deal with the Melissa incident first. It was a straightforward example of accent-related social snobbery and class prejudice. The commonly heard retort that *accent doesn't matter anymore* is feeble-minded, self-justifying to the point of delusion and in many respects simply false. A comprehensive list of commentators from different social backgrounds would appear to agree with this assertion. Ferdinand Mount (upper class), for example, maintains that 'class distinction in voices is the most painful subject' and believes 'our speech and manners have not converged as much as we pretend'.[1]

Kate Fox (middle or upper-middle class judging by the criteria she sets out) alludes to George Bernard Shaw's infamous barb – 'It is impossible for an Englishman to open his mouth without making some other Englishman hate him or despise him' – before insisting: 'We may like to think that we have become less class-obsessed in recent times, but Shaw's observation is as pertinent now as it ever was.' She goes on to say that 'class in England has nothing to do with money, and very little to do with occupation. Speech is all-important ... There are other class indicators ... but speech is the most immediate and most obvious.'[2] This reinforces the observation made in the previous chapter that it is sheer folly to elevate an individual into the 'middle class' on purely economic grounds.

There are others who are not afflicted with what Fox calls the 'phenomenal capacity for collective self-deception' of certain English people when it comes to analysing the true state of affairs relating to accent hierarchy and snobbery.[3] Despite speaking it himself, A.A. Gill insists that Received Pronunciation (RP) is 'such a smug mask for the English' – and lists accent as 'the last great cause of prejudice and distinction.' He elaborates further, claiming:

> Accent is the last great redoubt of prejudice. The race relations industry, that inquisition of fairness and sensitivity, doesn't protect against discrimination by funny voice. You can mock an accent with impunity, and everyone does.

Accent and pronunciation then, in concomitance with their close relation class, form a deeply ingrained triumvirate of acceptable prejudices still rooted in everyday English life. Gill also maintains that accent and pronunciation 'are a never-ending source of subtle snobbery and fury for the English', and suggests that the primary motivation for RP coming into existence in the first place was simple snobbery and the yearning for distinction. Analysing the spiteful, verbal-status-related pastime invented by Nancy Mitford, he refers to it as 'a game of mockery. The way others spoke, the knowing smirk'.[4] A knowing smirk passed down through the decades that briefly flickered on Melissa's face on the evening in question.

Do you think any of these commentators from upper, upper-middle, or middle-class backgrounds would be accused of having a chip on their shoulder for voicing such uncomfortable truths? No, I don't either. Okay, well let's look at the artist Tracey Emin's explanation of why, according to Sean O'Hagan, her work 'was a repository for all the philistinism, mean-spiritedness and class snobbery of modern Britain' for a time:

> 'It's the way I speak, innit?' she says, exaggerating her accent, which would once have been called working-class, 'People take the piss out of my accent all the time. They don't seem to like my voice. In fact, I think a lot of people in this country wish people like me didn't have one, full stop.'[5]

Although speaking before getting in to bed with the Tories by voting for Boris Johnson as London Mayor, and the Conservatives at the 2010 general election (a skankier bed than her detritus-laden effort, some might feel), I don't know. She's being a bit *chippy*, isn't she?

Bringing it a little closer to home, what are we to make of BBC Breakfast's business presenter Stephanie McGovern, from Middlesbrough, claiming in July 2013 that she was 'viewed by some in the organisation to be "too common for telly".' Recalling how at the end of one BBC job interview a manager said to her: 'I didn't realise people like you were clever', McGovern also revealed that 'there are still some viewers who can't accept that someone with my accent can have a brain. It means that I regularly get abuse about it. I've had tweets questioning whether I really did go to university because surely I would have lost my accent if I did; a letter suggesting, very politely, that I get correction therapy; and an email saying I should get back to my council estate and leave the serious work to the clever folk.'[6] Tssk. Typical *chip-on-her-shoulder* northerner, eh? Always whining and moaning.

Of course my reactions to Emin and McGovern are facetious and ironic. A simple attempt at highlighting the irrationality and hypocritical inconsistency of such clichéd claims, and the 'double-bind' people from working-class backgrounds who have accents often find themselves in. McGovern's observations are no different from Kate Fox claiming 'your position on the class scale will always be identifiable by your speech, unless you painstakingly train yourself to use the pronunciation and vocabulary of a different class'; or from Cristina Odone assuring us that unlike in other countries, 'in Britain [a regional accent] reveals not only where on this island you were raised but also where in the social hierarchy you belong'; or indeed Oscar-winning American screenwriter William Goldman acerbically avowing that all Brits 'have in their blood: a murderous sense of class. All they need is to hear you speak a few words and they know everything about you. It is their least appealing trait.'[7]

Reacting to Goldman's comment in a piece of work written near the end of my MA course in 2002, I wrote this:

> I have experienced this excruciating phenomenon first hand many times myself. You can see it in their eyes and their body language as they struggle in vain to distinguish between *what you are saying* and *how you are saying it*. Many times have I endured an uncomfortable glare, avoidance of eye contact, or condescending comments from people with an inferior intellect to my own, as they have struggled to come to terms with the fact that Received Pronunciation is not my mode of verbal address.

Lynsey Hanley, author of *Estates: An Intimate History*, would clearly identify with this. Writing in *The Guardian* about McGovern's comments, she insisted:

> For those who know what it's like to open your mouth and see the person opposite dock your IQ by 40 points, McGovern is a hero for breaking ranks. She's shown up her employer for its institutional classism, and its viewers for swallowing whole the idea that the only acceptable public voice is that which matches the uniform drone of the professional elite.[8]

No doubt she and McGovern understand, as I do, that unlike commentators from different social backgrounds who make similar observations, we open ourselves up to the instinctive 'chip on shoulder' accusation at least partially because, as Harry Pearson has pointed out: 'The stereotype of the Northerner with an inferiority complex is so pervasive in English society that a whole book could be written refuting it without budging it an inch from the national psyche.'[9]

Melissa's little aside can be put in a broader historical context of snobbish disdain towards regional accents. Alistair Moffat and George Rosie identified the Cheshire monk Ranulph Higden, a chronicler writing in the 1300s, as having written what they call the 'first recorded sneer' about North-East speech: 'All the language of the Northumbrians ... is so sharp, piercing, rasping and unformed that we Southerners can rarely understand it.' They also point out that J.B. Priestley concurred six centuries later in *English Journey*, when he whinged: 'To my ear it still sounds a most barbarous, monotonous and irritating twang', with the speech of Geordie men and women being 'equally objectionable.'[10] Melissa's jibe simply illustrated that such attitudes still prevail today – indeed are embedded in the psyche and behaviour of certain individuals from certain social groups.

Furthermore it exemplified the accusation levelled at such speech snobs by Andrew Taylor, author of *A Plum in Your Mouth: Why the Way We Talk Speaks Volumes About Us*, in which he maintained that they are:

> saying that their own speech, their own way of life, is at the centre of the world ... anything that is unfamiliar is bizarre, vulgar, or degenerate. By criticizing the way that other people speak, they are implicitly declaring their own superiority.

An interesting example of what Taylor goes on to call the 'search for certainty and the aching desire to demonstrate superiority' occurred in the now defunct *Observer Sport Monthly* magazine (October 2006 edition), when editor Jason Cowley seized upon Alan Shearer's opening sentence in the previous weekend's edition of *Match of the Day*.[11] It's worth dissecting Cowley's comments to understand the subtleties of such linguistic condescension.

The general gist of his *Editor's Letter* revolved round the issue of sports broadcasting in Britain being 'dominated ... by individuals whose only qualification for their roles is that they once played professional sport themselves.' As such, it is a reasonable piece of analysis. The perceived inadequacies of Sky Sport's cricket broadcasting team during that summer's abandoned Test Match versus Pakistan are referred to, and the broadcasting credentials of Chris Bailey, who fronted the same channel's US Open tennis coverage that year, are also called into question. Then Cowley turns to Shearer. Why, he wails, is Shearer an analyst on *Match of the Day* 'when is he is [sic] neither articulate nor insightful?' Being a tolerant sort of person on such issues, I'll give him the benefit of the doubt on the superfluous 'is' and assume it was a typo or suchlike.

But Cowley affords Shearer no such tolerance. Because what prompted him to switch off the television when Shearer was speaking was not his perceived lack of insight, but a word he used and how he used it. He recounts how Shearer's opening sentence was "Chelsea done today what they do better than any other team", before going on to sniffily proclaim: 'I may be a pedant or even a snob but that 'done' was enough to prompt me to switch off.' Had Shearer standardised his sentence presumably Cowley would not have been so offended. What distressed him so much was not Shearer's Geordie accent *per se*, but his failure to use Standard English.

According to Simon Elmes, who oversaw BBC Radio 4's *Voices* survey, this way of speaking is 'not a question of accent: Standard English is a variety of our language that can be spoken with any number of accents. Rather it's a matter of grammar, vocabulary, spelling and punctuation'. We can only speculate that Shearer's deviation from Standard English upset Cowley's grammatical equilibrium because he views it in much the same way as 'BBC English' used to be viewed: 'as an absolute standard, from which any local variation, regional terminology or irregular syntax were seen at best as quaint and often formally as 'wrong'.'[12]

Renowned Cambridge don Raymond Williams would probably have agreed, having described Standard English in *Keywords* as 'a selected (class-based) use' which 'attempted to convict a majority of native speakers of English of speaking their own language "incorrectly".'[13] This, in my opinion, is what lay at the heart of Cowley's righteous indignation. Perhaps he should read Andrew Taylor's book, which takes as its subject the different ways in which we speak. When discussing Geordie speech patterns, Taylor notes: 'There are also particular survivals of grammar and syntax which would be unfamiliar elsewhere … and there are distinctive past tenses of many verbs'.[14]

Shearer was simply speaking in the idiom of his home town. As current editor of *New Statesman* magazine Cowley is a leading luminary of the left, yet his petulant protest can be interpreted as an example of the prescriptivist clamour for grammar and standardisation in spoken as well as written English more typically associated with the right. A molecular part of the larger crusade-like campaign to civilise the grammatical heathens – the sometimes evangelical zeal of which denotes nothing more than bigoted and narrow-minded intolerance of linguistic difference. Oh, and should Cowley still be wondering whether he is a pedant or a snob, let me reassure him – in this instance, as I see it, he was both.

*   *   *

So Melissa's actions can be seen from an historical perspective of disdain for non-standardised regional accents and dialects, while Cowley's contempt for Shearer's sentence suggests such intolerance remains prevalent in English society. The underlying motivation of both seems clear. But what about my friend's motivation for his more forthright condemnation of how he perceived I was speaking at the wedding? He obviously felt that my monitorial ring was failing in its duty. Well he too was simply following a well-established, if more modern tradition of certain people in the North-East lambasting anyone who leaves the area and is perceived to have lost or changed their accent. For instance, on his website *www.myersnorth.co.uk*, the late literary translator Alan Myers bemoaned the fact that 'Northerners like Kevin Whately … [etc.] are now heard to say 'pass' and 'fast' southern fashion', and maintained that 'John Murray and Jack Charlton try to speak in a posh Geordie.'

Footballers also provoked the ire of Harvey Taylor who, in his chapter entitled *Sporting Heroes* in *Geordies*, commended Jackie Milburn for 'never changing his accent, unlike many of the area's recent footballing exports, whose response to media attention has been variable grotesque attempts at BBC vowels. Paul Gascoigne has only recently succumbed to this new language.'[15] His attitude to accent change by those who leave the area appears to be shared by North-East media figure Malcolm Gerrie, who was involved with iconic Newcastle-based music show *The Tube*. Endorsing the credentials of former Radio 2 boss Lesley Douglas when welcoming her to the board of trustees at Sage Gateshead, he eulogised: 'She's passionately loyal to the region, still gets her backside up here and most importantly has kept her accent.'[16]

If being accused of trying to speak 'posh Geordie' or mangling your vowels isn't enough, how about the serious implication of betraying your own and traitorously aligning yourself with the 'other side'? This is what seemed to be implied by a headline accompanying the lead letter in the *Evening Chronicle*'s *YOUR SHOUT* section on January 2nd 2006, which read: 'I've no time for accent turncoats'. Responding to comments by Peter Arnold (then leader of Newcastle City Council), in which he claimed it was '"deplorable" and "complete nonsense" that Geordies should need to change their accent to get ahead in life",' the letter writer, Mick Bidewell from Kingston Park, regretted that many of them do. Clearly a music aficionado, Bidewell accused three Geordie figures from the music industry (pictures of whom accompanied the letter) of committing accent apostasy.

According to Mick, Sting 'was speaking in broad Geordie' when he saw him at a gig in 1977, but was 'talking like Noel Coward' two years later in a television interview. Pet Shop Boy Neil Tennant 'speaks like a Bond Street jeweller but almost strangles himself trying to keep his Geordie accent in check during interviews', whilst Jimmy Nail is accused of providing 'the supreme example of a Geordie accent being abandoned (albeit short term) … in his *Spender* and *Crocodile Shoes* days'. The letter ended with this defiant assertion:

> Speaking Geordie shouldn't hold back anyone's career but any Geordies who achieve success, only to then abandon their unique accent while at the same time banging-on about their wonderful home town, had better not sit next to me on a bus. In my best Geordie accent I'll tell them exactly where to go!

The complaints of Myers, Taylor and Bidewell, and the tetchy admonition of my friend, hint at an instinctive reaction of contempt felt by some Geordies when they perceive others to have changed their accents. It's a reaction seemingly underpinned by a sense of disappointment, hurt and betrayal, which emphasises the claim that there remains a 'powerful emotional connection between how we speak and where we live'.[17] However, although that might possibly be true of Tyneside more than any other place in the country, it's not always as straightforward as some of the complainants seem to imply.

The derision heaped upon 'accent turncoats' is primarily fuelled by antagonism relating to geography and class. Alan Titchmarsh has touched on this:

> when you've lived down south a bit and you go back up north, everybody thinks, 'Oh, you've gone all posh from being down there.' So you suddenly find yourself torn ... I do notice myself when I go back up north slipping more into northern speak.[18]

Where the criticisms are sometimes misguided, is when the implicit assumption is that all individuals whose accents have altered somewhat have made a conscious class-related decision to change the way they speak. The word *turncoat* conjures up the idea of a conscious act of treachery worthy of the Judas chants once reserved for local footballers who left Newcastle United for pastures new. The underlying allegation is that the speaker is making a conscious, class-related decision (hence Myers's use of the word 'posh'), motivated by notions of social class aspiration; speech being such an integral part of the whole charade of social class, as we have seen.

An arguably quintessential example of this is provided by broadcaster Sue Lawley, a fellow alumna of Melissa at Bristol, who allegedly shed her Midlands accent whilst at the university. Her former colleague Michael Buerk claimed in his autobiography that she had a favoured line when they both worked at the South Wales Echo, in which she said she'd arrived at the paper with a lower second English degree but a First in RP. Lawley and fellow BBC presenter John Humphrys (who lost his Welsh accent and advised Andrew Taylor: 'If you say I have a Welsh lilt, I'll bloody kill you') can, of course, reasonably cite professional expedience; Humphrys has claimed 'you didn't get anywhere in the BBC of 35 years ago if you sounded like you had a coat hanger in your mouth.'[19] Nonetheless, the linguistic mimicry is plain for all to hear; they played the class game, choosing to convert rather

Mark Akenside was born in Newcastle upon Tyne in 1721, the son of a butcher, and he became a physician to royalty and a poet.

Akenside Syndrome is a condition of feeling ambivalent towards Newcastle or Tyneside despite often retaining a strong emotional bond with and/or sincere affection for the area.

On Butcher Bank was the birthplace of Mark Akenside, the son of one of the butchers on the steep street. Born in 1721 he later attended the Royal Free Grammar School and became a leading poet and physician. Different historians' views on his merits, however, vary considerably.

R J Charleton said of him that "His character is not a pleasant one to dwell upon ... his appearance is described as unpromising, if not grotesque ... he had no sense of humour, was peevish and sententious and took a joke very ill. He is said to have been ashamed of his native place, so that "he would sneak through Newcastle when occasion called him thither". Despite his reported faults his name lives on in the name of Akenside Hill and Akenside House, built in 1912 to the design of Marshall and Tweedy. Whilst Akenside's birthplace survived the Great Fire of 1854, it was swept away in the great changes which took place around the Quayside following the construction of the Swing Bridge in the 1870's.

SIR
CHARLES MARK PALMER
———— BARONET ————
BORN AT SOUTH SHIELDS
NOVEMBER 3RD 1822.
FOUNDER OF THE PALMER
WORKS & OF THE TOWN OF
JARROW OF WHICH HE WAS
FIRST MAYOR IN 1875.
ORIGINATOR OF THE FIRST
STEAM SCREW COLLIER
BUILT AT JARROW IN 1851.
MEMBER OF PARLIAMENT
FOR NORTH DURHAM FROM
1874 AND SUBSEQUENTLY
FOR THE JARROW DIVISION.
THIS STATUE ERECTED IN
1903 BY THE WORKMEN OF
PALMER'S COMPANY & A FEW
FRIENDS. COMMEMORATES
A LIFE DEVOTED TO THE
SOCIAL ADVANCEMENT OF
THE WORKING CLASSES. THE
PROSPERITY OF JARROW
& THE INDUSTRIAL
PROGRESS OF
TYNESIDE.

It has been suggested that Newcastle's 'value system, politics, myths and symbols are essentially working-class.' ABOVE: Unveiling of the Palmer Memorial in Jarrow. BELOW: Gearwheel of a ship being made on Tyneside, 1946.

'Our fathers worked on the railway, in the factory, in the shipyard, most of them, and you get the scale of it for this area if you reflect that a factory or shipyard employing five thousand men would be unlikely to count more than two hundred and fifty middle-class folk among them.' An extract from *Kiddar's Luck* by Jack Common. FROM TOP: Swan Hunter shipyard, Wallsend, 1973; Riveting squad at Armstrong's, Elswick, 1915; Pit lads at Charlotte Pit, Benwell, 1929.

The lyrics of Geordie anthem *The Blaydon Races* celebrate Tyneside's ordinary citizens, reinforcing the idea that it is a place of the people.

Class and accent are closely entwined, like the helical chains represented in Charles Jencks's *The DNA Spiral* in Newcastle's Times Square.

As books such as *Larn Yersel' Geordie* and *Todd's Geordie Words and Phrases* demonstrate, many people on Tyneside are proud of the way they speak, but is the perceived unintelligibility of Geordies actually true? Ant's accent is stronger than Dec's, and the way Alan Shearer speaks upset *New Statesman* editor Jason Cowley.

LARN YERSEL' GEORDIE

SCOTT DOBSON

TODD'S
Geordie words and phrases

... an aid to communication on Tyneside and thereabouts

ALAN SHEARER TESTIMONIAL 2006

The Bigg Market area of Newcastle has long been a place of communal gathering, but Stuart Maconie recently described it as 'a gladiatorial arena devoted to orgiastic alcohol consumption, moral licentiousness and sexual excess.' ABOVE: Bigg Market, 1820.

Erected by Temperance agitators in the nineteenth century, the red-brick water fountain in the Bigg Market has seemingly failed to convert many Geordies to its cause.

© ncjMedia

Alcohol courses through the cultural bloodstream of Tyneside and the ongoing commitment to communal congregation in pubs can act as an agent of social cohesion and integration. ABOVE RIGHT: Sir John Hall on the Newcastle Brown Ale production line at the now demolished brewery site near St James' Park.

According to *Times* journalist George Caulkin, Newcastle is 'a city where football and socialising remain indelibly linked … whose rhythms are defined by sport and alcohol.' LEFT: The famous Strawberry pub sign and the magpie mascot on the former Newcastle United Supporters' Social Club. BELOW: Wor Jackie's pub in Byker preparing for the 1996 FA Cup Final.

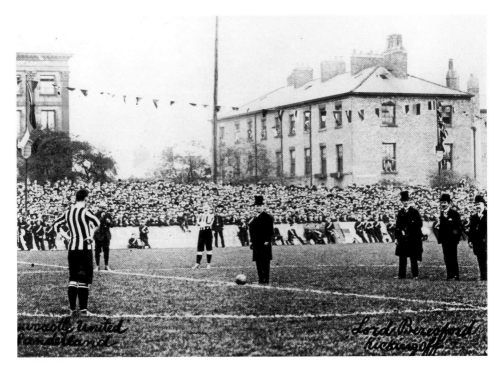

Harry Pearson has said that historically 'football became inextricable from existence itself' for some North-East people. ABOVE: Kick-off at the Newcastle v Sunderland derby, 1904. LEFT: Newcastle United cup-winners parade, 1932. BELOW: Scene from a game in 1950.

St James' Park dominates the Newcastle skyline. The Taylor Report, by Lord Chief Justice Peter Taylor – born and bred in Newcastle and seen here receiving the freedom of the city in 1992 – led to today's all-seater colossus (right). ABOVE: The stadium viewed from the west in 1975.

LEFT: The outpouring of grief following the death of Sir Bobby Robson exemplified football's capacity to unite people on Tyneside and beyond. ABOVE: Members of the Magpie Group including Sir John Hall (centre) and Malcolm Dix (right) pictured alongside the renovated St James' Park gates. Football is said to be a religion for many Geordies, and the decision to temporarily rename the stadium the Sports Direct Arena aroused divine dissent from nearby St Andrew's Church.

The late novelist Gordon Burn talked of walking against the crowds streaming out of St James' Park to do homework when he was a boy, insisting that it 'seemed a reasonable direction in which to be heading.' And when Barry Rogerson was filmed punching a police horse following Newcastle's defeat to Sunderland in 2013, it prompted the *Chronicle* to ask: 'Does this make you ashamed to be a Tynesider?'

than subvert, unlike Humphrys' fellow Welsh news-reading colleague Huw Edwards, who, despite also experiencing prejudice and barriers due to his accent as he rose through the BBC ranks, 'took a decision not to change it … because I felt it was an important part of my identity.'[20]

As Simon Elmes, who in a neat reversal of both the BBC and Bristol dynamic harbours a 'lifelong regret' about having a Bristolian accent drummed out of him as a child, has said:

> attitudes to accent and to an extent to regional vocabulary have much to
> do with feelings about social class, and a 'purer', less regional speech has
> for 200 years been seen as the essential concomitant of self-improvement.[21]

It would appear that some Geordies are not immune to this phenomenon – Harry Pearson has identified 'that vibrato nasal voice some North-East-erners affect because they think it makes them sound posh.'[22] Meanwhile Chris Donald has talked of how he thought the Newcastle bar owner Joe Robertson, 'developed an accent to match the superficial refinement of his 'hay clarse' drinking establishments', and A.A. Gill has observed that 'Received Pronunciation is … the second accent of more British people than any other. Very few Geordies train their voices to Somerset'.[23]

The Geordie who Charles Jennings encountered in Newcastle's Turkish baths during his tour of 'the North' provides a particularly stark example of Gill's point: 'in 1980 I took elocution lessons and became a Con*sor*vative and since then I've never looked back.'[24] It would seem the lessons weren't entirely successful. Andrew Taylor has opined that Received Pronunciation 'might often just as well stand for Really Pretentious … [and] continues to hang like a damp fog over the whole subject of how we speak.' According to him, the expansion of public schools in the nineteenth century fostered the conditions in which people: 'Instead of speaking with an accent which revealed their geographical background … began to speak with an accent that revealed their social class … The whole point of RP is its geographical anonymity.'[25] Clearly many people still attempt to adapt their accents moti-vated by these often interwoven desires: hiding their geographical roots whilst proclaiming their social class aspiration and perceived superiority – think Hyacinth Bucket.

As Tyneside remains a predominantly working-class area where lots of people are overtly proud of their geographical origins and the way that they speak, it is not difficult to see why umbrage is sometimes taken with those who seem to have changed their accents for these reasons. Some in the North-East see it as negative, false and an act of disloyalty; a point illustrated by David John Douglass's use of the words *collaborator, sneak* and *crawler*. It is seen as being un-Geordie-like – the perceived affectation involved is incompatible with the dominant ethos of the area, as Phil Sutcliffe implied in his 1991 interview with Sting. This way of thinking is not unreasonable. By and large I agree with it. However, these are by no means the *only* reasons for people's accents changing, and to lump everybody into this category is short-sighted and inappropriate. But before looking at the multiple influences that can affect the speech of those who leave the region, it's worth examining the changes and differences that can occur, or rather have occurred, within the confines of Tyneside itself.

Comparing the Geordie voices recorded for his survey in 2004 with previous recordings made on Tyneside twenty-one years earlier in 1983, Simon Elmes noted: 'What's immediately striking about the recordings ... is the change that appears to have taken place in the [intervening] years'. Following on from this, he infers:

> To an extent ... there's ... been a degree of reconstruction in the language. Broad accents remain, but much of the old Geordie talk is being supplanted by a vigorous, but different blend of humorous metaphor and terms borrowed from other sources or adapted and made new on Tyneside. The transformation seems vaguely in keeping with the city's recent metamorphosis.[26]

An inevitable consequence of globalisation, the digital mass media age and previously unthought-of geographical mobility, Elmes's findings corroborate Taylor's claim that accents 'are always under pressure: that's how they change and develop.'[27] Elmes relates how neither of the sets of people interviewed from the Newcastle area in 2004 had particularly broad accents, but describes how one interviewee 'grew broader in his speech by the second' as he became animated whilst sharing an anecdote.[28] It's an incident which clearly demonstrates how we can all modify and modulate our accent depending on the situation we find ourselves in and whom we are speaking to.

Andrew Taylor maintains that we all speak differently at different times and believes that most people 'who were brought up with any sort of regional accent can slip in and out of it almost without a thought.' From a pragmatic perspective, he also contends that '*changing* an accent is something that most of us do all the time, and it is likely to become an even more common skill in the next few years.'[29] An assertion that Mark from Ashington, a schoolboy interviewed by Elmes in 2001, clearly had a keen awareness and appreciation of:

> naouw a lot of pe'ple my eige are star'n' a speak maw cleeahly withou' as much of an accent; as things like the industries are cheingin', as you ha' to communicate with different pe'ple in other paahts of the coon'ry, an' still meik yourself un'ahstood.[30]

The many Geordies who work in call centres would no doubt empathise with Mark's perceptive sentiment, familiar as they are with utilising a gently modified Geordie accent for economic purposes (that they have to do so in light of the area's industrial decline is another matter altogether, not within the remit of this chapter).

Added to this, we have to consider that not all Geordies speak with the same breadth of accent or use the same amount of dialect words to start with. To imply that there is an absolute verbal Geordie norm ignores the evolutionary aspect of language, and does not allow for the fact that 'most people have several different grades of speech into which they can slip without even noticing it.'[31] Geordie prescriptivists, whose hackles rise at any perceived deviation from a supposed (i.e. imaginary) 'Standard Geordie', do not seem to accept that many accents are, in modern-day reality, a wide spectrum of varying breadths incorporating differing degrees of dialect usage. There is no such thing as *pure* Geordie. Within Tyneside itself accent breadth and dialect usage fluctuate on an individual basis. Teachers, more often than not, will speak differently from factory workers; locally-born newsreaders employ a fairly standardised form of English with dashes of

Geordie thrown in – Ant even speaks differently from Dec, for crying out loud! They all speak Geordie though. Just in subtly different ways.

If we accept that spoken Geordie is a spectrum and recognise the constant pressure on our accents which has seen them evolve *within* the geographical confines of the North-East in recent times, then a fuller understanding of accent change within individuals who have left the region might be easier to achieve. Many develop what Taylor calls bilingualism in English, the primary motivation for which is often simply to make themselves more easily understood and accepted in their new environment.[32] This mode of dual address can be quite dramatic and not clearly delineated in some; to my ear the journalist and broadcaster Carole Malone often fluctuates between the broad Geordie of a North Shields fishwife and a kind of affected theatrical 'posh' within the course of a few sentences. For others it is more subtle.

When I first moved to Guildford I worked part-time in Marks and Spencer, and whilst I often got a positive reaction to my accent from customers, I was also asked to repeat myself on occasions (incidentally, I was also sometimes asked which part of Ireland I came from). It reminded me of an episode of *Family Fortunes* many moons ago, in which the question put to the hundred people surveyed was something like: *Which British accent is the most difficult to understand?* A surge of defiant pride rushed through my chest as Geordie was revealed as the top answer. Nevertheless, after a while it becomes irksome and irritating if you can't always make yourself understood in a new environment, and for some – consciously or otherwise – little concessions begin to be made in certain situations. A slowing down and more deliberate use of speech here, a more standardised pronunciation there, and a gradual lessening of dialect usage in day-to-day exchanges generally (the extent of which will obviously depend on where you were on the Geordie speech spectrum to start with).

Relating the story of Bobby Thompson, a Northumbrian champion horti-culturalist and public speaker who had difficulty making himself understood in High Spen, Simon Elmes explained that his dialect was impeding compre-hension. The adaptations Thompson had to make represent for Elmes, 'the typical story of dialect change. When the message can't get through, you have to modify the medium to one both sides can understand. Linguists call it 'levelling'.'[33] And despite Tom Hadaway's defiant rallying call in *Geordies*

– 'Of course, there are problems of access and understanding. Concessions need to be made. Then let 'Them' make them. There are more of 'Uz" – when you are the person in the new environment, if you feel levelling is necessary, naturally enough it has to be made predominantly on your side.[34]

Levelling is what many Geordies who leave the area seemingly feel compelled to do, at least to some extent. The longer an individual spends away from the place of her or his upbringing, the more likely it becomes that a marked levelling of verbal address will occur. But is the perceived unintelligibility of Geordie speech accurate? Were the hundred people surveyed right? Isn't this just a ready-made excuse for those who change their accents for snobbish reasons but are too cowardly or lacking in self-awareness to admit it? Well, we'll continue to look at this as we go on, but for now while there are certainly some that delude themselves as to why their accents have changed, there is evidence both from within and without that the Geordie accent and dialect have been historically difficult to understand.

In her book *The Wire in the Blood*, later made into a TV series starring Robson Green, Alnmouth resident Val McDermid describes the difficulties of a young female character from outside the region passing through Newcastle Central Station for the first time:

> Changing trains wasn't quite so much fun. It was growing dark, and she couldn't understand a word anyone on Newcastle station tannoy said. They didn't sound like Jimmy Nail or Kevin Whately off the telly. They sounded like aliens.[35]

Stuart Maconie and Charles Jennings approach the issues of 'Northernness' and the North/South divide from diametrically opposed viewpoints, yet both have similar things to say about how Geordies speak. Talking about the first northerner he'd ever met (whilst at university), Jennings recalled him coming from Tyne and Wear:

> to my suburban London eyes, he looked and sounded ridiculous ... this caricature out of *The Likely Lads*, a fellow countryman of mine whose manners and customs were so alien to me he might as well have come from Alabama. He was working class

Despite later asserting that the Geordie accent is 'wonderfully beguiling', he also maintained that on occasions 'Geordie sounds like ordinary English spoken backwards', and recalled a World War Two veteran telling him that Geordie regiments campaigning in North Africa didn't have to use the same code-words or radio security as other regiments. This was supposedly because 'since most of what they said was incomprehensible to other English speakers, it was presumed to be completely unintelligible to the Germans.'[36] Sid Waddell might have begged to differ.

Unlike Jennings, who sets out to denigrate the North, Stuart Maconie's driving motivation in *Pies and Prejudice* is the affirmation of 'Northernness'. Yet he too recalls an incident during the 1980s in which he encountered a Geordie at a college bar and had some communication problems:

> Basically, I can't understand a word he's saying ... I can grasp the odd word here and there ... But the overall sensation is a torrent of alien sound ... stretched vowels, random emphasis and arcane dialect flow from his mouth and right over the top of my head. I feel acutely uncomfortable. This is the sort of difficulty an effete fop from Purley or Esher would have but not a kindred spirit.

Echoing Jennings in sentiment again, he goes on to say that Geordies 'sound lovely, while having by far and away the strangest accent in England.'[37] All three observers, you will notice, employ the word *alien* (or derivatives thereof), emphasising the sense of 'otherness' with which Geordies are often viewed by people in other parts of the country.

From the other side of the equation Paul Gascoigne has spoken of the initial discomfort, self-consciousness and alienation that can be felt by some Geordies when they are in an unfamiliar place. Talking about Bobby Robson being manager of Ipswich at the time of his first football trial, he remembered: 'I liked the idea that he was a Geordie and could understand what I was saying.' He loved being in the England squad with Peter Beardsley partly because 'at least he understood my accent', and, when contemplating whether to go to Manchester United rather than Spurs, a major consideration was the fact that when playing for England Under-21s, 'a lot of the southern lads couldn't understand my accent, or so they claimed.'[38]

All of which appears to lend credence to Sting's proclamation that Tyneside's powerful regional identity is buttressed by the Geordie dialect and accent, which many fellow Britons struggle to comprehend. If Peter Griffin, the potty-mouthed patriarch of American animated sitcom *Family Guy* is to be believed, this may affect Sting's singing style too. In an episode entitled *We Love You, Conrad*, Griffin asserts that only the last three words of any Sting lyric are understandable. However, bearing in mind what he said to Phil Sutcliffe and Andrew Marr, and if snarky 2010 song *Here Comes Geordie* by Richard Thompson – formerly of Fairport Convention – is accurate, this could be because his inflection is closer to Jamaica than Jarrow. It's not officially about Sting you understand, but, well, listen to the lyrics and make of it what you will.

The list goes on. Talking to a retired shipyard worker from Wallsend wasn't easy for Harry Pearson, because as well as being a bit deaf his accent 'was as thick as a plumber's mate'.[39] If none of these observers possess enough gravitas, then how about a man who has been described as the region's most prominent social historian; respected academic and one of the doyens of Tyneside-focussed social history, Dr Bill Lancaster? He too has talked about the 'impenetrable dialect' of Tyneside.[40] But before getting lost in a self-fulfilling vortex over our own perceived unintelligibility, we'd do well to stand back and apply a little linguistic and historical perspective. And to remember Brendan Healy's astute assertion that when it comes to perceptions of Geordie speech people can be stupid.'

The first thing to point out is the difference between dialect and accent, as the two are often erroneously used interchangeably. Andrew Taylor has pointed out the separation that ought to be made but regularly isn't:

> Dialects have their own vocabularies and grammatical structures – different past tenses and the use of a direct instead of an indirect object, for instance, so they say *I give it 'im*, rather than *I gave it to him* – while accent is concerned only with the sound of the words and the rhythm and intonation of the sentence.[41]

To say that historically the North-East *dialect* has been difficult for people outside the region to understand seems perfectly reasonable. To say that the modern-day Geordie *accent* is any more unintelligible than any other accent, regional or national, is utter nonsense. When David Almond, author of *Skellig*, appeared on Radio 4's *Desert Island Discs* in March 2013, his accent was distinct, authoritative, perfectly understandable and unapologetically Geordie. The millions of people who watch the likes of Sarah Millican, Ross Noble, Ant and Dec, Si King of the *Hairy Bikers*, Charlie Hardwick, Chris Ramsey and Matt Baker on television, seem to have little problem comprehending them. And you're far more likely to hear people around the country complaining that they can't understand call centre workers from India rather than Tyneside.

On numerous occasions down South I've had someone comment on my accent in conversation – be it complimentary or cutting – before going on to say how they can't understand the Geordie accent, whilst never once asking me to repeat myself. Saying Geordies are unintelligible is a deeply ingrained national cliché; part of the Geordie stereotype, the Geordie brand. It's like saying Scotsmen are tight, Yorkshire people are bluff, scousers are frizzy-permed moustachioed thieves, West Country folk are yokels, the Welsh shag sheep and southerners are all posh snobs. It's outdated and lazy. And while I understand the defiance of wearing this perceived unintelligibility as a badge of regional pride, to some extent it plays into the hands of those who would insist we must change our accents to get on in life. In some ways it is the sound of the bullied nervously agreeing with the bully, cowering in the corner (of the country), not wanting to be laughed at. Concurring when we should be contradicting.

For Barbara Ellen, bullying was at the heart of what she took to be a prevailing lack of sympathy and sense of *schadenfreude* when Cheryl Cole was dropped from the American version of *X Factor* in 2011, allegedly because of – you guessed it – the unintelligibility of her accent:

> if we say we are fine with what happened to Cheryl Cole, then we're also fine with myriad forms of bullying, not least cultural, regional, and professional … There is nothing uniquely unintelligible about the beautiful Geordie accent, no more than, say, the equally lyrical Scottish or Scouse. When the Beatles took America by storm and Lennon said: "Give peace a chance", no one said: "Eh? What did you say? Could you repeat that?" Similarly,

the likes of Sean Connery and Billy Connolly have worked in America for decades. All this, but they can't cope with a bit of Geordie? You're having me on, pet.[42]

The latter observation is all the more galling because, contrary to the country-wide perception, in terms of historic language migration and spread Scottish people talk like Geordies – not the other way round. There is no foundation in logic or common sense for supposing that Val McLane is any less intel-ligible than Val McDermid, or that Alan Shearer is harder to understand than Alan Hansen.

Despite all this, anyone who can't accept that change in the voices of those who left the area in the past sometimes occurred – often unconsciously – due to the simple necessity of being more easily understood in a new envi-ronment, is being a bit thick. This brings us nicely on to the next motivation for accent change. As Lynsey Hanley and many others including Jimmy Nail have observed, in England a person's social class is not the only factor that people think they can ascertain from an individual's accent: a simultaneous estimation of their intelligence – or lack thereof – is also often made.

A recurring sketch in the recent *Harry and Paul* shows, co-starring Harry Enfield and Paul Whitehouse, featured the latter as a thick, unintelligible, working-class Geordie called Clive. Even allowing for the fact that a fairly jaundiced representation of class and accent foibles permeated the whole series, the lazy, uninspired use of this Geordie stereotype seemed to me as anachronistic and dated as Bernard Manning telling jokes about 'Pakis', or Alf Garnett fulminating about 'wogs' and 'faggots'. I am not implying that Whitehouse or Enfield are racist, but unlike one of Enfield's previous Geordie characters (between them they have done a few over the years), Buggerallmoney, this new creation had no satirical edge or geopolitical subtext. Buggerallmoney also had the distinct and rather more important advantage of actually being reasonably funny.

Whitehouse's use of this hackneyed Geordie cliché demonstrated not only his waning comic perception (Enfield's withered and died long ago, regardless of what BAFTA like to think), but also the fact that the way Geordies speak is still thought of by some as primarily comedic. Catherine Tate's sketch show included the character 'Geordie Georgie' speaking with a caricatured Geordie accent, and Omid Djalili's show featured him playing an unreconstructable Geordie who, despite efforts to change, keeps reverting to chauvinistic outbursts in a broad Geordie accent. Countless stand-up comedians have done Geordie accent segments as part of their routine.

Comic Dialect is actually the chapter heading of Tom Hadaway's contribution to *Geordies*. In it he expressed the fear that entitling the chapter this way could be seen as an affront, 'as though it were … a kind of rustic frailty, funny because it is the vocabulary of idiots'. He went on to suggest that 'language is power, and having our dialect tolerated as merely amusing is one way of rendering us powerless – one way of denying us a share.'[43] Although some would argue the joke is on the upper-middle class characters that treat Whitehouse's Geordie as a pet, Hadaway's sentiment resonates throughout the sketches featuring this one-dimensional character.

For those who move away from the North-East wariness of ridicule, not being taken seriously and being judged can be strong: particularly when the move made is to another part of England. They are conscious of the fact that people 'expect the way we speak to reveal who we are. Or rather, they expect it to slot us into one of a series of preconceptions.'[44] The inability of some people to see the person behind the accent can be mind-numbing. Although there are positive associations with Geordie accents, as various polls have shown (attractive, warm, friendly, trustworthy, down to earth, reassuring), Whitehouse's representation reminds us that they coexist alongside negative ones such as unintelligent, uncouth, simple, inarticulate and working class in a derisive sense. When you find yourself surrounded by people who do not speak the same way as you, the necessity of making yourself understood can at times be accompanied by a simultaneous desire to be respected, taken seriously and not be seen as simply a novelty figure.

As always, the extent of this need will vary between individuals. For some it will be an unconscious desire, while others will be acutely conscious of it and deliberately modify their accent in certain situations or when communicating with certain individuals. Taken to extremes it can smack of pretension, insecurity or snobbery. But for many whose accents modify for this reason it will be part of a deeper, multi-layered psychological and emotional yearning to be accepted in their new surroundings. When geographical relocation is added to the assertion that a majority of people 'in an unconscious effort to please the person they are speaking to, will adapt their accent slightly to suit the circumstances', the development of a dual or multi-address verbal capacity seems almost inevitable.[45] Also inevitable is the fact that these subtle shades of vocal manipulation will at times overlap, a bit like an impressionist inadvertently allowing a hint of Frank Spencer into his Tony Blair.

Some will know Geordies who have emigrated to different parts of the world and developed, say, an Australian or American twang. Conversely, many Tynesiders will know of someone who has moved to the area and whose speech is now embellished with a few Geordieisms. Interviewing Newcastle United's Italian defender Davide Santon for the *Chronicle* in 2013, Lee Ryder approvingly related how 'he now speaks with a Geordie twang, occasionally slipping an "aye" or a "like" into conversation.'[46] According to fellow journalist Emma Brockes the accent of actor Jamie Bell, who played Billy Elliot in the film, was 'all over the place' when they chatted, which he attributed to 'living out of a suitcase since I was 15.'[47] Robert Rowell, a polyglot accountant born and raised in Gateshead but who has spent many years living in European countries such as France, similarly talked in *Back Lanes and Muddy Pitches* about how, whilst at college in Sheffield, he 'pretty much adapted to all the … Sheffield expressions and customs'.[48]

If people who attempt to change their accents while still living on Tyneside are thought of as primarily snobbish, those that leave sometimes suffer the added indignity of being accused of trying to hide their geographical origins. The former, thinking herself a superior Geordie, may be a snob but at least she is a Geordie snob. The latter's perceived misdemeanour is more heinous – that of trying to deny the very fact that he's a Geordie altogether. In reality it's rarely that simple or straightforward.

My own accent may have mellowed a little but I've never said 'ba*h*th', 'gra*h*ss' or 'cla*h*ss' in my life. Delivering post in Woking, Surrey at the start of 2007, the person at the other end of an intercom sounded confused and quizzically repeated a word I had just said: "Purst?" In 2008 at the Pitcher and Piano pub on Newcastle's Quayside, the southern wife of a Gateshead born-and-raised mate struggled to hear what I was saying above the general din. She tetchily likened me to none other than the Paul Whitehouse character! After being introduced to a new work colleague in Havant, Hampshire in June 2010, she stated that I didn't seem to have a very broad accent; yet as I was measured for a suit in Winchester later that year, the assistant apologised for taking my name down incorrectly because of my "thick Geordie" accent.

Speaking on the phone at the end of 2007 to the same friend who'd angrily upbraided me in 2002, he actually complimented me on *not* losing my accent. But in 2013 a Newcastle accountant said I'd lost my accent and a young Dutch tour guide expressed surprise that I didn't have one. I patiently corrected them by offering a condensed version of the themes discussed in this chapter. The former revealed that family members sometimes accused her of "going posh", but said it was simply the nature of the job to be able to adapt it a bit. Bemused by the latter's observation – made on the viewing platform of the Westerkerk in Amsterdam – I asked to whom she was comparing my accent. She said the cast of *Geordie Shore*. Hmmm. Later in 2013, a dreadful snob of an accountant in Hampshire haughtily pretended she couldn't understand a word I was saying because of my accent when I rang, denying me three times before transferring me to a colleague, who had no problem whatsoever.

At a family gathering in Portsmouth at around the same time, prompted by southern relatives commenting on the fact that I'd still kept my accent despite living away for so long, I mentioned the first two anecdotes. They were genuinely incredulous that anybody could think I didn't have a Geordie accent. Make no mistake about it – your accent will always be in the ears of the person listening to it. As Geordies we are perpetually on that verbal tightrope. Melissa would no doubt still find much to snigger about in the way I speak today but whatever she, my friend, or anyone else might think, my mode of speaking will never be exactly the same as it was before I left Newcastle. And frankly, *Ah divvent give a shite.*

*   *   *

Class and accent are so intimately entwined that a diagram of the two might see them represented as helical chains wrapped round the axis of a double helix, something akin to Charles Jencks's sculpture in Newcastle's Times Square. Consciousness of both remains deeply embedded in the cultural DNA of the English, to the point where it has been suggested that 'our obsession with regional accents [is] simply class warfare by another name'.[49] That American regional accents often permeate across vast distances and embrace all socio-economic groups is routinely commented upon. Similar claims have been made about Newcastle, bolstering the city's boast of being a largely classless conurbation where a high level of cultural convergence has evolved. The received wisdom appears to be that although the accents of the middle classes on Tyneside may not be as broad as their working-class brethren – and they almost certainly use less dialect – they still talk a recognisable form of Geordie.

At first glance this seems a reasonable claim. As we have seen, the Geordie accent, like all others, is an ever-evolving spectrum. It is not a standardised, inflexible, monotone entity. It's more like a colour-coded paint chart, with different hues of the same colour ranging from the pale to the vivid. Few born and bred Geordies may speak 'pure' RP, but the claim that many people 'speak some form of modified RP which reflects their native accent' is true of Tyneside too. Similarly, amongst Geordie emigrants there will be 'those who retain some aspects of their regional accents but modify others', which in turn exemplifies the assertion that 'the vast majority of people *do* retain that echo: relatively few want to cut themselves off entirely from their roots.'[50]

Despite all this, Tynesiders are not somehow immune to the divisive residual influence that centuries of verbal prejudice has rooted in the national consciousness. And it isn't just one-way traffic. Rob Colls has discussed the emergence of Geordie dialect as a 'regional badge', insisting: 'what is crucial here is that if the dialect was construed as regional and open to all, its true guardians were the working class … it was the other classes who were invited to join the workers'. When he goes on to maintain: 'Even today, a middle-class Geordie sounds wrong', it obliges us to acknowledge the Akenside Syndrome implications for those whose voices are located on the paler end of the Geordie accent chart.[51]

Even allowing for the possibility that Colls was referring to the general idea of middle-class Geordies being wrong, rather than specifically the way they speak, it nonetheless broadens the potential avenue of ambivalence speculated on in the previous chapter. In an exchange of e-mails with Chris Donald about the themes to be explored in this book, he talked of always having felt 'half Geordie and half not Geordie.' It's an unquestionable expression of ambivalence which, of course, consists of 'the coexistence of two opposed and conflicting emotions, etc.'[52] At school kids would say that he didn't have a Geordie accent and was posh. It's a scenario many will recognise and further exemplifies the English working-class strain of a universal human tendency to dichotomise, in which the population is composed of 'us' and the 'posh'.

Although some might argue that the majority of working-class Tynesiders are instinctively inclusive and accept people with weaker accents as bona fide Geordies regardless, as with any social or human group the reality is always more complex. The quote by David John Douglass and the experience of Chris Donald certainly hint at historical speech-based social division on Tyneside. Speaking of earlier times, Jack Common's Kiddar has this to say about his 'middle class' acquaintance Edmund: 'his speech, and his way of dressing, the atmosphere of him, was so strangely different from our own you tended to set him down as a sort of girl of another species.'[53]

Instances of people reacting with instinctive hostility towards someone who speaks RP, or simply has a less pronounced accent than themselves, are by no means unheard of on Tyneside. Accusations of them being 'posh', 'stuck-up', and thinking they are 'better than us' may accompany such outbursts. It's a defensive reaction that can involve feelings of inferiority and low self-esteem, alongside not wanting to be judged. Although understandable and not without justification at times, when it evolves into a default reaction to those who speak differently it becomes futile, divisive and self-defeating. It can be seen as the flip-side of social class-related accent snobbery (i.e. inverted snobbery), or as a conditioned, combative response to the centuries of accumulated prejudice against regional or 'working-class' accents. Both impulses pronounce loud and clear: 'They don't sound like us, so they aren't like us: it's all about belonging.'[54]

Feeling unsure whether you belong to a certain group, society, class, city, region etc. can bring with it multiple anxieties: *Do I fit in? Am I accepted? Am I one of them? Do I talk like them?* These are major considerations when contemplating Akenside Syndrome and the dismal ubiquity of accent prejudice in England has to be factored into the equation. Because the so-called dominant ethos or prevalent atmosphere of a place does not necessarily inoculate individuals from alienating experiences – in fact it can have precisely the opposite effect. But we must move on now from what comes out of Geordies' mouths to what goes in them. Anyone fancy a pint?

If there's one product that defines Tyneside,
it has to be the dark-brown beer which the
world knows as Newcastle Brown Ale.
*TYNESIDE: A History of Newcastle and
Gateshead from Earliest Times*

[Newcastle has] an ability to party unmatched in Europe
Lonely Planet guide to Britain, 2005

Newcastle's deeply rooted devotion to drink
amongst some has regularly captured the most
attention and continues to this day as an integral
part of the city's cultural image, promoted
in its sanitised form as 'Party City'.
Brian Bennison *Drink in Newcastle*, in
Newcastle upon Tyne: A Modern History

Newcastle has a drink problem ... We need to
wake up to the fact that we are in the middle of an
alcohol crisis and that new approaches are needed ...
It's only recently that we've steered the debate
away from city centre issues and started to look
at the real problem, alcohol in the home...
Nick Forbes, leader of Newcastle City Council,
addressing a national drink conference in Manchester,
quoted in *The Journal* 19th May 2012

Getting drunk all the time, to escape feeling
depressed, now that I did like, no question ...
I didn't like waking up in the morning, not
remembering what had happened, feeling
ashamed and filthy and guilty, feeling crap.
Paul Gascoigne in *GAZZA: My Story*

PILLAR THREE

Drink

EVER SINCE RESEARCHING THE TEMPERANCE MOVEMENT ON TYNESIDE whilst at Newcastle College, I've found the red-brick water fountain in Newcastle's Bigg Market appealingly anomalous. Erected by Temperance agitators in the nineteenth century, its abstinence-advocating inscription 'WATER IS BEST' seems utterly at odds with its surroundings – the Bigg Market having been recently described as 'a gladiatorial arena devoted to orgiastic alcohol consumption, moral licentiousness and sexual excess.'[1] As proselytising public monuments go, its ability to convert Geordies to teetotalism has proved as effective as a sculpture proclaiming 'Monogamy Works' in Amsterdam's red light district might have been. Whereas the first two pillars of Geordie identity examined who we allegedly are, the following two explore what we supposedly do. And what we are renowned for doing, indeed what we are Europe's finest proponents of it would seem, is getting pissed.

Although a country becoming synonymous with a particular drink is not unusual, either through historic consumption and/or effective marketing (e.g. Russia/vodka, Scotland/whiskey, Australia/Foster's, Ireland/Guinness), it is hard to think of another city, certainly in the UK, whose association with an alcoholic drink is so deeply entrenched. And if the cultural symbolism of Newcastle Brown Ale is emblematic of a broader dynamic, whereby 'Newcastle's long relationship with Bacchus ... [and the city's] passionate, unswerving attachment to drink in some quarters' continues to form an integral part of the area's culture and identity, then any potential link to Akenside Syndrome is worth investigating.[2]

Newcastle's seemingly unquenchable thirst for alcohol can, of course, be viewed from a national perspective. Contemplating his fellow countrymen, Jeremy Paxman wondered why 'a minority of the English population think that the only way to have a good time is to get disgustingly drunk'; while A.A. Gill has postulated that binge-drinking 'is the English calamity. Not just bingeing individuals, but bingeing communities.'[3] Statistics from two independent reports released in 2006 supported the claim that binge-drinking is a national malaise, but also confirmed that Geordies can't help going the extra yard (of ale). Based on statistics collated between 2004-2006 and set against a national average of 18%, a report by The Centre for Public Health showed Newcastle to be the binge-drinking capital of the country, with 29.2% of the population drinking at least double the daily recommended level at least one or more times per week.

While that statistic may bring a proud tear of pure alcohol to some Geordies' eyes, when we consider that the Government's Health Profile of England report, published later in 2006, demonstrated that 'the North-East was the worst region in England for smoking, drinking, life expectancy and deaths from cancer and circulatory disease', and also statistics quoted in The Journal in 2009 suggesting the North-East had 12 of England's top 20 bingeing communities, some might want to give the Bigg Market fountain's inscription a little more thought.[4] Further statistics released at the end of 2012 led to claims that the high self-harm rate in the North-East may well be linked to above average alcohol consumption, and the obvious question is this: why do so many Tynesiders feel compelled to console themselves through drink to the extent that for some it becomes tantamount to self-harm in itself?

Beyond the regional and national outlook lies a broader human dimension to drinking alcohol. According to Sigmund Freud the human condition, whereby our natural aggressive instincts are in constant tension with the prohibitive, censorious forces of civilisation, ensures:

The life imposed on us is too hard for us to bear: it brings too much pain, too many disappointments, too many insoluble problems. If we are to endure it, we cannot do without palliative measures … Of such measures there are perhaps three kinds: powerful distractions, which cause us to make light of our misery, substitutive satisfactions, which diminish it, and intoxicants, which anaesthetize us to it. Something of this sort is indispensable.

Clearly the need for altered states of consciousness is innately human, and as they deal with everyday existential dilemmas many Geordies apparently opt for the third of Freud's measures. He goes on to state:

The effect of intoxicants in the struggle for happiness and in keeping misery at a distance is seen as so great a boon that not only individuals, but whole nations, have accorded them a firm place in the economy of the libido … We know, after all, that by 'drowning our sorrows' we can escape at any time from the pressure of reality and find refuge in a world of our own that affords us better conditions for our sensibility. It is well known that precisely this property of intoxicants makes them dangerous and harmful.[5]

Although the Geordie Nation certainly accords alcohol a firm place in the economy of its collective libido, we must remember that we're not talking about all Geordies. It's worth reiterating that we are simply observing qualities and behaviour patterns common or marked enough to be noticeable and significant.

Nonetheless when Paul Gascoigne, who spent five weeks in an American rehab centre in early 2013 amidst fears for his life, talks about never even liking the taste of alcohol and only drinking to numb his brain and achieve oblivion, and Jimmy Nail – a teetotaller for many years – recounts in his autobiography the at least partially drink-related problems of his younger years, it's hard to escape the impression that the heavy-drinking culture of Tyneside may be viewed by some with ambivalence symptomatic of Akenside Syndrome. But before this persistent talk of drinking to alleviate existentialist angst drives us all down town for a treble, it's important to acknowledge a more positive aspect of Newcastle's drink culture.

Alongside a strong sense of classlessness, Bill Lancaster believes a 'carnivalesque atmosphere' to be the city's other most important modern characteristic. When discussing what he describes as 'Newcastle's unique form of urban sociability', he also notes the 'deep historic continuities' that underpin 'the present-day noise, banter, affability and exuberant sense of social ownership of the city's central area'.[6] Viewed this way the enduring commitment to communal congregation assumes a political or ideological dimension, exemplifying an egalitarian ethos. And although the more exclusive Diamond Strip has emerged in recent times, stretching from Swan House roundabout to Collingwood Street and indicative of the city's American-style money system leanings, the fact that it is directly adjacent to the Bigg Market area could be interpreted as financial reality being absorbed into the inclusiveness of the city's drinking culture, rather than the opposite being true.

There will always be an element of idealism and generalisation in such assertions. Nevertheless, there are reasonable grounds for identifying a symbiotic link between the first and third pillars of Geordie identity – class and drink. Talking about the essence of pubs and clubs in Newcastle after the Second World War, Brian Bennison, former president of the city's renowned Literary and Philosophical Society (located just off the Diamond Strip), maintained that its human dimension – 'participation in an unpolished democracy of mutual support and beery argument' – was of primary importance.[7] When we also consider Kate Fox's observation that '*all* drinking places tend to be socially integrative, egalitarian environments', and that 'the specific unwritten rules and norms governing the use of alcohol in different cultures invariably reflect the characteristic values, beliefs and attitudes of those cultures', we can see how this sits nicely with the perception of Newcastle as a people's city where mutual empathy exists between different social groups, and an aura of classlessness tacitly promotes social cohesion.[8]

Seen in this light Tyneside's penchant for pubs becomes a declaration of togetherness: shooters and shorts signifying solidarity and pints promoting proletarian pride of place. If journalist Ruth Sunderland (from Middlesbrough) is correct in claiming that a 'love of alcohol as a relaxant, a social lubricant and a disinhibitor is one of the few things that unites our class-ridden nation', then this can only enhance the connection.[9] But issues relating to class are rarely so simple. And while the claims of Fox and Sunderland are broadly accurate, although it is increasingly open to all, historically the true guardians of Newcastle's exuberant city centre drink culture have been, as with the Geordie accent, the working classes.

Recent statistics have shown that the highest proportion of people whose drinking is considered hazardous are to be found in affluent 'middle-class' areas such as Surrey. Though application of such statistics, as indeed with binge-drinking statistics, necessitates caution, they go some way to dispelling the persistent historical myth that alcoholism is the exclusive domain of the feckless, debauched working class. Dr Gray Smith-Laing, a liver specialist whose objectivity is surely beyond question, has reinforced this point: 'Alcohol is a totally classless disease. It may be more discreet among the upper and middle classes, because they do a lot of it at home. But it causes harm across all social classes'.[10] Therefore when Chris Donald talked of the working classes getting pissed down town whilst the middle classes bought up their property in and around the Jesmond area, it wasn't necessarily a barb about working-class drinking.

In reality it was an accurate observation about the popular pub-drinking culture of the city centre near to which he grew up, whose primary participants would have been predominantly working class. The drinking culture of Newcastle provided a backdrop for the exploits of memorable *Viz* characters including Brown Bottle and Sid the Sexist. Donald understood that drinking was inextricably woven into the working-class culture of Tyneside and mercilessly parodied its scatological extremes. However, although characters such as Sid the Sexist, the Fat Slags and Biffa Bacon have been described as 'all Geordies and all cretins; violent, pathetic, sexually loose cretins to boot', and Eight Ace and Brown Bottle labelled 'essentially hopeless drunks', you'd be hard pushed to find many working-class Geordies who would castigate the *Viz* writers for their portrayal of drunken Geordie life.[11] Donald has described the standard formula for creating certain *Viz* characters as 'taking a recognizable stereotype and exaggerating it', and few would argue with his claim that the inspiration for characters such as Sid the Sexist and Biffa Bacon was rooted in reality.[12]

Drink then is an integral, deeply ingrained aspect of what many Geordies believe they are about. It's part of who they are and has been a staple of their popular culture for centuries – that many consider it 'their birthright of a 'good neet in the toon'' is undeniable.[13] Yet both the comic creations of *Viz* and the academic musings of people like Lancaster and Bennison acknowledge a less appealing aspect of 'Party City'. As Chris Donald's brother Simon has said: 'Tyneside's a brilliant society, but like a lot of great cities it's got a real sort of dark side to it. And certainly in the 70s ... there used to be a lot of street violence and drunkenness and so on.'[14] Examples of Jeremy Paxman's belief that: 'Far from being ashamed of their behaviour ... [part of the English population has always seen] fighting and drunkenness as part of their birthright. It is the way they proclaim their identity', can certainly still be found in Newcastle.[15] Indeed, drinking and fighting have been referred to by one observer as 'Geordie life skills'.

That drink-fuelled aggression on Tyneside may cause wariness, perhaps ambivalence, in individuals less inclined to pugilism seems a reasonable speculation. It would be easy to caricature such people as weak, or effeminate, or as killjoys, but to do so would ignore the fact that being on the receiving end of an indiscriminate twatting by a Biffa Bacon-like bonehead in Newcastle of an evening, has been a very real fear over the years. Take Brian Bennison's overview of how different people regard the modern-day drinking culture of the city:

> For some observers there is an enviable gusto about such hedonism: it is carnival. For others it is the revival of a local identity in 'the playing out of what it means to be a Geordie'. For the less enthusiastic, however, it merely teeters on the edge of rowdyism and disorder.[16]

The latter view was endorsed by figures published in 2012 showing that paramedics are called out to an alcohol-related incident every 17 minutes in the North-East, with one, Richard Ilderton, claiming: 'I have been assaulted, both verbally and physically, as have most of my colleagues.'[17]

Bennison accumulates statistics illustrating the historic inclination of certain Newcastle residents toward heavy, irresponsible drinking, before concluding that in the modern day: 'whilst a majority of the citizenry display a responsible, if un-newsworthy attitude to drink, a sizeable minority ensure Newcastle's reputation for heavy drinking persists.'[18] Clearly believing the behaviour of a sizeable minority *was* newsworthy, on 20th December 2007 the *Evening Chronicle* front page headline read: 'Vomiting, violent attacks, public sex acts, anti-social behaviour, criminal damage, urinating and fighting ... Just a night on the town'.

Reporting on undercover researchers' findings based on observations made around Newcastle in October of that year, the paper's editorial comment section employed similar language to Bennison. Expressing concern that 'a significant minority threaten to undo much of the good work being done to promote the region to visitors', it suggested 'more needs to be done for people to enjoy rather than endure our city's nightlife.' Not so much urban sociability as urban anti-sociability. Two days later the *Chronicle* also carried a report on the Friday before Christmas – the busiest night of the year for paramedics that many Geordies know as 'Black Eye Friday' – which referred to the Bigg Market as 'infamous'.[19]

Pascal Fulgenzi, whose Italian restaurant Roma on Collingwood Street closed in 2008 after 43 years of business, agreed with the *Chronicle*'s sentiments. Saddened by the closure he regretted that the atmosphere in town was 'not conducive to our clientele any more ... it can be intimidating with all the people going from bar to bar ... It's a shame that it's happened like it has. In the last couple of years the city has really gone down market.'[20] Former chief constable of Northumbria Police, Mike Craik, suggested near the end of his tenure that the area suffers from its party image. Having declared: 'The party's over for drunkenness, violence and disorder', he went on to complain that the 'behaviour among many of the people who patronise pubs, bars and nightclubs has reached a shameful state.'[21] Though his use of the word 'many' would be questioned by, well, many, whether it is a sizeable, significant minority or otherwise, there can be little doubt that the associated anti-social behaviour of Tyneside's drink culture may prove as alienating for some as the actual act of drinking itself.

So why do certain Geordies believe that drinking and acting like a bell-end is not only acceptable, but inevitable and even *expected* behaviour? Even allowing for the broader national and human perspectives, Newcastle's historic drinking and drink-related behaviour provides a fairly rarefied sub-cultural climate. Any hope of a comprehensive, all-encompassing answer to such an open question naturally fluctuates between negligible and non-existent. But in order to scratch the surface, referring back to Bennison's allusion – 'the playing out of what it means to be a Geordie' – may offer us some insight. Bearing in mind that in relation to notions of Geordie identity a primary aim here is an examination of how far one definition of stereotype – *a standardized image or conception of a type of person, etc.* – may have morphed into another: *an idea, convention, etc., that has grown stale through fixed usage*, will also prove useful.

There is a condensed description similar to Bennison's for those Geordies whose drinking, and to some extent thinking, appears to conform to a preconceived notion of what it is to be a Geordie. Simply 'playing the Geordie'. Michael Collins has discerned how some white working-class Londoners, 'either searching for an identity or clinging to a past they never knew, have taken on the mantle of a caricatured cockney'.[22] It seems likely that particularly amongst the post-war generations, as deindustrialisation gathered pace, some Tynesiders similarly sought refuge in a performative 'one size fits all' display of playing the Geordie. As drink is such a fundamental facet of many Geordies' sense of their cultural identity, it is therefore interesting to contemplate the extent to which drinking begets Geordieness, or Geordieness begets drinking.

In the early evening of Black Eye Friday, 2007, I found myself in The Red House bar on Newcastle's Quayside with one of my oldest and closest friends, who boasts the quintessential Geordie name of Robert Stephenson. We bumped into a group of male acquaintances and whilst chatting to them I observed how several incessantly performed what I perceived as their pre-conditioned Geordie roles. All in their thirties, those acting up most energetically seemed intent on realising the fears of Colls and Lancaster by fulfilling the role of Geordies as 'stereotyped joke figures, usually daft males'.[23] The type of Geordie male who, like Simon Donald's most famous *Viz* creation Sid the Sexist, is doomed to a state of perpetual adolescence.

As the most exuberant member of the group displayed his bountiful reserves of lairiness, he half-jumped, half-fell off a raised platform in the pub and landed heavily on the floor, his head missing the wrought-iron base of a table by a matter of centimetres. Chastened and in a mild state of shock he picked himself up sheepishly, with a look flickering across his face that seemed to say: *What the fuck am I doing?* The overall impression I got was that he wasn't really being himself and the drinking culture of Newcastle – and no doubt the restrictive dynamics of his group of friends – was almost compelling him to play the Geordie. It showcased a Tyneside version of the broader English whole observed by Kate Fox: 'Saturday-night … drunkenness, where we are merely acting out a prescribed social role, a sort of hammy caricature of what we think uninhibited behaviour ought to look like.'[24] If to be a Geordie is to drink, then drinking also seems to induce a conditioned, protective layer of stereotypical Geordieness in some individuals.

Although being aware of this may take the fun out of believing we're spontaneous comedy mavericks acting with a heightened sense of comic improvisation whilst out on the lash, taken to extremes, the tension between an individual's 'beer persona' and who they actually are – or want to be – can be problematic. Fans of celebrated American sitcom *Friends* will be familiar with the incidental character known as Fun Bobby. A laugh-a-minute prankster whose legendary charisma and humorous antics are talked up by Monica, the *Friends* gang look forward to his attendance at a party, eager to bask in the glow of his infectious *joie de vivre*. However, when he arrives it emerges that he has given up drink, is plagued with crippling emotional issues, and is in fact crushingly dull and boring, much to the gang's disappointment.

It's a latent fear that must be keenly felt by those who have cultivated an exaggerated sociable drinking persona: the depressing possibility that their 'character' and 'personality' are all a drink-induced façade. Contemplating his own problems with alcohol, Paul Gascoigne identified the destructive pressure of maintaining a drink-manufactured social role as part of the problem, saying he was 'living a plonky life, being a plonky person, being Gazza instead of being Paul Gascoigne.' In his autobiography he also recalls how the thought of waking up sober 'produces another fear. If I stay sober, will I turn into a boring person? I was always fun when I was drinking … what if the penalty, the by-product, is to become a sensible, dreary, boring twat?[25] Stripped of the persona-forming social lubricant of alcohol, and an accompanying compulsion to play out the hammy caricature of a Geordie stereotype, how many of the sizeable, significant minority would have to confront the disturbing possibility that the chasm between their beer persona and who they really are is similar to that of Fun Bobby's?

The personal development of some who endure a troubled relationship with Bacchus may be greatly hindered not just by the drink itself, but also by the attendant superficial veneer of performative Geordieness. Gascoigne recalls getting drunk for the first time aged only fourteen and lists the first three major problems he's faced in life as beer, wine and vodka. In 2008 clinical psychologist Oliver James said:

> He's got a weak sense of self resulting from a poor early infancy and subsequent traumas. That's meant he isn't very good at forming stable relationships, other than with drunken companions ... He lacks a social network and identity and so is just floating around in some horrible, horrible state.[26]

Whether that is the case or not, a suspicion persists that an inability to extricate himself from a fragile, culturally conditioned Geordie beer persona has played an underlying role in his woes. That he might have to add Akenside Syndrome to his ailments seems inevitable.

The height of Gascoigne's fame coincided with the zenith of *Viz* magazine's nationwide popularity; the pair combining to sear a perception of Geordies as hapless, if at times endearing pissheads into the national consciousness. Despite his flaws he remains very much one of our own. According to Henrik Ibsen, 'A man shares the responsibility and the guilt of the society to which he belongs,' and the thought that we contributed to his formation, and by extension his turmoil, should perhaps provoke a tweak of the collective Geordie conscience.[27] But he is far closer to being an exception rather than the norm. He is not representative of the vast majority of Geordies, nor even of the area's professional football fraternity.

For confirmation of this we need look no further than the likes of Alan Shearer, Chris Waddle, Lee Clark, Michael Carrick, Shola Ameobi and Peter Beardsley. Though possessing similar sublime football skills to Gascoigne, Beardsley represents his polar opposite in drinking terms (at least historically). He too disliked the taste of alcohol when trying it as a youngster, but was comfortable enough in his own skin and mentally strong enough to reject it altogether. Likewise fellow teetotaller Shola Ameobi. Proof that the Bigg Market fountain's rallying cry has not fallen entirely on deaf ears, and that the concept of Geordies embracing teetotalism is not altogether ludicrous.

However, people who abstain on Tyneside may be aware of a certain antipathy that drinkers can hold toward teetotallers, observed by Ruth Sunderland. She abstains herself and has suggested that teetotallers 'are not an appealing bunch', believing that one reason why 'people hate teetotallers is they suspect them of being proselytisers.' While it's unlikely Beardsley and Co. will instigate a fountain-erecting public subscription appeal any time soon, Sunderland's experience of pressure flowing the other way is instructive. She insists that she has 'no desire to lecture anyone or to try to stop them drinking, but there is plenty of pull in the opposite direction', and claims that choosing not to drink is seen as 'unsettling, almost subversive' to the 'social consensus' that unites the classes in alcohol consumption.[28]

Perhaps that's another reason why the Temperance Movement enjoyed little sustainable long-term success. We all want to fit in and be accepted in some way or another and pressure to conform to the drinking habits of an area like Tyneside, where alcohol courses through the cultural bloodstream, is surely great. Like a Geordie without an accent, a Geordie who doesn't drink is somehow compromised – not quite a *proper* Geordie. A Geordie-*lite* at best.

An examination of selected staples of Geordie identity and the potential of the cultural whole to cause feelings of ambivalence within certain individuals is another primary aim of this book. It seems appropriate then, that countries with a drinking culture such as England's are described by anthropologists and social scientists as 'ambivalent' cultures. These cultures have 'an ambivalent, morally charged, love/hate, forbidden-fruit relationship with alcohol, usually the result of a history of temperance movements', and experience far higher levels of "alcohol-related' social and psychiatric problems' than countries whose relationship with alcohol is more relaxed and straightforward.[29] This clearly imbues the Bigg Market fountain with an extra layer of interpretation.

Though there is much to enjoy and admire about Tyneside's enduring commitment to sociable drinking, the less attractive aspects seem stubbornly ingrained. In March 2014 plans for the North-East's first 'dry' bar in Newcastle's Cross Street were said to be gathering pace, and the same month saw Northumbria Police commissioner Vera Baird revealing tax incentives for bars that ditch happy hour deals. It is perfectly plausible to suggest that the antics of a sizeable, significant minority contribute toward the reluctance of certain people to live within the city's boundaries. That historically some have found elements of the local drinking culture and its associated anti-social behaviour embarrassing is also entirely probable. But perhaps others from all social backgrounds simply see it as unappealing, aggressive, intimidating, not particularly relaxing and not their idea of a party. As many have alluded to, a night out in Newcastle can at times be a test of endurance.

Questioning the authenticity of a perceived modern day 'working-class swagger', Ferdinand Mount wondered: 'doesn't all this seem a little like bluster, a boisterous façade concealing a deep-lying uncertainty and lack of self-worth?'[30] Speaking more generally, and across classes, Wilkinson and Pickett have suggested that behind misleading recorded rises in people's self-confidence lies:

> a picture of increasing anxieties about how we are seen and what others think of us which has, in turn, produced a kind of defensive attempt to shore up our confidence in the face of those insecurities. The defence involves a kind of self-promoting, insecure egotism which is easily mistaken for high self-esteem.[31]

Although impossible to quantify in any meaningful way, perhaps for some who adopt an exaggerated Geordie beer persona, and for a high percentage of the sizeable minority, drinking heavily and acting anti-socially simply provides temporary respite from the paralysis of low self-esteem and lack of confidence.

Underlying economic factors will, of course, also have been historically relevant including to this day. For his book entitled *Danziger's Britain: A Journey to the Edge*, Nick Danziger spent time in Newcastle in the mid-1990s and concluded that Geordies: 'come in taxis and by the minibus load [to the city centre] to drink and forget their dull jobs, if they have one'.[32] Furthermore, in 2007 a national newspaper study revealed that five of the top six areas for annual spend per patient on anti-depressants were in the North-East, with three on Tyneside itself (Gateshead #2, Newcastle #4, and North Tyneside #6).[33] More recent research showed 8 of the top 10 in the North-East, and a similar survey published in 2011 placed Newcastle and Gateshead in the top five of English primary care trusts for prescription of antidepressants, with an astonishing combined total of almost a quarter of a million prescriptions issued throughout 'Newcastle-Gateshead' in 2009 to 2010 alone.[34]

Even allowing for obligatory caution concerning statistics, when the fact that the North-East has some of the highest suicide rates in the country is also taken into account (15% higher than the national average for males), it's impossible to imagine that Tyneside's drinking culture is not a significant contributory factor in all of this.[35] If the statistics bear scrutiny, then it would appear that the most drink-sodden corner of the country is also the most depressed and prone to suicide. This is fertile terrain for Akenside Syndrome to flourish in. Illustrating the often marked separation between the social self and the true person within, Erich Fromm uses the example of a man who has been at a party engaging in much laughter and convivial conversation. On leaving, the instant after closing the door his friendly smile is replaced as there 'appears on his face an expression of deep sadness, almost of desperation.'[36] We can only speculate as to how many Geordies have experienced a similar sense of deflation on returning home from Party City. Cheers.

In the North-East people wound the strands of their everyday life around it – childhood, youth, work, friendships, relatives, experiences, memories – until football became inextricable from existence itself.

Harry Pearson, *The Far Corner*

If there is one single image that conjures up Newcastle to the outside world it is St James's Park with the Geordie crowd crammed into the vast terraces of the Gallowgate and the Leazes ends.

Richard Holt and Ray Physick, *Sport on Tyneside*

Following Newcastle is a birthright, a religion, a warm-up before the knees-up of a night out. On the Geordie check-list of must-do activities, watching the Toon ranks alongside breathing.

Henry Winter, *Daily Telegraph* 24th October 2006

[Newcastle is] a city where football and socialising remain indelibly linked ... whose rhythms are defined by sport and alcohol

George Caulkin, *The Times* 27th November 2010

In most other big cities, there are now other distractions and the game is not all-consuming like it was years ago. On Tyneside football is still king ... There can be nobody in the city who doubts the affiliation of the supporters to the club. It is a total identity.

Kenny Dalglish, former Newcastle United manager

The obsession for football is overwhelming and sometimes I used to get quite frightened of the responsibility we had for people's lives ... I realised, in a sense, we've got our businesses, we've got our jobs and we've got our interests but to them that was their whole life. And it's a strength and a weakness. It's a strength – the passion – great for the club. But it's a weakness that we haven't moved beyond it intellectually. And it sums up the area in some ways. There *has* to be something more than the football club ... *there has to be a lot more, if we're going to progress forward.*

Sir John Hall, former Newcastle United owner and chairman

PILLAR FOUR

Football

T HE INTERDEPENDENCY OF THE THIRD AND FOURTH PILLARS OF Geordie identity was neatly illustrated in the title of a recent book by *The Mag*'s Billy Furious: *And They Wonder Why We Drink? Newcastle United – The Quest for the Intertoto Cup.* The club itself enjoyed a close relationship with the recently demolished neighbouring brewery for many years. In 1992 Kevin Keegan was dramatically unveiled as the new Newcastle United manager on brewery premises, and his much-heralded team of entertainers sported the Brown Ale logo on their shirts for the majority of that first managerial stint. It seems entirely appropriate to suggest that when people from outside the region think of Geordies, the image often conjured up will be that of Newcastle fans sporting their colours (Newcastle East MP Nick Brown has alluded to this: 'If you ask anyone about Newcastle, the first thing they will say will be either Newcastle United or Brown Ale.').[1] The fact that Holt and Physick employ similar language to Moffat and Rosie when asserting that Brown Ale defines Tyneside – *If there is one single image that conjures up Newcastle/If there's one product that defines Tyneside* – reinforces the impression that both activities occupy a central role in the area's cultural life.

Some Geordies' relationship with the club could certainly be described as a total identity. Rob Shepherd has expanded on the issue, alongside others already explored on these pages: 'Newcastle ought to be England's equivalent of Barcelona, a football club at the head of a nation within a nation, one with its own identity and causes.'[2] And if it's true that some Geordies' relationship with Newcastle United amounts to a total identification, then we can perhaps see how the comments of Sir John Hall, supported by A.A. Gill's insistence – 'Investing that much emotion in a game that you have no control over, that you don't play in ... that offers so much unproductive disappointment and triumph, is cultural suicide' – open up an avenue of investigation regarding Akenside Syndrome.[3] Likewise the observation of football broadcaster and journalist, Gabriele Marcotti, 'Viewed from afar, you get the sense that Newcastle fans are a monolithic bunch of infantile fools.'[4]

Returning to live on Tyneside in autumn 2008, I noted an advert plastered around Newcastle United's official club shops. Simple but effective, the word *'belong...'* sat above an enlarged club crest, with the words '... *always united'* underneath. It brought to mind the Newcastle-born novelist Gordon Burn, who left the city when he was 18 and never moved back before his death in 2009, aged 61. Reflecting on his days as a grammar-school boy growing up in Newcastle's West End, he admitted to having been an 'intolerable snob' and, as we have already seen, felt he was 'culturally, and in class terms ... a displaced person.'[5] The notion that Burn was 'an unofficial Geordie ambassador in "the smoke"' appears to be undermined by the writer's own musings.[6] It's an ambassadorial role he seems to have been oblivious of – his acute experience of Akenside Syndrome apparently remaining internalised and dormant, until self-diagnosis late in life led him to abandon the rather odd belief that coming from Newcastle had nothing to do with who he was.

Admitting to the city's claim on him in 2005 (an admission somewhat tainted by his speculation that this was partially down to 'what Orwell called *nostalgie de la boue'* – nostalgia for the mud or dirt), he occasionally applied himself to football matters. In *Living memories* he talked about how Newcastle United's team 'is crucial to the fabric and self-image of the city', and, relating this to his late father, suggested that 'the city – its local detail; the particularity of place – was central to who he was. He belonged.' Burn clearly did not feel that he himself belonged – 'I didn't think coming from Newcastle had anything to do with who I was for many years' – and employed the image of the hordes leaving St James' Park to illustrate this.

He recalled that whilst walking home from poetry-oriented 'cultural jam sessions' at Morden Tower (a medieval turret that is part of Newcastle's city walls), he would sometimes encounter:

> the crowds streaming out of St James's Park. To get to where I was going – back home, to do homework – I'd have to go against the flow. This always seemed a reasonable direction in which to be heading.[7]

The image Burn conveyed of a lone poetic warrior resisting the crush of the football-supporting mass, and the subsequent subtle alignment of himself with both Lawrentian characters and George Orwell may be telling. Talking about Orwell's trouble with rationalising the mass, Oxford professor John Carey suggested his problem 'was that he identified the masses both with freedom and with dirt. He believed in freedom, but dirt repelled him.'[8] This connection might offer us a deeper understanding of Burn's experience of both *nostalgie de la boue* and Akenside Syndrome.

In another article Burn talked about 'the love of sport as an expression of the love of place', and the sentiment will resonate powerfully with many Tynesiders.[9] Newcastle is, after all, a one-club city. Whereas citizens of places like Bristol, Nottingham, Sheffield, Liverpool and Manchester are afforded the opportunity of supporting one of two clubs, for most people in Newcastle there is no choice at all. Although having more than one club in a city does not necessarily negate supporters expressing love of place, it surely dilutes it, with neither club's fans enjoying unique representative status.

Tempered by the parochialism of being civic top dog, having numerous rivals in the same conurbation surely erodes the love of place factor even further in vast cities like Birmingham and London; pride in their patch overriding love of the city as a whole. And we can safely assume that Manchester United's notoriously large southern fan-base is not motivated by Mancunian civic pride. Though they could be cited in support of Kate Fox's theory that the English 'are not obliged to support [their] local team', such a concept would seem unnatural to the vast majority of football supporters on Tyneside (with the obvious exception of South Shields, equidistant as it is from Newcastle and Sunderland).[10]

The historic importance of football to communities in the North-East noted by Harry Pearson – *football became inextricable from existence itself* – had not diminished by the turn of the last century according to Holt and Physick:

> The love of sport as an expression of the love of place – industrial or post-industrial – seems to burn as brightly [on Tyneside] today as it did in the century that spanned Harry Clasper, Hughie Gallacher and 'Wor Jackie'.[11]

So what are we to make of this unflinching devotion to a club whose post-1950s trophy-winning history has been, bar the 1969 Fairs Cup, an unremitting narrative of failure?

Holt and Physick also insist that Newcastle's fans have become more famous than the team; listing their loyalty, passion and patience among the reasons. A few former managers may disagree with the validity of the latter quality, but it is true that the primary basis on which Newcastle can currently consider itself a 'big' club is its large fan-base and financial turnover (conversely the only reason it cannot be considered a 'big' club is its lack of trophies). That the team's performances and results can affect some Tynesiders' sense of well-being, individually and collectively, is also assured. Moreover, as with Newcastle's drink culture, factors such as solidarity, communality and camaraderie – in a nutshell, football as an agent of social cohesion and integration – can all be added to the equation when considering the football ethos that prevails on Tyneside.

However, as we have already examined such issues in relation to drink, it would serve little purpose to re-tread the same turf here. Of one thing we can be sure though, love of Newcastle United means much more than a simple love of football itself. On returning to the club for an ill-fated second stint as manager in 2008, Kevin Keegan averred that while people down South might prefer to go to the theatre to be entertained, Geordies watched football for the self-same reason. Sid Waddell made a similar analogy: 'watching Newcastle is … working-class theatre. Fans are more concerned with being entertained than they are with winning.'[12]

And taking it one step further, psychoanalyst Chris Oakley has likened the mental state experienced by football fans at a match to a form of madness:

> The desire to go on tilt. Mad, less on the side of something regressive, but more a progress narrative suggesting an eagerness to throw aside the constraining carapace of identity ... football offers us the possibility of manageable doses of this self-elected madness.[13]

This correlates with the escapism element of Newcastle's drinking culture. Football as a drug, an altered state of consciousness, with Newcastle fans the hopeless junkies still addicted to their football fix despite a long history of bad trips. For some Geordies going to the match is as much about immersing themselves into a collective whole – whilst simultaneously getting out of their heads – as getting lashed down town is for others.

But the assertion that entertainment takes precedence over winning is by no means unequivocal. Questioning the homogenising caricatures of Newcastle fans, Gabriele Marcotti goes on to state that of the dozen or so he knows personally, 'there are only two who remotely fit the cartoonish description'; and a trawl through Newcastle United fans forums revealed 'the same kind of range of opinion you might find on any fans forum: some idiots, some lunatics and a majority of posters who represent a variety of views.'[14]

From a local perspective, railing against what he perceived as the misinformed representation of Newcastle fans by national newspaper journalists in the aftermath of former manager Sam Allardyce's departure, then *Sunday Sun* columnist Neil Farrington insisted that the alleged demand for 'champagne football' was: 'Plain lazy mythology – what Tyneside wants is a winning team, whatever it takes'. Playing to the area's sense of separatism and pride in its one club city status, he maintained:

> few outsiders have ever really understood Newcastle United. How can people who pick their football club like they would a settee pass judgement on those who had it chosen for them at birth?[15]

The allusion to a mandatory, pre-ordained obligation to support Newcastle United from birth is of particular interest when contemplating football-related cases of Akenside Syndrome, because obligation can be restrictive, stifling and oppressive.

Added to the psychological impact of investing so much emotion into a club whose trophy cabinet would not look out of place in Miss Havisham's parlour, it's difficult to disagree with Michael Calvin's observation that disappointment is Newcastle fans' birthright.[16] If Farrington is right in asserting that most supporters crave the vicarious thrill of their team winning trophies as much as the fans of any other club, you have to wonder whether, beneath the veneer of eternal optimism, the unrelenting disappointment endured by the last few generations has embedded a deep sense of fatalism. They can't think like winners because in their lifetime they never have been, thus chronic self-doubt lurks just beneath the surface. Being emotionally aligned from birth with a team renowned as habitual losers simply cannot be good for collective self-esteem on Tyneside.

So why do so many Geordies persist in wearing their Newcastle United replica shirts? If we accept not all of them are motivated purely by entertainment requirements, and that those who crave vicarious association-related status-boosts have endured nothing but disappointment for generations, then there must be some other reason for what could be interpreted as masochism masquerading as loyalty. Another observation by Fromm in *The Fear of Freedom* affords us some insight. His claim that 'nothing is more difficult for the average man to bear than the feeling of not being identified with a larger group' is illuminating, because as Professor Gavin Kitching has similarly said: 'People need something bigger than themselves and football does it in the North East'.[17] Seen as such, Newcastle fans' penchant for wearing their colours – likened to walking into a 1930s film by Harry Pearson and to a herd of baying zebras by Sid Waddell – can be interpreted in a number of ways.

On one level it's a straightforward act of affiliation denoting loyalty and solidarity. It speaks of togetherness and states loud and proud *I belong*, a fact not lost on Stuart Maconie during his visit to the city: 'Everyone in Newcastle supports the Magpies with a unity of purpose that borders on mass hysteria'.[18] Viewed from a different perspective, however, it could be said that for some it is an act of unquestioning, sheep-like conformity. For if the sheer volume of people who wear Newcastle tops or related merchandise is seen as a regional eccentricity, then we must consider that 'what most people think of as English eccentricity in dress is really the opposite: it is tribalism, a form of conformity, a uniform.' This in turn can be seen as indicative of 'a deep-seated insecurity about dress ... [and a] desperate desire to fit in and conform' that informs many of our sartorial selections. Like the sportswear favoured by some lower down the socio-economic scale and the gaudy trousers worn by upper-middle-class males, the Toon top tendency on Tyneside thus reduced to the donning of 'tribal-sub-culture uniforms'.[19]

In 1998 Newcastle's former chairman Freddy Shepherd was infamously recorded talking about how cheap the club were able to produce replica tops before selling them on to fans at a huge profit margin. During the uninspiring managerial reign of Graeme Souness, appointed by Shepherd, a mocked-up image appeared behind the bar of the Rose and Crown pub on Newgate Street in Newcastle. It depicted the two of them as Laurel and Hardy, both saying to one another: *'That's another fine mess you've got me into!'* Humorous and apt, it was an image that could be interpreted as symbolising Shepherd's stewardship of the club. And yet the initial folly of the Mike Ashley era (which prompted Northumberland Brewery to produce an ale called Another Fine Mess, accompanied by an image of Ashley and Dennis Wise as Laurel and Hardy this time) seemed to provoke a ripple of counterintuitive nostalgia for the former chairman. But in my opinion, and perhaps for some other fans, Shepherd's tenure coincided with the club's demise from being the nation's favourite second team to the laughing stock of English football.

As if to literally illustrate this, when Michael Owen signed for Newcastle in 2005, *The Sun* ran a cartoon on its editorial comment page which echoed the WHSmith ads starring Nicholas Lyndhurst. It depicted a Geordie couple disembarking a flight from Madrid. The woman has a 'TOON' tattoo on her upper arm, while her partner is chronically obese, also sports tattoos, is carrying big bags of duty free (booze and tabs probably) and has a Newcastle United replica shirt stretched tautly across his huge beer gut. The woman barks: *'Take off the shirt! People are going to think you're Michael Owen.'* Whether we see it as lazy, cheap-shot regional stereotyping or a harmless piece of tongue-in-cheek fun, it is emblematic of how the image of the beer-guzzling, replica shirt-wearing, daft Geordie seemed to intensify in the nation's consciousness during Shepherd's tragi-comic reign.

Reinforcing this impression an article headlined 'OUT OF TOON' appeared in *The Observer Sport* a few weeks before the *Sun* cartoon, with a subtitle that asked a simple question about Newcastle United: 'COMEDY CLUB?' Let's be honest, nobody enjoys being laughed at and systematically cast as pathetic figures of fun held up for national ridicule, yet the ill-judged return of Kevin Keegan under Mike Ashley unleashed a surly combination of scorn, derision and contempt that transcended mere mockery. It was the outpouring of a festering animosity sensed by Stuart Maconie, whose otherwise eulogistic appraisal of Newcastle and its inhabitants nonetheless also noted: 'a sneaking resentment of the Magpies ... fermenting of late', due in part to 'Newcastle United's absurdly inflated sense of self-importance' and the 'self-mythologising name' of Toon Army.[20] A sneaking resentment that later, in April 2009, led one *Guardian* journalist to ask: 'Why does everyone dislike them *so* much?'[21]

Keegan's return prompted some outlets of the national print media to exhume a plethora of hackneyed analogies and glib observations. Newcastle was a 'soap opera club'; their fans a 'sect', 'hopeless romantics' and a 'circus crowd' not concerned with winning trophies. Keegan, given his association with a Soccer Circus enterprise, was inevitably cast as the ringmaster of this black and white big top. On learning of his reappointment, according to Paul Hayward writing in the *Daily Mail*, there was an instinctive countrywide outburst of laughter.

For Patrick Collins, of sister paper *The Mail on Sunday*, the subsequent appointment of Dennis Wise ratcheted up the laughter decibels even further. Paul Wilson of *The Observer* seemingly agreed. Under an article headed *Ashley's odd cast at theatre of the absurd*, he argued that with the appointment of Wise Newcastle had 'staggered into the realms of the surreal', having previously labelled NUFC 'a pretend football club', and later deriding the celebratory chants following Keegan's first victory as a chorus from 'the most easily pleased supporters in the world'. In an article ostensibly praising Newcastle fans later in 2008, he referred to their 'almost pathetic willingness to worship anything in a black and white shirt'.[22]

Paul Hayward has also claimed that in 'defending their club against "southern" critics some Newcastle fans have acquired quite a persecution complex', so let's be absolutely clear about this.[23] Much of the copy produced by Wilson et al consisted of even-handed, astute analysis, and the subsequent implosion of the management structure at Newcastle United fully justified their broader observations. But what we're interested in here is perception. How Geordies, and in this case Newcastle United fans specifically, are perceived; one of the problems being that the two often appear interchangeable in the national consciousness.

Hence in February 2009 BBC reporter Robert Peston, in my view at least, both trivialised and patronised his Tyneside audience of Northern Rock shareholders who had been critical of his reporting on the bank's crisis – some of whom had suffered life-changing financial loss – by entitling his blog on the meeting *Toon army v me*. We're also interested in how this perception from without, added to notions of self-definition from within, might influence Akenside Syndrome. Because Wilson's condescension and Collins's sense of *schadenfreude* (as I see it) is symptomatic of something broader. The dismissive, resentful attitude towards Newcastle United and their fans noted by Maconie goes far beyond the insular world of London-based sports columnists.

Consider this contribution to a BBC website notice board in the wake of Keegan's return:

> I think the so-called 'Geordie nation' are living in a dream world – they are a complete laughing stock ... Newcastle United – the North East branch of Jongleurs – a genuine comedy club ... if you Geordies actually believe [Mike Ashley's] phoney 'I'm one of the lads' routine, then you're as stupid as you look.[24]

Perhaps the contributor had seen the *Sun* cartoon and read the *Observer* article a few years earlier. A riposte to Newcastle fan Rob Smith's letter in which he had denounced the 'non-Geordie' response to Keegan's appointment as 'boringly typical: patronising scorn about our 'comedy club'', wasn't much more forgiving:

> The reason the rest of us are bemused, bored and yet highly amused at the goings on in Newcastle is the parochialism and laughable belief that only 'Keegan or a Geordie' could possibly understand this huge, replica shirt-flogging, trophyless club.[25]

And though the short-lived second coming of Keegan as a manager feels a long way off now, it's useful for us here because of the latent animosity it brought to the surface. One charmless response to the question in 2009 (Why does everyone dislike [Newcastle fans] *so* much?), insisted it was because 'they're witless fools who believe whatever they read.'[26] Proof, as if it were needed, that the Geordie brand is firmly embedded in the national consciousness, and not necessarily always in a positive way.

Asserting that the football dimension of Geordie identity has suffered a degree of brand contamination over the last fifteen years or so is a safe bet – in fact I'd put a lot of wonga on it. Back in 2008 a thought occurred to me as I walked around the Hampshire market town of Petersfield wearing a Newcastle United waterproof jacket. With the club crest on the front and the Northern Rock logo on the back, it suddenly dawned on me that I was inviting scorn and ridicule from both angles. A comedy club sponsored by a comedy bank – both prone to seismic, self-inflicted collapses. It was the sartorial equivalent of putting myself in stocks in the market square. Yet for some which club's crest was on the jacket would have been irrelevant. Because football has its uglier aspects, and they can engender a belief in certain people that the entire sport is irremediably contaminated. The implications for Tyneside, where supporting Newcastle has become so routinely aligned with the perception of Geordies, are obvious.

It's easy to forget that only around 50,000 people from the Newcastle city region (population over a million when including parts of Northumberland and Durham) actually attend games at St James' Park on a regular basis, though many more consider themselves supporters nonetheless. A.A. Gill's observation that football terraces 'are really, really funny and really, really horrible, both at the same time', suggests an ambivalence also observable in Louise Taylor's rumination on football's 'simultaneous ability to enthral and appal'. Taylor's conflicting feelings for the beautiful game were roused by what she called 'the moronic behaviour of some Newcastle fans' during the away game versus Middlesbrough in 2007. According to her the fans in question subjected Boro's Egyptian striker Mido to a persistent stream of 'vile and ignorant Islamophobic abuse', in which he was 'stereotyped as a terrorist bomber in a barrage of anti-Arab abuse'. Any temptation to caricature Taylor's disdain as politically correct, leftist sanctimony (she writes for

The Guardian), may be undermined by a similar reference to 'sick terrorist taunts' in *The Sun*.[27]

For a majority of Geordies such bigoted behaviour would more likely prompt toe-curling embarrassment rather than a chorus of *If you're proud to be a Geordie, clap your hands*. Some Tynesiders may feel a desire to distance themselves from such people, their behaviour, and the sport that has come to be seen as emblematic of what Geordies are all about. That is to say, they may experience football-related symptoms of Akenside Syndrome. Certainly anyone who has attended matches regularly will instantly recognise the type of fan that Harry Pearson encountered at St James' Park during his tour of North-East football grounds. The imbecilic infantilism of the three fans in question provoked a strong response from the otherwise genial author. Their actions were 'a concentrated display of idiocy', he said, with the ringleader's crass behaviour and comments suspected of being 'simply the product of abysmal ignorance, woeful insensitivity, and arrested mental development.'[28]

Similarly, when a few hundred Newcastle fans invaded and vandalised football pitches used by amateur side Wigan Cosmos in March 2013 – during a game – it provoked negative national headlines, prompting respected fans' website *www.nufc.com* to regret that 'incidents of this nature … play into the hands of those seeking to portray Toon fans as brainless, drunken louts.'[29] But even this was surpassed only a month later when, amid the disorder after Newcastle's derby day defeat to Sunderland, 45 year old Barry Rogerson of Bedlington – clad in a retro Newcastle top and a club scarf covering his face – was filmed punching a police horse outside St James' Park. Scenes which prompted the *Chronicle* to ask these questions on its Facebook page: 'Do you think Sunday's events have brought a negative image on the city? Does this make you ashamed to be a Tynesider? Do you worry that Geordies will all be 'tarred with the same brush'?' They might have added: 'Did such scenes provoke symptoms of Akenside Syndrome within you?'

These people can be compared to those whose stereotypical Geordieness is exacerbated by drink. When I asked avid Newcastle fan Chris Donald whether some Geordies had historically internalised the stereotypes around the word, compelling them to play the Geordie in a preconditioned way, he offered a football-themed response. "You do definitely see people … they think there's a way that they should act, possibly," he reflected. "My only real experience of going anywhere with Geordies is when you go to away football matches, and you'll stop in places and you'll see people assuming their sort of Geordie roles that they do. There is this role-playing – I think they have a perception of how they should behave rather than simply behaving the way that they [would normally] behave. They think they've been given a part in life that they have to play and they feel obliged to do it." Though he went on to say that cockneys and scousers can be found doing the same thing, we can see how for some fans the compulsion to live up to the daft, drunk and/or aggressive Geordie stereotype when donning a Newcastle top is hard to resist.

This type of fan sprang to Brendan Healy's mind when I asked if he'd ever experienced Akenside Syndrome, whether he'd ever felt ambivalence toward the culture of Tyneside. After reinforcing his loyalty to the area – "I'm still here and I still love it … there's too many things I would miss [if I moved away for work reasons]" – he went on: "Ambivalence, yes. When I was in Orlando airport and I sat at the bar and a bunch of guys came in with black and white shirts on and the barman went, 'Oh Jesus, the zebras.' I felt really, really embarrassed to be a Geordie. Because this barman in America who doesn't even know what the football team is … and his reaction was 'Oh Jesus, the zebras.' And I thought what sort of way of flying our flag is that? And they were just wrong uns. There'd be other guys who would turn up and would be lovely guys, but obviously he's got a thing about us and it *really* shocked me. Sitting at that bar thinking this guy on the other side of the world doesn't like guys in black and white shirts. So yes, there's an ambivalence, if you like."

Ruminating on the issue further, he continued, "I don't like overplaying the Geordie thing, do you know what I mean? I think people overplay it. I was on holiday walking down the main street in Nice and some geezer shouts at me 'Hey, Geordie!' – top of his voice so the whole café turns round, and I just thought: 'Well, I'm just on my fucking holidays!'" When I asked him to confirm that he felt some overplay the whole Geordie thing, Healy's response was emphatic: "Oh *yeah*. Geordies abroad are murder, aren't they?" and was corroborated by an observation from opera singer and Newcastle United fan Graeme Danby. "I feel very proud to be a Geordie," said Danby, before adding: "Like anybody else sometimes I'm embarrassed but that has more to do with the situation that you're in, the place in Europe that you're in, or the place in the world that you're in. There's nothing worse than walking along a nice street in Barcelona and some Geordie is smashed out of his head peeing in the corner."

Like Chris Donald, Healy and Danby were keen to point out that people from other parts of the country can be found behaving in these ways too, and, as with drink, it's essential to acknowledge the perception-distorting minority of Geordies – or in this case Newcastle fans specifically. For instance, a poll held in Cardiff resulted in Newcastle fans being voted the friendliest visitors to the Millennium Stadium whilst it hosted big games during Wembley's revamp. The opinions of more than 500 bars, restaurants, hotels and other establishments were canvassed, and of the 40 teams (over two million fans) who visited the city it was the Toon Army who came out on top. Ed Townsend from the Cardiff Initiative, who organised the poll, said:

> Newcastle fans just have an aura of friendliness about them. There was a special buzz about the place when they came here and even though the result didn't go for them, they still had a good time without a hint of any trouble.[30]

As someone who was there and thoroughly enjoyed the Welsh hospitality, if not the football, I couldn't have put it better myself.

So if the Cardiff poll offers a view of Geordie fans on an away day *en masse*, what about the Toon Army and city of Newcastle as football hosts? In a supplement marking the start of the 2007/8 season, a fans network in *The Observer Sport* voted for the best Premier League away ground experience. Top of the pile was St James' Park, the only club to receive a 9 out of 10 rating. A ringing endorsement of the ground and city – by away fans remember – concluded with this observation: 'Doesn't get much better than this. Massive ground, city-centre location, huge range of pubs and usually ultra-friendly, in a non-cheesy way. It's a must-visit.'[31] There's nothing self-mythologising about these polls. Geordies generally and Newcastle fans specifically have every reason to feel proud of them. And it's also perfectly plausible to cite them as being more representative than the juvenile chants of a few hundred away fans, the buffoonery of those who invaded the pitches in Wigan, and the thuggery of those involved in the 2013 derby day debacle – many of whom had not actually been to the game.

Nevertheless, the darker side of football clearly still exists on Tyneside. In May 2013 Kick it Out chairman Lord Ouseley talked of a need to tackle the 'nastiness' in football, suggesting, 'The tribalism and the way people seek to express their frustrations in football is quite unique', and, as with binge-drinking and drink-related anti-social behaviour, football's associated evils permeate on a national level.[32] Evidence of this can be found on the periphery of almost every club's fan-base and Newcastle United is no exception.

But taken together, if both football and drinking are seen as definitive aspects of an area's culture, informing the sense of identity of many individuals within that area, then the potential for feelings of alienation must exist. The aggression and anti-social behaviour – albeit at the extremes – of both the football and drinking cultures of Tyneside surely increases the cultural unease of some Geordies, who might feel that Gordon Burn's crowd-opposing direction of travel was perfectly understandable. And while the correlation between the third and fourth pillars of Geordie identity is as obvious as an Alan Pardew head-butt, the ubiquitous issue of class also demands attention.

Pardew caused a bit of a stir in March 2014 by asserting that his old club Southampton has a more successful youth system than Newcastle in part due to having a more middle-class catchment area, and the levels of educational attainment of the respective players. Whether you feel his observation has merit or not (bandwagon-jumping political populists on Tyneside unthinkingly dismissed it out of hand), the claim that football was 'the overwhelming obsession of North-East working men throughout the twentieth century' highlights both the game's historical association with the working classes, and the all-consuming hold it has enjoyed over a hefty proportion of the area's male population.[33] Few would question the unifying effect of such a resonant shared symbol, or doubt football's constructive role in encouraging social integration, but the fact that it can be described as an overwhelming obsession of working-class men over the course of a century provokes pause for thought.

The family of former *Granta* editor Ian Jack were anti-football, believing it had 'drugged Scottish working-class life … [and was or would be] a brake on social progress'. Jack quoted James Hamilton Muir – 'The best thing you can say for football is that it has given the working man a subject for conversation' – and in 2005, twenty years after he had suggested to Derek Hatton (in the wake of the Heysel disaster) that 'perhaps the people of Liverpool cared about football too much, in the absence of anything else,' Tim Adams repeated the question to the former political maverick. Hatton responded by saying: 'If anything it has got worse in that way. At least, when we were around, people in pubs would debate the state of the city finances as well as football. Now it's football or nothing.'[34] Any number of quotes encountered in my research could be cited at this point, all running along the lines of Geordies think/care/talk about football to the exclusion of almost everything else.

We'll make do with just one from the late, great Sir Bobby Robson: 'Not much matters more than football in the North East'.[35] Certainly it is arguable that Tyneside's proud history of radicalism and anti-establishment dissent coexists with an occasional tendency towards political lethargy. Chartist-inspired mass participation on Tyneside has been described as 'never better than patchy and ephemeral', the area was surprisingly slow to embrace trade unionism, and in recent times the overwhelming votes of *No* to both a regional assembly (2004) and an elected mayor in Newcastle (2012), spoke for some of an enduring undercurrent of political indifference and timid conservatism.[36] Though it would be naïve to lay too much emphasis on Tyneside's twin obsessions of drink and football in all this, it would be equally ill-judged to suggest that they were not an underlying factor. When I asked Glenn McCrory why a region with a reputation for casual pugilism had produced only himself as a world champion boxer, he stated without hesitation: 'Football. Football. You know, everything, *everything* takes second place to football.'

Similarities between Liverpool and Newcastle, scousers and Geordies, also consistently cropped up throughout my research, and employing such a comparison seems particularly apt in this instance. Former Liverpool defender Jamie Carragher has said that 'in Liverpool we probably see ourselves as an island', and Phil Redmond, the creative force behind television programmes such as *Grange Hill*, *Hollyoaks* and *Brookside*, has described Liverpool as 'a city village and if you don't come from the place you won't get what it's about.'[37] Sound familiar? Redmond's description could just as

easily be applied to Newcastle. When Harry Pearson talked of the village-
like atmosphere that prevails, he emphasised that it manifests itself most
obviously in the city's relationship with football. The experience of living
in an overwhelmingly collectivist environment has already been examined
in relation to Akenside Syndrome, and the prevalence of an all-consuming,
myopic obsession with football may well exacerbate the condition in some
individuals.

Being brought up on Tyneside to be traditionally middle class may also
have caused historic discomfort of a different nature. Jeremy Paxman has
declared that 'no honest member of the English middle class would deny
a fear of what the football mob may contain', and bearing in mind the
interdependent relationship between class and accent, A.A. Gill's avowal
that people who speak RP 'sound stupid at football matches' is likewise
illuminating.[38] Take as an example Robert Rowell, who has written about
how he did everything he could to hide his Geordie accent whilst studying
at Sheffield Polytechnic. Perhaps unconsciously cognizant of Gill's theory,
it was only during a televised FA Cup tie featuring Newcastle that he 'felt
confident enough to turn my Geordie accent back on for the occasion'.

In further suggesting that 'you can't expect your child to have brains in his
feet *and* in his head', and 'possessing a brain and following Newcastle United
are two things that clearly don't go together', Rowell inadvertently illustrates
that football remains a popular target for social, cultural and intellectual
snobbery.[39] Therefore Michael Collins's claim that in the early twentieth
century football became 'the one national sport that was representative of the
masses' should not be lost on John Carey.[40] He is a master at pricking the
pretentious pomposity of artistic and intellectual elites. According to fellow
author Steven Pinker, his well-known book *The Intellectuals and the Masses*
demonstrates 'how many 20th-century literary intellectuals had a contempt
for ordinary people comparable to Hitler's.' Pinker maintains the book is
worth reading 'for the chastening continuity it shows with today's "social
critics", down to their despising fast food and popular entertainment.'[41]

In it Carey notes the virulent condescension of cultural commentators
such as Clive Bell and George Steiner toward the popular pastimes of the
masses including football. It was therefore somewhat disappointing to
discover Carey himself opining:

Football is sad. It is such an illusion. People feel they have achieved some-thing when their team wins, but of course they haven't. They're just desperate for some sense of achievement. Also, it is mindless, and the fact that it occupies such a central place in our culture suggests what a desperate state we are in.[42]

No evidence of empathy emanating from the academic ivory towers towards football's twin towers in that summation. Paraphrasing Carey exposes the limitations of such a reductive critique because although his view isn't wholly false, it is certainly incomplete.

Deriving vicarious pleasure is an assured aspect of following any team sport, but to reduce it to no more than that suggests a narrowness of perspective. The late Cardinal Basil Hume, former leader of the Roman Catholic Church in England and Wales, whose bronze statue overlooks Newcastle's Neville Street, presumably did not feel that football was sad when he made a retirement request to Pope John Paul II in order to dedi-cate his remaining years to, amongst other things, his beloved Newcastle United. He clearly had no problem reconciling his religious calling with being a passionate follower of the team. In a similar vein Graeme Danby, a Professor of Music and former principal bass of English National Opera (whose electrifying rendition of *The Blaydon Races* at St James' Park before the derby against Sunderland in 2008 was a joy to behold), clearly enjoys a richly diverse cultural life whilst readily acknowledging that he 'bleeds black and white'.[43]

Such evidence contrary to their own prejudice rarely troubles dedicated anti-football snobs. Indeed Brendan O'Neill recently wrote an article for *The Spectator* entitled *An acceptable hatred: The last politically correct form of prejudice is against football's working-class supporters*. He complained of a 'petit-bour-geois push to clean up footie', in which the alleged liberal perpetrators had turned against 'white working-class football fans, whom they look upon as childish, inferior, tribal and monkey-like … The view of working-class fans as a peculiar tribe is widespread.'[44] And yet football has already moved a long way from its roots as an almost exclusively working-class game (*Financial Times* journalist Simon Kuper insists that 'Football, once "the working man's ballet", has become the joy of all classes and ages, of women as well as men'), and research has shown that many middle-class people are both interested in and happy to attend football matches.[45]

Former Tory advisor and Chelsea fan Daniel Finkelstein of *The Times*, who was appointed to the House of Lords in 2013, is one of them. However, he has observed that football is not considered an acceptable profession by certain sections of the middle class. Propounding a theory that England's social class structure and attendant prejudices play a part in diminishing the country's chance of winning the World Cup, he insisted 'English football is boycotted by the educated middle class' in a way not familiar to more successful footballing countries.[46] Viewed through this prism, we can see how vitriolic comments by a notorious critic of football such as Michael Henderson – who believes the game 'is infested by small armies of mediocrities and few men of substance' and 'produce[s] woefully inadequate human beings' – can be interpreted in much the same way as Rod Liddle's 'monkeys and morons' jibe about Geordies.[47] For though ostensibly concerned with a particular sport, in my opinion the subtext pulsates with class contempt.

Football, footballers and football fans inspire eulogy and opprobrium in equal measure, in a way that epitomises the very essence of ambivalence. The game's capacity to provoke feelings symptomatic of Akenside Syndrome is plentiful. Take the letter by 'A Walton' from Burnopfield that appeared in the *Sunday Sun* on 12th October 2008, under a strap line imploring: *Look forward not back*. Talking about the upheaval at St James' Park in the wake of Kevin Keegan's departure, and responding to another reader who had written in answer to a previous letter he'd had published, he argued:

> In ignoring the irony and missing my point, he succinctly confirmed my premise that our mask of fierce regional identity hides a mass head in the sand mentality.[48]

For me this hints at broader frustration with a perceived inward-looking and insular mentality in the area, and is a quintessential example of football-induced Akenside Syndrome.

Newcastle fans sing about being *'the loyalest football supporters the world has ever seen'* and it brings to mind Harry Pearson's observation that football 'is the only subject that can induce a bloke to swank about his fidelity.'[49] Taking the analogy further, being obliged to support Newcastle United from cradle to grave means that unlike being in a loveless marriage, a disillusioned Toon fan is not permitted to have an illicit fling with, say, Manchester United or Chelsea, in order to put a bit of oomph back into his or her football-supporting life. Robert Rowell has resigned himself to this, acknowledging that he is 'lumbered with Newcastle United for the rest of my days, to honour and to hold, to love and to cherish, till death us do part.'[50] When it comes to for better, for worse, and excepting the tremendous excitement of the Sir John Hall/Kevin Keegan era and Sir Bobby Robson's gallant efforts, the last few generations of fans have endured almost entirely the latter, with bitter recrimination and an Ibsenian sterility seeping into the relationship for some.

Fashion designer Angy Morton has recognised this sense of claustrophobic despair. After creating a wedding dress out of her and her husband's Newcastle tops that she had ripped up in protest (representing fans' ambivalent feelings for the club after Keegan's then recent departure), she stated:

> Newcastle United fans have a real love-hate relationship with their team at the moment ... Many fans are finding it difficult to wear their shirts with pride with the way things are going at the moment, but ultimately there's no escape because they are really married to football and the team.[51]

Her sentiments retain an on-going resonance. Outrage at the decision to temporarily 'rebrand' St James' Park as the Sports Direct Arena and the subsequent sponsorship deal with Wonga – not to mention the fury generated by Joe Kinnear's short-lived reappointment as Director of Football – clearly confirmed this. Divorce papers being served on the club citing irreconcilable differences due to a prolonged bout of Akenside Syndrome not being an option, some fans may be in urgent need of intensive relationship counselling. Let's say it together: *What irritates me most about my relationship with Newcastle United is...*

*   *   *

So there they are – the *Four Pillars of Geordie Identity*: class, accent, drink and football. On one level these selective cultural characteristics simply represent the popular Geordie stereotype or brand, exaggerated portrayals of which can be found emanating from within and without the area. Such representations arguably cast us in the role of the nation's village idiot; unfashionably working class, burdened with a funny accent, and inveterate alcoholics hopelessly addicted to supporting a losing football team. Tolerated, even liked in some quarters, but not really respected or taken seriously.

An example of this can perhaps be inferred from *The How To Be British Collection Two*. A light-hearted book of skits and cartoons anatomising the perceived foibles of British social manners and etiquette (though tending more toward the English side of things), the front cover has an illustration of the British Isles with recognisable stereotypes dotted around it. Some are general types; a man doing DIY, two raucous women on a hen night and a vicar walking his dog. There are national types also. An Orangeman and Irish Republican gesticulate at each other in Northern Ireland; in Scotland a red-haired, kilted Scotsman prepares to toss his caber, and astride Wales a rugby player and woman in Welsh national dress are united in song. Southern England finds representation in the form of a snobbish, uptight-looking old couple; the woman drinking tea with her pinkie out as her bowler-hatted husband struggles with his brolly. Nearby, in Nigel Farage's neck of the woods, another grimacing couple (dressed for Henley Regatta) peevishly prod mainland Europe farther away from Blighty with a bargepole.

Only one caricature that represents a city – or city region – appears on the map, and, sure enough, it is in the shape of a couple of Geordie blokes. One arm around each other's shoulders, they are wearing black and white striped shirts and clasping half-empty pint glasses, thus confirming their devotion to pillars three and four. They appear to be jigging about, being lairy, with their mouths wide open – probably in the middle of a football chant, perhaps *The Blaydon Races*. Whatever chant they're reciting, it's fair to assume that it is being belted out with strong Geordie accents. Taking into account all that has been examined so far, there can also be little doubt that they were conceived as working-class characters, or even if they weren't they will be perceived as such by those who cast eyes upon them.

Any scepticism on this point is dispelled by observing that the laces on the left shoe of the obese, shaven-headed Geordie (ring any bells?) are undone. Although a seemingly innocuous feature, it is instructive that the only other two characters in the book who share this slovenly trait are a 'commoner' at the bottom of a social hierarchy chart (who's also picking his nose), and a lairy-looking woman among a group of undesirables taunting morris dancers outside a country pub. The illustrator clearly utilises undone shoe-laces as a visual signifier of lower or working-class characters. Beyond any reasonable doubt all four pillars of Geordie identity are embodied within, or can be inferred from, this depiction of Tynesiders.

It's intended as light-hearted humour, of course, and should be treated exactly as such. No group wants to be seen as being overly sensitive about generalising cultural misrepresentation, and puritanical political correctness, funnily enough, did not feature on the list of possibilities when composition of the *Four Pillars* was being contemplated. Be that as it may, depictions such as this, alongside the WHSmith adverts, the *Sun* cartoon, the Paul Whitehouse, Omid Djalili and Catherine Tate characters etc., suggest concerns voiced in the early 1990s that the nationwide perception of Geordies may degenerate into 'stereotyped joke figures, usually daft males', were not without foundation and are still relevant more than twenty years later.

Despite this stereotypes are not always entirely artificial constructs and many have at least a basis in truthful observation, however vague and distorting. A form of regional, civic and cultural identity *does* exist on Tyneside of which class, accent, drink and football are integral components. And that culture is fundamental in the process of forging a sense of Geordie identity which, though positive, harmless and comforting for many, causes certain people to develop Akenside Syndrome. What now needs to be addressed is who this strong sense of Geordie identity has naturally included and who it might have alienated. In the following section groups believed to be in the high-risk category of experiencing Akenside Syndrome are assessed by applying what we have explored thus far.

An inevitable element of arbitrariness and subjectivity played a part in the categories chosen. Many were considered but didn't make the final cut. Of those that remained my objective was clear and simple: to explore with the help of people who have personal experience of which I have no access to, how one particular strand of their identity (e.g. gender, ethnicity, private schooling) has related to their sense of themselves as Geordies. Whether in the petri dish of personal identity the two components reacted benignly or malignantly, creating a harmless fizz or a disruptive, fragmentary explosion. Clearly no claims to representative status are made for those I interviewed; in academic terms anecdotal evidence is rarely sufficient and the samples are small. But this work is not conceived of as an academic thesis or a classical Hollywood narrative. Asking questions and stimulating debate takes precedence over proffering half-baked, simplistic conclusions. Embracing Harper Lee's advice I invite readers to think for themselves.

It was never going to be easy securing interviews for such a project and so it proved. Had there been no element of critique, no sensitive or controversial topics tackled, perhaps it would have been more straightforward. As it was, getting sufficient Geordies to engage with a certain critical detachment often proved a thankless task. Plenty weren't up for it. And yet slowly but surely against this backdrop of timidity and diffidence a more confident, self-assured group of people came to the fore. Understanding the broad aims and themes of the research, they readily took time to offer their thoughts, insights and experiences. All interviews took place between 2008 and 2010, and as the input of such contributors was seen as essential to the integrity and credibility of the whole project, I owe them a debt of gratitude.

There is also a sense of duty not to misrepresent. It's therefore essential to emphasise from the outset that it is not my intention to portray any of the contributors in a pre-conceived fashion, and specifically not in a negative way. They are subject to selective quotation, naturally enough, and a mere fraction of what each of them said makes it on to these pages. For instance in an engaging hour-long conversation with Lawrie McMenemy, he frequently expressed pride in and loyalty to the region of his birth and upbringing. But it might be inferred from the excerpts included here that we had a brief chat in which he had little positive to say about being a Geordie or his experiences on Tyneside. Such an inference would be wholly misguided.

The same sentiment applies to all the interviewees, all of whom had positive things to say about Geordies, Newcastle and Tyneside. Nonetheless, the nature of the book's aims, and the themes explored in relation to Akenside Syndrome, meant that an unflinching position had to be taken when including more uncomfortable observations. It's possible that the necessity of adopting such a position unintentionally results in an imbalanced representation of individuals, despite every effort to avoid this. A cautionary illustration can be elicited from two more contributors, Val McLane and Sir John Hall. Val regards herself as "A born and bred Geordie" and when asked if she is proud to be a Geordie, responded: "Oh yeah – absolutely! … I love the North-East and I love the North-East people," while Sir John Hall affirmed that "the Geordie character, in essence, is basically a lovely, charming, hospitable, caring person."

But both are strong personalities, unafraid to speak their minds, and they possessed the strength of character to address and comment upon less complimentary facets of Geordie culture also. So when both independently expressed similar sentiments about a particular issue, the obvious differences between them – gender, political outlook etc. – seemed to add weight to their observations and made their inclusion a no-brainer. Similar examples could have been used from all of the contributors. With this in mind I urge readers to be mindful that where uncomfortable excerpts and quotes are utilised, they should always be understood in the broader context of the individual's contribution, the majority of which does not appear here. And remember that these people were bold enough to express opinions and share their experiences when many others weren't.

AKENSIDE SYNDROME

Group Therapy

The Bigg Market is not a male drinking binge. Women are there
in equal numbers … But there is nothing debauched or sexist in
this phenomenon. Indeed, the Bigg Market is a curiously feminist
experience. The women equal the men in behaviour as well as
numbers … Their participation signifies their emancipation.

Bill Lancaster, *Newcastle – Capital of What?* in *Geordies*

… a region notorious for its incontinent, marauding masculinities –
the football, the drinking … Andy Capp, the Toon Army and *Viz*
magazine, the signifiers that infused Geordie identity with misogyny

Beatrix Campbell, feminist writer and former Newcastle resident (quoted by
Gordon Burn in *Living Memories, Guardian Review* 11th June 2005)

There again the different worlds of Da and Ma.

Observation by Willie Kiddar in *Kiddar's Luck*

Historically, there has been a strong differentiation in terms of
gendered identity in the North-East based on the traditional sexual
division of labour and persisting even into the post-industrial present.

Hilary Fawcett, *"We Gotta Get Out of This Place": Fashion, Gender and Identity
in the North East in the 1960s* in *Made in Newcastle: Visual Culture*

Tyneside's women have achieved through work an
economic and social revolution without waging cultural war.
Sid the Sexist may roam between Tuxedo Royale and Bentley's,
but the Fat Slags have beaten him at his own game.

Elaine Knox, *'Keep Your Feet Still, Geordie Hinnie':
Women and Work on Tyneside* in *Geordies*

Feminism may be a dirty word for those who see
wearing skimpy clothes, drinking heavily and
maintaining a McJob as a triumph for modern woman

Mariella Frostrup, *The Observer* 23rd December 2007

WOMEN

Y'alreet, Pet?

I S TYNESIDE THE LAND THAT FEMINISM FORGOT OR A POST-FEMINIST cultural oasis of gender equality? One of the first essays I had to write as an undergraduate posed the question: *There is no such thing as feminism, only feminisms. Discuss.* It invited students to contemplate the notion that feminism is not a monolithic, homogenous critical theory, but rather a loosely woven patchwork of disparate opinions, the composition of which creates a fragmented whole knitted together in awkward, often competing coexistence. So if the quotations above appear contradictory and paradoxical, that is to be expected. Nonetheless, one thing most observers – male or female, feminist or otherwise – would probably agree on, is that the historical concept of Geordie identity embodied in the *Four Pillars* has been unashamedly masculine. When former Newcastle United idol Malcolm Macdonald lists the three great loves of Geordies as being football, beer and women (in that order), we can safely assume that he is referring exclusively to Geordie men and not identifying Tyneside as some sort of Sapphic haven.

Similarly, though things may have changed slightly with the visible rise of women such as Cheryl Cole, Sarah Millican and Denise Welch, when people from outside the region think of Geordies it is often men that they instinctively envisage. The cultural representation and stereotyping of Geordies already examined exemplifies this. Therefore it was not surprising to discover that when Stuart Maconie listed twelve people in the public eye who have contributed to Britain being 'conditioned … to think of Geordies as kindly, funny, roguish, tough but not nasty, bluff but warm', every single one of them was a man.[1] Unsurprising because Elaine Knox's argument that 'Work, leisure, union activity and protest form the single-gender lens through which … [Tyneside's] past is viewed', is surely accurate and resonates residually to this day.[2] And although the intricacies of feminist theory are beyond the scope of this chapter, aided by the Geordie women I spoke to an exploration of the opening observations seems attainable.

The *Geordies* collection is comprised of ten essays of which Knox's is the only contribution by a female, thus making it only nominally more gender-balanced than Maconie's all-male example. This statistic was not lost on the co-editors, who expressed regret that they had:

> little success in finding women writers who felt they could contribute to what we were trying to do. Suffice to say that their reluctance raises another dimension to regional identity which this book has not been able adequately to explore.[3]

Fifteen years later in *An Agenda for Regional History*, Bill Lancaster declared: 'Women in the region await their historian', but in his own personal contribution to *Geordies*, Rob Colls went further.[4] With regard to the historical tendency toward shaping Geordie identity around masculine notions of self-definition, he wondered how much life was left in this 'male response'. After questioning how strong said male response remained, he answered his own rhetorical question: 'in reality the male response has gone and is not likely to come back.'[5] All of which could be seen to complement Beatrix Campbell's assertion that the area's 'incontinent, marauding masculinities' have, at least in the past, infused Geordie identity with an undesirable misogynistic element.

Nevertheless, while we might expect to find football, drink and Andy Capp on Campbell's index of shame, the inclusion of *Viz* provoked wary scepticism in me towards so-called radical feminists, who tend to hurl the

word *misogyny* around with dubious justification at times. Misogyny means
hatred of women, and hatred is a polarised extreme which precludes interpretation and the potential for ambiguity. We need look no further than *Viz*'s
own Millie Tant for a stereotypical caricature of those on the far left whose
ideological intransigence and po-faced piety often invites ridicule. That's not
to suggest that the portrayal of women in *Viz* is particularly flattering. Far
from it. But the portrayal of men is equally as damning at the very least,
and it would be ludicrous to argue that this is indicative of misandry (hatred
of men). If you're going to go down that road, an observation of underlying
misanthropy would be the most balanced evaluation; after all, Sid the Sexist
cuts a far more pathetic figure than the Fat Slags – a fact clearly not lost on
Elaine Knox.

As well as claiming that the women of Tyneside had engineered an
economic and social revolution without waging cultural war against men,
Knox also suggested, at the time of writing in the early 1990s, that the area's
men had:

> survived this social and economic earthquake with many of their illusions
> intact. Role models for Andy Capp and Sid the Sexist still abound ... the
> comfortable assumptions of the past still remain.[6]

In the same book, whilst exploring the historic exclusion of women from
sport on Tyneside, Harvey Taylor reinforced this belief: 'it is surprising just
how tenacious the old culture has been ... there is abundant evidence of the
continued strength of a masculine, working-class, regional identity.'[7] And
you don't have to fit the emasculating caricature of a SNAG (Sensitive New
Age Guy) to empathise with women *and* men who might feel a certain
unease, inhibition and ambivalence living within what is still on some levels
an overtly aggressive masculine culture. To this day you don't have to walk
very far round Newcastle city centre before encountering some bloke being
loud, lairy or aggressive. As renowned Newcastle born and raised fitness
coach Steve 'Blackie' Black has insisted: 'there's only one set of people that
Geordies revere more than their sports stars and that's their hard men.'[8]

It's doubtful whether commentators such as Campbell and Frostrup would
agree that nocturnal Bigg Market antics represent a feminist experience,

curious or otherwise. But added to the assertion that the Fat Slags have beaten Sid the Sexist at his own game, it does suggest certain Tyneside women have achieved a sense of equality of sorts. It's a version of equality that appears to work along the lines of Lad and Ladette culture (conservative commentator Peter Hitchens has labelled it 'the raucous equality-in-grossness of the hard-drinking and lewd 'Ladette"), whereby assimilation and imitation carry more value than subversion, self-definition and reinvention.[9] How fulfilling this notion of equality is for those who don't regard aping masculine ribaldry as the apex of feminist self-assertion is highly questionable, and the probability of a gender-related strain of Akenside Syndrome seems strong.

Val McLane is perhaps best known on Tyneside for her portrayal of Norma, sister of Tim Healy's Dennis character in the second series of *Auf Wiedersehen, Pet*. However, alongside her acting career she has assumed various other roles including that of author, broadcaster, university drama leader, and campaigner championing causes such as the anti-apartheid movement and women's rights. Recalling her days on local radio she remembered being "noted at Radio Newcastle for being such a strong feminist", and her commitment to giving women a representative voice has produced two books; *Women in my Past* (which culminates with the lyrics of her song *Women of Tyneside*) and *Xhosa Women's Voices*, focusing on women from the Xhosa tribe in South Africa's Eastern Cape province. For Val a typical Geordie woman is "strong, caring and loving and has a sense of humour."

Having also played another iconic North-East female character – Andy Capp's wife Flo no less – in London's West End, she seemed a good person to ask whether Beatrix Campbell's claim that Geordie identity has been historically infused with misogyny was accurate. She replied, "I suppose it did, yes. And I suppose you could see it that way. I mean I have come across quite a lot of misogynists in my time, especially male bosses. And I've had dealings with them where I have not been able to cope with it, and I've had to leave two jobs. I left two jobs in the course of my early career because I was working for misogynists." Although that was back in the 1970s when overt sexism was more prevalent nationwide, Val also expressed concern about present-day problems encountered by some women on Tyneside and beyond: "I have talked to a lot of the girls that I've taught about [misogyny/ sexism etc.] and they say it still exists."

BAFTA-nominated film director Sue Clayton grew up in and around the Newburn area of Newcastle, and freelance writer Jo Chipchase was brought up in Walkerville in the city's East End. Both generally agreed that Campbell's claim is historically accurate. Sue mentioned historic statistics relating to drink and domestic violence (Andy Capp used to give Flo a slap now and again, of course, leading to Homer Simpson's ironic line in an episode of *The Simpsons* in which, laughing fondly while reading the comic strip, he talks of him as a 'wife-beating drunk'), and this evoked an earlier era on Tyneside described in *Kiddar's Luck*: 'They were like many a wife in our parts who regularly wore a black eye because her husband was given to an untidy belligerence when drunk.'[10]

Jo left Newcastle in the early 1990s and currently divides her time between Brighton and the Sierra Nevada region of southern Spain. She recalled that "since leaving Newcastle, I've met a couple of Geordie men who seem to be acting the part of one or all the aforementioned characters [on Campbell's misogyny-infusing Geordie identity list]." Referring to a "self-styled hard man from North Tyneside" whom she believed to be "a definite misogynist", she said, "Unfortunately, he reacted badly to beer: it made him violent. This didn't stop him from drinking the stuff, as it was clearly part of his perceived 'male Geordie identity' ... I'm sure he couldn't shake off his 'beer and a scrap' attitude which was hardly appropriate in a quiet Spanish town." She was likewise unimpressed with another male Geordie ex-pat, describing him as "a definite misogynist. He tends to make insults towards women and then pretends it's a joke, in line with the Tyneside regional culture."[11]

All of which appears to further endorse the assertion that for some men on Tyneside, both historically and perhaps to this day, an at best dubious attitude towards women is incorporated into their sense of masculine Geordie identity. However, when asked whether the perceived dominance of working-class culture on Tyneside still holds women back, with gender roles more clearly delineated (described historically by Hilary Fawcett as 'the gender polarisation endemic in the region'), both Val and Jo gave more nuanced responses.[12] Val agreed, "Yes. Yes it does," but added: "It's not just working-class. We're talking about women in general being held back by misogyny." And Jo maintained that she had "witnessed much more sexism

in London," especially in the City, and avowed that "sexism and male dominance are hardly restricted to Tyneside."

Developing the notion that issues of gender reach beyond the regional and
class-based (though these are clearly vital factors to be considered), Jo went
on to say: "I'm not certain that this prevailing attitude of male dominance is
peculiar to Tyneside. And surely it's partly generational." In relation to the
possibility of Geordie women experiencing a gender-related strain of Akenside Syndrome the reference to a generational element, considered earlier, is
important. It echoes a sentiment expressed by the youngest woman I spoke
to, Charlotte (pseudonym requested by contributor), then in her early twen-
ties. When asked if she agreed that the marauding masculinities associated
with Geordie identity have infused the concept with misogyny, she reasoned:
"I'd say that there's something kind of macho and masculine about it but
I don't know if I'd go as far as misogyny, that's slightly too strong. But then
again it might be one of those generational things … growing up that couple
of decades later might just make a general difference." Quite a contrast from
Val's experience, whereby she maintained: "women of my own era have told
me regularly that they have felt dominated by the male sex."

The male ex-pats whose behaviour Jo described could be seen as representing two popular Geordie stereotypes – or archetypes depending on
your point of view – exemplified by *Viz* characters Biffa Bacon and Sid
the Sexist. The former with his 'beer and a scrap' mentality and the latter
with his incessant sexist remarks symbolise a certain historic social and
cultural male conditioning on Tyneside. They were in effect playing the
Geordie roles which they felt their culture demanded, respected and valued,
unhindered by the fact that they inhabited a different country with different
cultural norms and customs. Geordie versions of the wince-inducing Little
Englander abroad. Nonetheless, while playing the Geordie is more typically
associated with men, women can feel the pressure of conforming to cultural
expectations and pre-conceived notions of Geordieness too. This has been
illustrated in an article on the BBC Tyne website entitled: *'She can drink,
she's a Geordie'.*

Focusing on report findings by University College London, revealing
North-East women aged 18-49 to be top of Britain's binge drinking
league tables, the article touches on the experience of Lynne, originally

from Blyth. A recovering alcoholic, she lived in London for over twenty years before her parents brought her home to rehabilitate having realised the extent of her alcoholism; a problem she blames partly on a North-East upbringing. Talking about her life in London, she told the reporter: 'Whenever there was anything bad in my life I used to go to the pub and drink because that's what we did up here, it was in my northern roots. They [friends and colleagues in London] always used to say 'Oh, Lynne can drink, because she's a Geordie.' I didn't mind it at all. In fact I thrived on it.' Also quoted in the article are statistics from Balance, Britain's first regional 'alcohol office' which for obvious reasons opened in the North-East in 2009, claiming that North-East women drank more units of alcohol per week than their male counterparts, up by 22% as opposed to a 14% decrease for men.[13] Little wonder then that during Charles Jennings's visit to Newcastle for his travelogue, he claims to have found the Geordie women he encountered in the Bigg Market 'uniformly dead drunk.'[14]

Ruth Sunderland has talked of 'the double standards around women and alcohol' and, as Charlotte pointed out, we need to be wary of gender hypocrisy when discussing the women of Tyneside's relationship with this particular pillar of Geordie identity: "One thing that does actually really annoy me is this kind of double standard about binge-drinking and women binge-drinking. That somehow binge-drinking culture is a huge problem *and* women are doing it! As if that makes it worse. I don't quite understand why this should be … it bothers me not that women get criticism, but that women get criticised for it *more* than men, for doing the same thing."[15] Touché. However, if Geordie women's drinking and drink-related behaviour is to be held up as some sort of emancipatory victory, then it doesn't seem unreasonable to question whether it is of the Pyrrhic variety. Research released in 2012 by The Office for National Statistics revealed that alcohol-related deaths in the North-East for men in 2010 was 40% higher per capita than the national rate – for women it was 36% higher per capita.[16]

Professor Ian Gilmore, who attended Newcastle's Royal Grammar School, is a liver specialist and former president of the Royal College of Physicians (an organisation of which Mark Akenside became a fellow in 1754), and he has stated: 'Women are more susceptible to the effects of alcohol. They are smaller, they metabolise drink less well and it affects their vital organs more.'[17] Journalist Tanya Gold, a recovering alcoholic, has meanwhile talked of alcoholism as 'a disease of the soul, a system of self-harming thought', and, reflecting on the fact that more than twice as many women drink themselves to death now than did in the early 1990s, wondered what response was necessary 'to this burgeoning mental illness in young women'.[18] Certainly whilst working as a Crisis Loan Decision Maker in North Tyneside in 2009/2010, I found it depressing, but unsurprising, hearing so many Tyneside women (and men) cite alcoholism or alcohol-related issues when asked whether they had any health problems.

Talking about the less attractive side of Tyneside's drinking culture generally, Val McLane said, "I think it's sad. People say it's giving the North-East a bad name, although this happens all over the country. I just think how sad it is that they want to be part of the tribe and to be part of the tribe you've got to behave like this, you know? You've got to get drunk; you've got to drink twenty shots in a night." So can the Bigg Market really be seen as a feminist experience? Can women's numbers, behaviour and participation realistically be said to signify their emancipation? "No. In a word," was Sue Clayton's initial response, before adding, "the 'community-ness' of those gangs of women is very good ... the drinking doesn't really prove anything else beyond itself." Jo Chipchase concurred: "Calling it a 'feminist experience' is pushing it somewhat! The Bigg Market is an example of Ladette culture fuelled by binge drinking. Feminism is not at the heart of it." When asked whether Elaine Knox's *Viz*-themed intimation of gender equality could be interpreted as assimilation rather than emancipation, Sue agreed: "It's a Ladette thing, yeah. It's very limited."

Having waded this far into the murky waters of feminist theory and gender studies (not to be interpreted as a phallic misappropriation of a feminine space or symbol), now is an apt juncture at which to enlist the help of an expert on such matters. North-East academic Dr Melanie (Mel) Gibson is one of the country's leading authorities on gender representation in comics, and in 2008 she appeared on BBC2 documentary *COMICS BRITANNIA (Anarchy in the UK)*, which heavily featured the phenomenon of *Viz*. On the show she expressed views about the Fat Slags that sit uneasily with more mainstream feminist readings: 'My reaction to *Viz* was actually one of enthusiasm at the time ... And you would have thought that I would assume it was offensive and problematic, but they were people I recognised and I was actually quite excited by them. I thought they were terrific ... You can read them as terribly negative stereotypes – or you can see them as women who do what they want, when they want, with whom they want, in any way they want, and that everyone needs to be frightened of them. Now that's actually quite empowering.'[19] Sue Clayton echoed this sentiment, "If you're going to be semiotic about it, the Fat Slags in one way were quite powerful."

Although happy to describe herself as a feminist, with such outspoken views I wondered whether Mel regarded women's Bigg Market participation as signalling their emancipation: "No, not necessarily. Possibly though. It's not a space that I want to be part of, but when you look at my costume I'm not Bigg Market style. But I do reserve the right to go out and drink as hard as the blokes if I so desire to. And to create as much havoc as the blokes if I so desire to." When I mentioned that this notion of equality appears to work along the lines of Lad and Ladette culture, and questioned how fulfilling it can be for those who feel aping the boorish antics of some Geordie men is not the pinnacle of feminist self-assertion (hinted at on a national level, albeit with a snobbish tint in my opinion, by Mariella Frostrup's 'McJob' observation), Mel referred to the work of another female academic, who "talks about the Ladette as a sort of reaction and appropriation which you wouldn't necessarily see as feminist, but you *can* see as an assertion."

Mel's reference to costume reminded me of former *Byker Grove* star Donna Air's belief that 'people have the stereotype of [Geordies as] these big, lardy *Viz* characters, or Andy Capp, and that all Newcastle girls are really up for it', perpetuated by Anthony Daniels who writes as Theodore Dalrymple in *The Spectator*.[20] Bemoaning what he sees as young British women's propensity for exposing 'their white-puddingy thighs to the freezing winds of two or three in the morning,' he added the aside: 'no one who has been to the centre of Newcastle on a Saturday night can fail to appreciate certain advantages to the burqa'.[21]

Despite this quite unpleasant observation, having earlier examined the relationship between choice of clothing and the desire to fit in and feel that you belong, it was interesting to note that Mel felt some positives could be derived from the clichéd image of the scantily-clad female Bigg Market reveller, while not ascribing to the minimalist sartorial style herself. "I have gone out in the Bigg Market but I don't find it comfortable because I know I'm different. But I think within the Bigg Market, within the culture in terms of dress codes – it's empowering. But from my point of view it's uncomfortable, because I don't fit the code, male or female."

Feeling that you're different and experiencing discomfort about not fitting in with dominant cultural codes are, of course, classic indicators of Akenside Syndrome. For Jo the donning of such attire can be interpreted in a similar way to the Toon top tendency. She suggested that "opting for a certain form of group behaviour – such as wearing the 'uniform' of short skirt and skimpy tops in all seasons, including winter, to get pissed in the Bigg Market – is a form of shrugging off personal identity. It's a case of fitting into the prevailing culture. That's what my friends and I did when we were 18," before adding "And, yes, I think Mariella [Frostrup] is having a dig at working-class women with little ambition beyond this sort of 'fun'."

Similarly summarising the issue of women and drink on Tyneside, Charlotte recalled how she felt her school in Jesmond "had this very narrow concept of feminism; that it basically involved being able to do the same things that men were doing, and nothing about re-evaluating the worth that our culture ascribes to different ways of doing things." As a concluding reflection, she maintained: "On the one hand it is in some senses a triumph … It is an equality. I suppose it's kind of whether or not that culture in itself is a good thing is the issue, rather than whether it's specifically women [participating in it]."

Whether we choose to analyse Tyneside women's relationship with drink moralistically or from a feminist viewpoint, see their participation as liberating or self-flagellating, it seems reasonable to appraise that modern-day men and women's interaction with this pillar of Geordie identity is, broadly speaking, of a similar nature. But can the same be said about accent? In *Talking for Britain* Simon Elmes recalls how his mother, 'like so many just-postwar parents, was keen to make sure her son didn't grow up using local dialect words and a local accent', and relates how time and again throughout the course of his research he encountered: 'a plaintive cry about school-teachers who 'beat the dialect out of me', the tale of parents – frequently mothers – who still today tell their children to 'speak properly' and not use slang or rough words'.[22]

Once again *Kiddar's Luck* yields up a valuable localised historical perspective. Remembering his mother reading to him as a child, Kiddar muses on 'her own pleasantly modified version of the Tyneside dialect,' and recollects how when he and his father were learning to read together she could be found 'now and then cleverly correcting his pronunciation.' Going to school for the first time, aged 5, he finds himself impressed by his teacher, Miss Greensill, 'a lady, not so much for the way she dressed ... but because she talked posh. All day. I'd heard the little girls imitating her ... It hadn't occurred to me that anyone could keep up that kind of lingo constantly and with ease.' When a fellow pupil called Freddy says, 'Please, teacher, Ah divn't knaa', Miss Greensill instructs him: 'You mustn't say "divn't", say "I don't know"', whilst Kiddar describes the speech of a girl in his class, Lizzie Heslop, as an 'affected rattle'.[23]

In his rumination on present day accent-related issues, Andrew Taylor reports how 'according to modern academic linguists, women are *more* likely than men to lose their regional accents', and explains that 'regional or non-standard accents are also seen as bringing with them elements of roughness, toughness and machismo.'[24] Considering Geordie is a man's name that has also come to describe the way Tynesiders speak, allied to the heavy industrial, masculine-focused historic construction of Geordie identity, it's easier to imagine a man feeling emasculated by not having, or having lost, a Geordie accent – remember David John Douglass's assertion that 'lack of accent meant softy' – than it is to imagine a woman feeling less feminine about the same thing.

So is pride in having and retaining a Geordie accent generally more of a bloke thing? Jo was in no doubt: "YES! I think so. It is all part of the 'toon army'/'my group' mentality: to be a real masculine man, you have to have a strong accent, enjoy football with the lads and drink beer. Possibly with a few tattoos thrown in for good measure!" She also felt that "a strong regional accent can sound a bit rough on a woman," while Sue believed that women "tend to want to fit in more wherever they go ... whereas an accent may be more fundamental to a man's identity."

Sue went on to say that "women are always more inclined to adapt in all sorts of ways culturally, although I can't really prove that." Charlotte, who studied linguistics at Oxbridge, elaborated on this theory. Referring to the view that language levelling proliferates more through women, she said, "men tend to identify more with work … there's often a class element to that; your culture, the people you work with, the pride that goes with accent." Furthermore, she cited gender conditioning as a potential factor in some women being more likely to lose a regional accent, it being a less important mainstay of their identity: "'people-pleasing' is one of the characteristics that girls are brought up to do more than boys; fitting in and pleasing other people and going along with other people is one of the traits that is encouraged in women." To illustrate the point she offered an education-based example: "So say when I went to university the theory would be that I would feel worse about standing out and less confident about my identity and myself. Whereas a bloke would have been encouraged to be very proud – so having a distinctive accent would be less of a stigma, in a way."

Although this complements Sue Lawley's alleged verbal conformity at Bristol, the accent-changing inclinations of Robert Rowell whilst studying in Sheffield offer a cautionary tale against crassly over-simplified gender assertions. Nonetheless, the sharply contrasting experiences of Sue Clayton and Sid Waddell at Cambridge University afford us an opportunity to put Charlotte's theory to the test. When Waddell attended Cambridge his accent led to aggressive encounters with public schoolboy contemporaries, yet he refused to buckle under the widespread societal pressure to linguistically conform, reflecting in 2007: 'the one thing I'm good at using is also the thing for which I've always been pilloried, my Geordie voice. It's because of that Geordie voice I'm now famous as the bloke on telly who screams about darts players and their salty tears.'[25]

Sue's vocal trajectory at New Hall, Cambridge, could hardly be more different. Interviewed for *The Guardian Review* in 1998 whilst promoting her film, *The Disappearance of Finbar*, she recalled first-term discomfort amongst RP-speaking, middle-class fellow students: 'They said 'buks', 'Yah', 'baaath'. I hated them thinking, 'What a funny little Geordie', so I learned words with 'aaas' in them, like Frascati and avocado, and practised in the mirror'.[26] Reading this tragi-comic anecdote both saddened and maddened me, and when I asked Sue if she felt proud to be a Geordie – one of my opening questions to all Tynesiders interviewed – she replied, "Oh, I do absolutely. I still consider it my true place," but soon came round to her time at Cambridge unprompted. "I wasn't [proud to be a Geordie] at first when I got to Cambridge. I definitely got the ambivalent syndrome because nobody could understand my accent. I had a very strong accent and they used to laugh in this very sniggery, patronising way … they used to always be either irritated or amused by it, or else they'd think it was very cute. So certainly for a couple of years I didn't feel at all proud, but that's the only time in my life when I wasn't."

Less inclined to accent-provoked pugilism than Waddell, she made an instantaneous decision to linguistically adapt, motivated primarily by one of the reasons for accent loss already examined: "It was an absolute fear of ridicule and I literally lost it in a day. For a few months I had this ridiculous posh accent because I'd just learnt it … What I find about the Geordie accent is people always think it's funny. Most middle-class southern people think all accents mean you're stupid. They always think it means people are stupid. But, in addition, they think that the Geordie accent is funny, and that's what humiliated me more than anything."

While it is essential to consider the class and educational aspects of this – Geordie graduates was considered as a full chapter theme and it seems safe to assume that attending Oxbridge intensifies such issues – of broader relevance is the fact that Sue left the North-East and has lived in the South for about forty years. Relevant because Akenside Syndrome particularly afflicts those Geordies who, like Mark Akenside himself, leave the region to live their lives elsewhere. Despite being brought up in Newcastle for the first twenty years of her life, Jo Chipchase no longer considers herself a Geordie and is at ease with having lost her accent: "I didn't deliberately lose my accent. It has simply faded over time. It wasn't especially strong in the first place and I never used dialect words or expressions." Viewing herself more as English or British whilst growing up in Newcastle, she maintained that she doesn't "identify with the 'traditional' Geordie traits (apart from drinking!) including loyalty to one's home town, football and being a paid-up member of the 'Toon Army'. I find the Bigg Market culture unappealing even though I used to participate in it when I was 18."

Asked whether she had any regrets about losing her accent, whether there was any sense of loss, Jo was equally unequivocal: "No. I am quite pleased about it as I like my accent the way it is now. I don't think of Newcastle as 'my own place' anymore and my lighter accent fits more with the South, where I have tended to spend more time." Sue on the other hand, remarked: "Oh definitely; a bit less so now. I find that people's accents in Newcastle seem to have softened a bit." She further recalled how on trips back from Cambridge in the 1970s, "it was like different languages. I would have to revert to broad Geordie to talk to my relatives, whereas now when I go back they're not so Geordie and I'm not so 'southern'. But for years I did feel terribly guilty – well except I don't regret it because I like to be anonymous, I don't like people to tag me. I don't want to reveal that much of myself to people I don't know."

Despite ostensibly opposing methods of losing their Geordie accents – Sue a conscious vocal revolution and Jo an unconscious evolution – Jo expressed similar sentiments, affirming: "People occasionally comment on the fact I've lost my accent, which I don't mind at all. I don't like the idea of being 'pigeonholed' according to accent anyway." In not wanting to be tagged or pigeonholed, both display a desire to deflect the crude accent-related judgements and prejudices that exist in England to this day, with linguistic standardisation the chosen means of evasion.

Another form of linguistic conformity that may distance some Tyneside women from the accent pillar of Geordie identity is more contentious, and can be inferred from the Whitley Bay estate agent in her mid-twenties whom Harry Pearson encountered when moving back to the North-East from London. Pearson recalls how she 'talked as if she was reading off an autocue in that vibrato nasal voice some North-Easterners affect because they think it makes them sound posh.'[27] Referring to what she calls 'The Marrying-up Rule' and associated issues concerning class aspiration and imitation, Kate Fox suggests that intelligent working-class men who 'marry up' 'can sometimes be a bit truculent and resentful about having to change their habits', and also (while acknowledging that there will be exceptions) asserts that: 'women who 'marry up' are usually more compliant, and make more of an effort to fit in. If anything, they can sometimes be rather too eager to adopt the accent, vocabulary, tastes, habits and manners of their husband's class'.[28]

Donna Air's accent hit the headlines in August 2013 when she gave an interview from Cowes yachting regatta, provoking various newspapers to comment on the absence of her Geordie accent and note a perceived 'plummy' affectation. Dating the brother of Kate and Pippa Middleton at time of writing, Air refutes allegations that she has had elocution lessons, so perhaps the upper class inflection in her voice can be interpreted as an example of Fox's theory, following her previous relationship with Damian Aspinall (though they didn't actually marry). Eliza Doolittle-like accent change as much to do with class aspiration or assimilation as geographic location, which she has previously cited as the reason.

When I asked Val McLane whether she thought it was true that women are more prone to the behavioural mimicry that social class aspiration often involves, she paused to reflect, before concluding: "The point is that there are far more women who marry into a higher class than there are men. So of course that must be true, what [Kate Fox] said must be true. But I don't think you can get a fair analysis here because there aren't enough men who do this to bring comparisons between male and female ... But I do understand and agree with her that women who marry above their class do mimic the husband's class." Jo thought Fox "might have a point," Sue felt "it is probably true" and Charlotte believed "there is some truth in it. I don't know if it's the whole truth ... It does tie in a bit to what I was saying about women wanting to please people and fit in." We have already explored how accent-related social snobbery, real or imagined, is generally frowned upon within the ritualistic cultural codes of Tyneside. And when a gender dimension is added to class and accent in relation to Geordie identity, the potential for Akenside Syndrome ambivalence can amplify, particularly for those women who leave.

Modern-day Tyneside may be unrecognisable from an era in which Rob Colls could say of Catherine Cookson: 'there was a conscious decision to leave the North-East and forget it ... As a woman, the region's masculine identity was not open to her in the way it was open to the men.'[29] Yet although Chris Donald has claimed that there are 'still Sid the Sexists and Biffa Bacons, but not as many as there used to be ... I think the underlying trend is towards better behaved men', gender issues remain perennially perplexing.[30] However, the fact that a number of contributors to this chapter also appear in subsequent chapters is another nod to the postmodern concept of fluid, fractured identities. Several understood Akenside Syndrome as something they could identify with personally but few cited their gender alone as the primary cause.

Responding to the question of whether she had suffered from or experienced Akenside Syndrome, Jo stated: "Yes, for sure. I don't think it's vital to maintain loyalty to a particular region/city just because you grew up there. I don't want to be labelled as belonging to somewhere I haven't lived since I was 20." Meanwhile Charlotte focussed on class rather than gender: "I think there is a kind of ambivalence about the strong regional identity and just the cultural confusion about can you be middle class and have a strong regional identity? I'm very aware of that."

Val, embedded in the region's consciousness as an archetypal strong Geordie matriarch through her acting roles, affirmed, "Yes, I've regularly felt like an alien," before laughing. Asked why that should be the case, she replied, "I've often said I feel like an alien, I'm so different … I mean obviously there must be a hundred reasons why this has happened, but I think one of the reasons that I've felt like an alien is because I'm outspoken." Taking a broader perspective on Akenside Syndrome, without citing specific personal reasons for feeling that way, Mel insisted: "I totally recognise it. That sort of ambivalence about the North-East. Both loving it and feeling uncomfortable about it, and not knowing where else to belong. And feeling perpetually displaced is, I think, inherent to the North-East."

Of all the contributors it was Sue who felt that gender had played the most significant part in her own experience of Akenside Syndrome. A descendant of Tyneside's 19th century world champion rower, Harry Clasper, she recalled growing up in a culture of clearly delineated gender roles and spheres. "The symbol for me was Harry Clasper and the five brothers. I used to say 'Was there a girl?' and finally I was told there was a sister who was called 'the maid'. I mean 'maid' traditionally just means young girl, like maiden, but also it has all the other connotations of she was the one that looked after them, and I don't think she married. So there was very much this idea that the woman could only be a bit player in the big story – you couldn't be the hero." It's a discomforting recollection, reinforcing Elaine Knox's claim that 'One half of the region's population has been omitted from its history', and Bill Williamson's suggestion that in the North-East's collective cultural memory, 'Women are largely written out of the script'.[31]

It's also a poignant anecdotal illustration of why the editors of *Geordies* struggled to enlist female contributors to their cause, and partial vindication of Beatrix Campbell's assessment: 'The north-east has suffered from the sense that its heroism is linked with industries founded on exclusion of women and black people – mining, shipbuilding, engineering. These things in the north-east's ideology constitute the north-east. Well, excuse me! What about all the mams and school dinner ladies – the women who make the world go round?'[32] Sue dealt with these internal anxieties by defining herself as different and Bohemian, and ultimately by leaving the region, a la Catherine Cookson: "I just kind of defined myself as different and opposite, but there again, probably more than I should have had to. I felt as different as if somebody had outed themselves as being gay or something. I felt that extremely different from the community. And looking back that was maybe quite a stress, you know."

I used to get spat at in school, beaten up,
my bag thrown on the roof ... It was a terrible campaign
of bullying and name-calling which I just had to deal with.
I didn't even know I was gay myself at that point.

Nick Forbes, leader of Newcastle City Council, talking about
his experiences at a County Durham comprehensive school,
The Journal 15th March 2008

Geordies were just about the last people to accept
homosexuality ... We were: "You'll never catch a gay
Geordie! Never had any of that, like." And yet there's been
loads of gay Geordies knocking about, and they're great
people too. They're no less [Geordie] because they are [gay].

Graeme Danby reflecting on the limitations of traditional masculine
notions of Geordie identity, and a perceived historic reluctance to
embrace other cultures on Tyneside

I feel sorry for anyone who grows up gay in them heavy
industrial estates in Newcastle, because you've got no
chance. I'd have more of a chance being the only 'Paki'
growing up there. But if you're gay you've got no chance.

Narinder Kaur, Tyneside-raised former *Big Brother* contestant

Tennis was considered a "puffs" game in our school ...
I'd ended up in a town full of puffs!

Robert Rowell reminiscing about his schooldays
in Gateshead and university life in Sheffield

Where I grew up, the notion of reading books didn't
make you a swot, but a poof. There's still a lingering
assumption in parts of Newcastle that your masculinity
must be in question if you choose to use your mind.

Billy Elliot playwright Lee Hall interviewed by Alfred Hickling,
The Guardian 25th September 2007

GAY

Black and White... and Pink?

FTER BILLY ELLIOT'S CROSS-DRESSING GAY FRIEND MICHAEL KISSES him on the cheek in the film, Billy tells him that just because he likes ballet it doesn't mean he's a *puff*, and, all things considered, it seems a fair bet that Lee Hall got called a *puff* on more than one occasion during his childhood in Newcastle. Robert Rowell's pluralized use of the word – once with criticism-deflecting inverted commas and once without – enhances the impression that on Tyneside it has been a commonly used term, sometimes with an abusive or derisive edge to it. As a descriptive word it's rougher, more direct and aggressively blunt than the southern version *poof*, which frankly sounds somewhat *poofier*.

Semantics aside, it seems reasonable to speculate that the industrialised atmosphere of Tyneside's past, allied to the social conservatism of the area's working-class culture, and the tendency to chauvinism and marauding masculinities observed by some commentators, could create a censorious and prohibitive environment for gay people to come out into. The points made by Graeme Danby and Narinder Kaur may be arguable, but if we accept that there is at least a degree of historic truth in their observations, then we can see how it may be an environment in which, as Sue Clayton implied, a gay person might feel extremely different from the community. And when an acute sense of difference and dislocation creates an aching vacuum within an individual's psychological and emotional make-up, Akenside Syndrome can seep in to the void.

When Nick Forbes was interviewed by Hannah Davies for *The Journal* in 2008, he had this to say about the general acceptance of gay people in the region: 'While a lot of people are a lot more accepting of gay people, there are still pockets of homophobia and prejudice around.'[1] Three years later, as the region's first openly gay leader of a local authority after Labour's victory in the 2011 elections, he made a similar though broader point in *out! northeast* magazine: 'Key to our vision for the future of Newcastle is a more equal city, with residents feeling that they are treated fairly and not disadvantaged by the old prejudices, which are breaking down, but sadly still exist in some quarters.' Eager to ensure that others did not have to suffer what he endured at school, he also said he was 'determined to stamp out homophobic bullying in schools', and wanted 'Newcastle to be a welcoming city for everyone.'[2]

Forbes represents the Westgate ward of Newcastle covering much of the city centre including John Dobson's Grade I listed Grainger Market, which opened in 1835. And it was in this unlikely setting that I met Shane and Neil, two gay Geordies for whom Forbes's drive to eradicate homophobic bullying in schools came too late. The Nelson Street end of the Grainger Market provides space for MESMAC North East, a support centre for Tyneside's lesbian, gay, bisexual and transgender (LGBT) community, which plays host to the Gay Men Tyneside (GMT) group. Billed as the North-East's longest established social group for gay and bisexual men, GMT promotes 'an interesting and entertaining alternative to the commercial gay scene', and it was at one of their weekly gatherings that Shane and Neil shared their experiences.

Born, raised and then still living in Jarrow, Neil was 27 when we spoke, and responded to being asked whether he was proud to be a Geordie a little defensively: "I'm proud to be me." Despite coming from the home of the iconic Jarrow March, for years a defining image and potent cultural and political reference point for Geordies, when asked to elaborate, Neil insisted: "I don't think being a Geordie defines who I am as a person really." Identifying instantly with the high school experiences of Nick Forbes, he talked of being similarly subjected to homophobic bullying at Hedworthfield Compre-hensive in Jarrow. So how did he cope with it? "I didn't really. I kind of like had a breakdown when I was about fifteen and that's when I left school."

Shane was born in Scotswood in Newcastle's West End where he spent the first twelve years of his life; moving to neighbouring Benwell for most of his teenage years. Aged 31 when we talked, he was living in Gateshead where he'd moved aged 19, and his initial response regarding whether he considered himself a Geordie was more positive than Neil's: "I consider myself a true Geordie, really. I think the West End has that kind of Geordie pride about it." However, this initial positivity began to dissipate when Shane identified a sense of camaraderie as a trait of Geordie culture, before then considering it in relation to himself: "I mean I don't particularly feel it myself. I think what's interesting with me here – it's the [feeling of] ostracism."

Again the correlation and empathy with Nick Forbes regarding bullying at school was strong; in Shane's case at Rutherford School, now Westgate Community College on Newcastle's West Road: "Yes, I was definitely bullied at school for my sexuality. But it was strange for me because I never actu-ally thought that I was gay at the time. But I did receive a lot of bullying, yeah. It would definitely be called homophobic bullying these days." Sadly, unlike Forbes, who transcended the bullying to secure a place at Selwin College, Cambridge, where he was elected president of the students' union (1994-95), Shane's experience was more reminiscent of Neil's: "I had a very bad schooling because of the bullying. It wasn't necessarily just the sexuality, but I would say I really left school at fourteen [years old]."

While reiterating that it would be inappropriate to claim representative regional status for any of the contributors to these chapters – this is clearly not an exhaustive and detailed survey – it is useful to acknowledge national perspectives also. In 2011 a sociology lecturer from Bath University, Eric Anderson, proposed that homophobia was dying out, particularly among students on university campuses, and also claimed: 'Young people have disassociated themselves from homophobia the way they once did from racism.' Pre-empting criticism, he added: 'When I say that homophobia is in retreat, people often point to one case and think every gay person is oppressed … We're very good at holding one case of bullying up as a belief that this is the common experience, but the common experience for gay kids is that they are treated just fine.'[3] But in the same year, in stark contrast, and far more in keeping with the experiences of Neil, Shane and Nick Forbes, Tim Franks of the British gay charity Pace expressed this opinion: 'Homophobic bullying in schools in this country is still epidemic. It's absolutely rife. Most British schools are not safe places to be gay.'[4] Forbes may well have his work cut out in his anti-bullying ambition.

Although Shane remained "very cautious about bringing my sexuality into play in any kind of social scenario" on Tyneside, as a mature student studying Philosophy at Newcastle University he hopefully enjoyed a similar experience to that of Forbes, who has recalled: 'When I went to university, people were more open. It is a time when people explore their lives more openly.'[5] Like any good scholar Shane enjoyed applying his evolving philosophical insights to the society around him, and rationalising the perceived culture he grew up in: "I feel that there was definitely that functionalist society feeling to the North-East. The nuclear family kind of feel. And there was such a negative attitude towards anything that was deemed alternative … that's the way I see it now: anything that was deemed alternative was considered wrong."

In addition, whilst reflecting on restrictive notions of masculinity on Tyneside perhaps contributing to a certain cultural narrowness and rigidity, he asserted: "This stereotype, well archetype male, sort of permeated through this functionalist society, [to the point where] it seems as if, if it's change in any way then it's an attack on some kind of sensibility in them. You know, you can't be any other way than this one type of male. And I think that's what something like a conservative mind-set would put you into."

The conservative mind-set Shane described can sometimes lead to what has been called 'homohysteria' – 'where men try to act in sexist, hyper-macho and homophobic ways to prove they are not gay'.[6] To some extent this mode of behaviour could be ascribed to the Geordie ex-pats Jo Chipchase encountered, and there are obvious parallels with the type of Tyneside manhood depicted in *Viz* characters Biffa Bacon and Sid the Sexist. Although not accusing him of homohysteria, in my opinion we can also reasonably infer a certain culturally conditioned conservatism from Jimmy Nail's recollection in his autobiography of a chance meeting with celebrated gay artist Francis

Bacon. Difficult not to envisage as a kind of Biffa Bacon meets Francis Bacon scenario, it was in London at the height of *Auf Wiedersehen, Pet*'s popularity in 1986, and Nail recalls being anxious because at that time he had had no socialising experience with gay people. As Bacon came on to him, suggesting they go back to his place so he could draw him, Nail brought the flirtation to an abrupt end by sending him packing with a volley of abuse, including a derivation of the word *puff*. He's fine with the gays now though.

I put it to Shane that perhaps the conservative mind-set he identified is a factor in continued use of the word *puff* on Tyneside. "I don't hear it very often. But I did hear it recently. A manager used it in a very derogative way," he replied, adding that functionalist societies "want you to be very much pigeon-holed into this definite masculine character." Gay rights activist Peter Tatchell was outraged when former Manchester United footballer Paul Scholes allegedly called the referee a 'fucking poof' during a live televised game in 2006, and demanded that the football authorities take action against such 'alleged homophobic abuse' if the case was proven.[7] I asked Shane if he believed *puff* is homophobic abuse – the type of language that should be stamped out on Tyneside. "Well yes, all bullying should be stamped out really, shouldn't it? It's a very nasty way of describing someone." Nonetheless, when I suggested that certain Tynesiders may use it unthinkingly because they have been culturally conditioned to consider it an acceptable term, and therefore it is not necessarily always indicative of rabid homophobia, he was inclined to agree: "Ah well yes, definitely, yeah."

Questioning Peter Tatchell's reaction to the Scholes incident, gay-focussed website *www.PinkNews.co.uk* queried whether: 'In the context of being (yellow) carded and angry, is the insult 'poof' really wilfully anti-gay, or just a throw away swear word?' Adding a comment on an online article covering the incident, one respondent wondered: 'Is 'poof' homophobic? I thought it had long ago been relegated to a mere insulting generalism to describe an ineffectual, incompetent or overly-sensitive individual'. And while I readily acknowledge a high regard for Tatchell's campaigning on a range of issues, and accept that many of his points were perfectly valid and well made, I must simultaneously admit that it was refreshing to hear that not all contributors to this chapter adopted a militant stance, denoting, I believe, a reassuring self-confidence.

Ken Hill was born in Wallsend in 1952 and lived in Jesmond until he was 6 years old, then moving to Newton Aycliffe followed by Darlington due to his father's work. Aged 32 he moved back to Wallsend in the mid-1980s, living there for eight years and 'coming out' when he was 34. Despite moving back to Darlington he retains close ties with the city of his birth, having previously run the North-East branch of Gay Outdoors Club and being an active volunteer at GMT for many years before stepping down in 2010. Now a practising Reiki therapist, Ken's experience of the word *puff* on Tyneside was different from Shane's, as were his beliefs on how it should be dealt with: "It's used a lot and it doesn't bother me. It doesn't have any value to me. It's not a word that shocks or even offends."

He remembered working for an organisation in Darlington who were "very politically correct regarding language" and particularly prescriptive about which words were acceptable and which weren't. "The gays don't do that," he declared. "We've taken on board all the words of [abuse]. We've absorbed it, we've made it our own, we've taken the sting out of it and we've given it value. And that's what I like." Neil, the most reticent and guarded of the contributors, agreed, insisting: "I use the word myself, you know, in a humorous way."

Tony from South Shields, at 18 the youngest of the gay Geordies I spoke to, responded in a similar fashion when asked if he felt use of the word *puff* was still quite widespread in the area: "Yeah, but I even say it and stuff … no word's [inherently] offensive; it's just how you use it." Displaying a maturity of insight beyond his years, he added: "It's just a word that's being used in context. They're not always trying to be offensive, it's just how they use it." But when I mentioned Tatchell's point of view to Ken, he conceded: "I suppose it depends how it's used," and Neil's response to whether *puff* is homophobic language that should be stamped out contained a comparable sentiment: "It depends on the way the person's using it. If they're using it in an aggressive way then yes. If it's done in a humorous way, it's alright by me."

Such counterintuitive and conditional reactions made me question whether their feelings about ostensibly homophobic chants (taken from the short-lived Toon Ultras website) would be as unequivocal as those of Cris McCurley about homophobic chanting generally. A solicitor and regular contributor to *out! northeast*, explaining the implications and intricacies of the

Criminal Justice and Immigration Act 2008 in the magazine, she insisted: 'Any of us who go to football matches on a regular basis will be familiar with the revolting anti-gay chanting that goes on against some players.'[8] Shown chants including the lines, 'I know a Mackem bastard, He comes from down my way, I know he is a Mackem coz he's big and fat and gay' and 'We hate Jenas, Because he takes it up the arse', Neil said: "It's quite funny," and when asked how he would feel if sitting at St James' Park surrounded by fans singing such lyrics, calmly remarked: "I would probably just laugh."[9]

Ken elaborated further but was equally dismissive: "Sounds typical. I think it's childish. Yeah, that's offensive but it bores me. My response wouldn't be to get angry; I just think 'Ah, grow up!' It's the sort of thing you'd expect kids to come out with." More inclined to analyse the implication of the words was Shane, who interpreted the Jenas lines by discerning: "Well that's interesting; you hate someone because he takes it up the arse. Fascinating why you would hate someone for doing that. But again I think it just picks up on the reasons why someone would dislike someone for being gay. Because it assaults their sensibility of this functionalist society. And that assault feels like an attack on them." Yet despite this incisive summary, he went on to say: "It seems like silly fun to me," affirming that if he was surrounded by fans singing such songs: "I'd probably just roll my eyes. I mean, it doesn't sound like there's any malice in it really. But maybe that's because they've put it into a rhyme."

If such balanced reflections came as something of a surprise, less surprising was the general attitude toward football amongst the contributors. Unanimous indifference was the prevailing theme, taking Tony as a starting point; "I can't stand football. I hate it. I just find it boring. I would hate it! [going to a Newcastle United match] ... just the whole atmosphere I would hate, for some reason; the aggression, and there's just people trying to drink and shout and start fights," moving on via Neil's succinct "I don't like football" to Ken's "football isn't an interest of mine – none of my gay friends are interested in football," and concluding with Shane's diplomatic disinclination: "I wouldn't say I supported Newcastle United but it's very nice to hear that they're doing well. But it doesn't make my day any better or worse!"

Although Ken used to attend games at St James' Park in the 1970s before he came out, even going to Wembley for a cup final, these days he's wary of going to straight bars in the city centre if there's been a match on, and he used to leave GMT meetings early if there had been a midweek game to avoid being on the train with football supporters. Explaining why, he said: "It's off-putting. I suppose it's the aggressive masculinity. It's like the herd instinct with them."

That there should be discordance between the football pillar of Geordie identity and Tyneside's gay community is obvious; sport generally has been described as 'the last great bastion of homophobia', and gay footballers have allegedly been advised not to come out because of football's historically homophobic culture.[10] Cris McCurley has insisted that 'campaigns such as Kick Homophobia out of Football could seriously do with a boost,' and on the surface it seems there are insurmountable barriers between gay Tyne-siders and this historically defining component of Geordie identity.[11] Our job here though, is to scratch such surfaces. And there seemed like no better man to ask about football-related gay Geordie issues than Pete McDonough, then chairman of Newcastle Panthers, the North-East's first gay-friendly football team.

The Panthers were formed in April 2008 by Rob Wood and Russell Potter, with Wood stating that he wanted people in Newcastle to become more aware of gay interest in football. The club's original website said the 'reasons why they both decided to set up a predominantly gay football team was that there is a general feeling of gay people not wanting to get involved in straight teams due to prejudice', something Pete recognised from first-hand experience. Talking about his playing days in Tyneside Sunday League football, Pete, 27 at the time of our conversation, recalled: "That's exactly the same position I was in. It was too over-violent and if it came out that you were gay then you would get even more victimised, and probably hit [tackled] even harder."

Becoming increasingly uncomfortable with the levels of violence and feeling victimised, Pete leapt at the opportunity to join the Panthers: "In Sunday League football you've still got issues of racism creeping into the game, and obviously homophobia is just another part that is sometimes overlooked a lot of the time. So that was one of the reasons why I wanted to move away from it, and I would imagine there are probably a number of gay players who are in the same position really."

Pete felt a self-preserving compulsion to keep his sexuality hidden whilst playing for straight teams. Although one or two team-mates knew he was gay, it was "kind of like a hush-hush thing … it's not as though I openly told them that I was gay, because I felt I might get victimised because of that. So it's not something you can openly admit to, sadly." The Panthers provide a space where gay players like Pete can enjoy playing the sport they love while not having to repress their sexual identity, as he explained: "They feel proud of the fact when they play for us; there isn't such an issue, there's not something they've got to hide because they'll be victimised." Though not without setbacks, the club's growth and success has been encouraging. Joining the national Gay Football Supporters Network (GFSN) league in 2009-10, in May 2011 the Panthers won the GFSN National Cup in Sheffield, beating London Falcons 3:2 on penalties after extra time – proving not all teams who play in black and white stripes from Newcastle are habitually averse to winning silverware.

Pete's love of football extends beyond playing – though no longer chairman he still plays for the Panthers – to supporting the better-known, silverware-deficient Newcastle team. A season ticket holder for many years, he has followed Newcastle United home and away including many games across Europe. Agreeing with Cris McCurley and Peter Tatchell that more should be done to rid football of its anti-gay elements, he observed: "You can see Show Racism the Red Card, which I think is a great cause, and I think they do really well in this country, but I think homophobia's overlooked somewhat in the sport itself." On a personal level he felt his 'straight-acting' traits and personality inoculated him from being targeted at Newcastle games, but believed that "if somebody was more openly gay or maybe looked overtly gay, then they probably would experience a lot more prejudice than I would. If you went with somebody who was quite camp then you probably would feel quite uncomfortable."

Shane, who attended a match at St James' Park once and found it "good fun to watch," despite being "quite disturbed by the racism" and maintaining "I wouldn't say I 'belong' there," offered a similar appraisal: "I didn't feel threatened in any way. I mean I don't think I would have necessarily made it a gay event. And I wouldn't necessarily say a party of feather-boa-wearing girlie-boys would be made to feel welcome there. So yeah, definitely there seems to be a macho kind of environment where you're in competition – I don't think that goes into gay lifestyle."

Excluding Pete there appeared to be mutual mistrust between what might loosely be termed football culture and gay culture, similar to that identified by Pete Farrow, then captain of another GFSN team, the Yorkshire Terriers. Cited though not directly quoted by journalist Philip Ottermann, Farrow suggested: 'the problem is not simply that footballers are uncomfortable with homosexuality ... The gay scene also has hang-ups about football. The Terriers ... offer not just an escape from the macho culture on the terraces, but also the sometimes over-sexualised atmosphere within the gay scene.' Farrow's team-mate Stephen Fenton added, 'I have always been a Middlesbrough fan, but a lot of my gay friends give me funny looks when I start talking about football.'[12]

Having listened to Farrow's and Fenton's views, Shane flatly rejected my proposal that the gay scene on Tyneside might have hang-ups about football too, contending: "I wouldn't say that they have hang-ups – I just don't think they really care. I think the hang-ups definitely come from the heterosexual side of things; and that they're the people who have the problems integrating with men who have sex with men." Tony's take on the issue was more equivocal, admitting: "When some of my mates have said 'I'm watching the match,' it still feels a bit weird." In his experience, "When gay people say they're straight-acting, a lot of gay people find that offensive and think: 'You're just watching football because you're trying to act straight,'" which suggests a stigma attached to football may ring true for some gay Geordies.

What better way to break down barriers between these two uneasy bedfellows than an openly gay player donning the black and white stripes for Newcastle United? Although professional sport has been called 'the final closet', research published by Ellis Cashmore, professor of culture, media and sport at the University of Staffordshire, revealed that 'almost eight out of 10 fans thought openly gay players would have the same positive effect on football as black players did in the 1980s and 90s when racism in the sport was tackled.'[13] But Shane was sceptical about the prospects of a day when an openly gay centre-forward could play at St James' Park and his sexuality wasn't an issue: "I couldn't imagine a time when that could happen, but I don't know."

Ken, remembering the misplaced doubts of his late partner about gay marriage and civil partnerships becoming a reality, was more optimistic, if cautiously so: "Yeah. I mean God knows when that will happen but you just don't know. To have an openly gay player at St James' Park – wow!" Pete, the most intimately acquainted with the rituals of fandom, was actually the most upbeat respondent, asserting; "Once you put the top on I think the fans are behind you regardless of sexuality, in the majority. I suspect that if he was scoring the goals and winning the competitions, I don't think any Newcastle fan would have an issue really," albeit then adding a reality check: "We're not there yet, no. Certainly not."

Given his straight-acting persona and footballing inclinations, I wondered if Pete felt that the macho, aggressive masculinity aspect of Geordie culture made it more difficult for gay people to fit in on a broader level beyond football. "It does," he confirmed, before elaborating while making reference to another pillar of Geordie identity – drink. Although happy to go to straight bars in Newcastle with work-mates, he maintained: "If I was to say to some of my gay friends 'Do you want to go round the straight scene?' they would not feel comfortable. I mean there are particular places like the Bigg Market and some of the bars in The Gate [a leisure venue on Newcastle's Newgate Street] that even I avoid because of that [aggressive masculinity]. You're going out socialising with your friends to have a good time and if you look the wrong way at somebody they'll take exception and not think twice about just kicking you within an inch of your life. And yeah, I try to avoid that. Somewhere instilled in these people is the fact they've got to think they're some sort of macho person, to prove to themselves and their friends and potential suitors that that's how they should behave."

Asked whether there were any bars or areas in Newcastle city centre that he would avoid, there was no hesitation from Shane either: "The Bigg Market. I would not feel comfortable. I've only ever felt comfortable in one bar in the Bigg Market and that was when I was out with a female friend who was quite mad. And that was fun, but otherwise no I would definitely not feel comfortable at all." Though perhaps difficult to envisage with the upgrading of Newcastle's gay scene in the past decade or so, there is a hint here of potential historic alienation between gay Geordies and the drink-related 'urban sociability' enjoyed by their heterosexual peers. Although unable to explore this complex concern in depth, former Northern Pride chair Tom Gorman has referred to a sense of social exclusion that some gay people on Tyneside can feel, and Louise Evan-Wong of The LGBT Foundation NE has likewise talked of the need to 'solve some of the isolation issues.'[14]

Teetotaller Neil felt this most keenly of the people I spoke to, acknowledging that he had experienced it himself: "Yeah, definitely, yeah. Before I started coming to GMT I went through a period of feeling very isolated living where I did." Unlike their straight female counterparts then, who have, depending on your point of view, liberated or assimilated themselves into the orgiastic epicentre of Tyneside's drinking culture, it seems from the overwhelming response of those interviewed that gay Geordies who are more comfortable with the drink rather than the football pillar of Geordie identity, much prefer to indulge it on Newcastle's burgeoning gay scene – in effect a form of socialising separatism.

It's perfectly understandable in many respects. The priority given to providing a clearly demarcated space in the city centre for the LGBT community is symbolic of a modern, maturing city for many, and several contributors pointed out that Sunderland, a nearby similar-sized conurbation, has no established scene. But I wondered if, from a wider philosophical perspective, the encouragement of separate social spheres might actually hinder integration between gay and straight Geordies. Acting as a restraint on the promotion of contact theory, whereby social interaction between previously estranged groups helps dispel stereotypical thinking and dissipate prejudice. Though not averse to such utopian thinking, Ken pointed out: "I mean, any element of society likes to have somewhere for them to go themselves, like a working man's club or whatever. So I think if gays say 'Well look, we would like to have our own bar,' that's fine. But I think there also should be bars where anybody goes in."

After saying he'd heard a lot of gay people on the scene in Newcastle complaining about 'straights' interloping on their patch, Tony advanced Ken's theory: "You want to be accepted but you can't have your own [exclusive bars]. If you want to be accepted you have to be the same as everyone else. For it to be accepted there would have to be no such thing as a gay scene, but I think it's gonna be a while." Shane contemplated the segregational implications of the term *gay*, briefly proposed getting rid of specifically demarcated gay bars, advocating a future where there was "a friendlier atti-tude to both sexualities [gay and straight] approaching someone," before concluding: "I don't think we should get rid of gay bars but I think there should be less homophobia in the 'straight' pubs if you are approached by another man; and I've heard this is happening a lot with the younger lads. Someone who is straight could say 'Well, thanks very much but I'm actually straight,' instead of saying 'You puff!' LAMP! Which I think happens more, possibly, in areas like this."

Despite such reservations, Shane definitely agreed that Tyneside has become less homophobic since he came out in the mid-1990s, and felt that attitudes towards diversity generally were improving: "I think it's getting better now which is fantastic. It's great to see such diversity being embraced in the North-East, but I do think it's taken a while and a lot of people have lost a lot of blood, sweat and tears through it." Neil seconded this view: "You're always going to get your arseholes who will say something, but I think as a whole people in the North-East are quite accepting of gay people really. I think people are a lot more open-minded now and are less fearful of it, if that would be the right word."

Nonetheless, Ken, who said he'd been sacked from two jobs due to his sexuality earlier in his life, felt it was still "more difficult for the working-class gay men to come out" on Tyneside. "A lot of the gay men keep it under wraps, they don't tell anybody. And it's just impossible for a lot of them to come out, but I think it's changing." An anecdote he shared reinforced a positive perception of change for the better: "When I used to go for my copy of *Gay Times* I used to go to this newsagents opposite the Central Station and she'd always say, 'Would you like it in a brown paper bag?' And I would say, 'Of course, of course.' That was the attitude then. If anybody asked me that now I know what they would get. So things have moved on a lot for me and I see things have changed a lot in Newcastle."

The same shop may well have stocked *Viz*, whose 12th issue in November 1984 bore the strapline: *THE MAGAZINE ONLY PUFFS DON'T BUY*. But judging the modern-day level of homophobia on Tyneside to be "prob-ably no different to everywhere else," Ken added weight to Shane and Neil's testimony that it has become a less homophobic society. "Yeah, definitely," he enthused. "The outward changes. I often think when I come up to

Newcastle, I will always find something different. My grandparents wouldn't recognise this place if they were here now, it's changed so much. And from a gay man's perspective, it's changed for the better. I feel very comfortable in Newcastle."

Pete, perhaps most familiar of the gay Geordies I talked to with 'straight' spaces on Tyneside, felt that use of the word *puff* was still widespread (though he imagined you "get it everywhere") and also believed homophobia was still prevalent. He indignantly recalled an incident that occurred only a few months before our meeting, at a Blockbuster store in West Denton, when a "charvy type" said to his female companion something like "Look at them two benders/fags" within earshot of him and his then partner. When Pete challenged the man he took his coat off, gave it to the woman he was with and went outside waiting for Pete to come out, leaving him to conclude: "When you confront these people they will actually want to fight with you because you confronted their homophobia."

Although estimating his assailant to be roughly the same age as him, he said of homophobic attitudes on Tyneside: "I think it's of a generation, person-ally. I think it's a generational thing. I think people of my age, slightly older, are probably more accepting." However, he also posited another dimension, one that other contributors made similar reference to: "I suppose it could be geographical as well. In the fact that I've worked in Durham and Durham is even more discriminating against anything really. Mining villages, they're in the middle of nowhere; anything that's different, anything that stands out from the norm, they're not happy [with] and they'll discriminate against – should that be race, colour, sexual orientation, they will discriminate. So it's not just a case of age, it's a case of where you live as well. Because it's just not so diverse in them places."

When I asked Pete whether he had experienced Akenside Syndrome, his response involved football. He no longer goes to Newcastle's away games and explained the reason why: "When I go to away matches I think some of the away fans – when following football you're quite ashamed that they are from Newcastle. In the fact that you get a lot of discrimination regardless of whether that's against women, religion, colour or sexuality. A lot of that makes me think: 'Yeah, I actually don't want to be part of this at all in the slightest.'" There was cautious vagueness from Neil; "I've questioned whether

I fit in or belong but that's just been sort of a 'me' thing really," whereas for Ken his sexuality was a factor but easily surmountable: "If I've ever had doubts about whether I fitted in, they would only be from the point of view of being a gay man. But those doubts were pretty soon dispelled so, no, I think Akenside Syndrome is alien to me."

At which point it's worth remembering that Ken, though his allegiance to and identification with his home city are strong and genuine, and his insights valid and valuable, has spent more of his life living away from Tyneside, including many of his formative childhood and teenage years. A crucial factor, I feel, in whether or not an individual is likely to experience Akenside Syndrome on the more pronounced and problematic end of the scale. Reflecting on how he lived in Newcastle between the ages of 6 and 18 before moving away for many years, playwright Michael Chaplin mused: "I suppose in terms of forming who you are and what you are it's probably the most crucial time ... coming to terms with all the issues that derive from the process of growing up and becoming an adult. And those formative experiences are of profound importance on all sorts of levels, but in particular working out where you feel at home, which I suppose is one of the most profound elements of your sense of identity – where you feel most comfortable."

Shane and Tony had spent their entire lives living on Tyneside, and their responses were markedly different to Ken's. Asked in the form of an open question, Shane requested clarification as to whether I meant due to his sexuality – to which I responded that the second part of the question was: 'How much of this has been to do with your sexuality?' "Yes, I would say *definitely*," was his forceful answer. "I felt ostracised from making friends at school [with boys] who were quite overtly masculine. And they pushed me away, yes. Because I was taking a different path in life. I was separating from the 'they' as they would say in philosophy." He further recollected that deviating from the perceived norm and doing things "a woman would normally do, pushed me away and definitely made me feel segregated, especially as a child. I don't think I felt it at the time. I didn't notice that I was being segregated, I just thought that was pretty much what people were like."

Shane's experience of Akenside Syndrome appears to be that of the individual who stays on Tyneside despite deeply held ambivalent feelings toward the culture; someone who develops coping mechanisms and rationalises their surroundings in order to alleviate the condition. But for some the tumultuous feelings are too much and the only remedy is to physically remove themselves from the environment they feel is provoking such internal agitation. The necessary simplicity of these chapter headings does not, of course, do justice to the unending multiplicity and contradictions of individual human experience and perception. Nowhere was this more evident than when contrasting Shane's assertion – "Nowadays a lot more people are wearing brightly coloured hair and alternative clothes, and they're quite accepted walking down the street in Newcastle, like Northumberland Street. But back in my day they would definitely have got some abuse" – with Tony's personal experience. It's also worth reiterating that Shane wasn't approaching retirement age when we spoke, but only 31 years old.

"Not feeling I belong here? That's why I'm moving," Tony insisted, yearning for a move to Brighton as a student after completing his course at Newcastle College. At an early but epochal stage of his Akenside Syndrome arc, asked why he felt this way he talked of being recently 'gay-bashed' by a male friend of his sister, and spoke with exasperation of running a daily gauntlet of derisive comments on the council estate in South Shields where he lived: "It's just generally the people in my area. I can't stand the way they go on, and the way people shout stuff." Feeling he could be himself more in Brighton, partially due to an inevitably romanticised view of a city described as 'the drug death capital of the UK' in 2011, and where, according to research by youth support charity Allsorts, 23% of those reporting bullying in Brighton secondary schools in 2010 said it was homophobic in nature, he went on: "Even now when I walk home, say when I leave the bus or metro, I always have to have my hood up. That's why I always carry my jacket, even in summer."[15]

Ironically, considering Shane's observation, Tony had bleached blonde hair with a blue streak in it, and said putting his hood up was "really to hide who I am," before backtracking slightly: "Actually it's not to hide who I am – it's to hide the way I look from them. Because they'll end up saying stuff and if I couldn't be bothered with it I don't want to end up getting in a fight so I'll just put it up." Proud of his Geordie accent but torn between a sense of loyalty and loathing towards the culture that has moulded him;

craving the opportunity to reinvent himself but feeling unable to achieve the desired metamorphosis on Tyneside, in Tony we witness someone at a particular point of what might be considered the classic Akenside Syndrome trajectory. British society may have come a long way since the time when Terry and Bob could be evicted from a pub because the manager suspected them of being 'fairies' in *Whatever Happened to the Likely Lads?*, but evidence suggests that Tyneside still has some way to go before it can declare itself truly black and white... and pink.

Even now when I come back to Newcastle, I still get the odd kid
saying 'There's that Paki off *Big Brother.*' It makes me wonder –
has anything really changed? I've been really saddened and deeply
shocked by some of the stories. You know what? I'd never bring
up my children in Newcastle. It begs the question – what is
being done to change these old-fashioned attitudes?

The conclusions of former *Big Brother* contestant Narinder Kaur, who was
brought up in West Moor, North Tyneside, in the 2007 *Inside Out (North East)*
documentary she presented investigating race relations on Tyneside

This one is a bit of a dilemma. Not being native to Newcastle
I believe that anyone coming to the city will be genuinely taken aback
by the warmth and humour of most people. However, being dark skinned
it is clear that there is still a disturbing minority of extremely ignorant
and stupid people living here. Whilst to a certain extent it seems
inevitable that every area will have such populations, what I do often
find disheartening is that a lot of people in the area attempt to minimise
racism and even imply that it is somehow the fault of the victim

Contribution by 'Mobin' to the *Inside Out (North East)*
message board reacting to Narinder's conclusions

I'm not sure whether racism is more prevalent in the
North-East than elsewhere … Certainly, though, racism exists
and at times the everyday friendliness of the region's people
make it more obvious and wounding when it does occur … In the
North-East, a place that prides itself on a justifiable reputation
for warmth and kindness, any display of truculence, racially
inspired or not, stands out like a turd on a trifle.

Harry Pearson, *The Far Corner*

The whole ethos of Tyneside working-class culture
was anathema to the bullying on which racism is built.

Barry Carr, *Black Geordies* in *Geordies*

RACE

Toon, Toon... Black and White are we?

L IFE HAS AN UNERRING CAPACITY TO PLACE US ALL IN SLIGHTLY awkward situations, and so it came to pass that just over two years after Narinder Kaur's damning assessment of perceived racism in Newcastle, local newspaper the *Sunday Sun* reported her homecoming. 'Newcastle has changed a lot since I last lived here. If I was worried about racism I wouldn't bring my children here', she told reporter Sophie Doughty, further enthusing, 'Newcastle is a lovely city and a clean city and I think it will be a great place to bring my children up.'[1] Considering Mobin's measured summation was accompanied by a number of irate reactions to the documentary, including sentiments such as 'incensed', 'disgusted', 'disturbingly offensive', 'extremely insulted', 'a damn disgrace', 'appalled and offended' and 'extremely disappointed [about the] inflammatory generalisations', there was perhaps a damage limitation aspect to Narinder's homecoming eulogy. Whether that was the case or not, it seemed to me that she was displaying classic symptoms of Akenside Syndrome.

We've seen how popular perceptions of Geordies paradoxically incorporate both friendliness and aggression, and from Harry Pearson's unappetising dessert-based rumination, Mobin's musings and Barry Carr's observation, we can infer a similarly uncomfortable juxtaposition; that of Geordies as warm and welcoming but simultaneously quite racist. In the same year that Narinder presented her documentary, academic Dave Renton published a book entitled *Colour Blind? Race and Migration in North East England since 1945*, in which he made a formidable attempt at addressing this quandary. At the heart of the book, he explained, lies 'a distinction between different kinds of responses to migrants and their descendants', and a constant theme explored is 'the contradictory experience of migration to the North East, and indeed to England in general.'[2]

Inevitably an analysis of the class pillar of Geordie identity permeates Renton's research, and when I spoke to Narinder Kaur at her Gosforth home five months after she'd returned to Newcastle, she maintained that growing up on Tyneside: "I felt very working-class; I felt very fitted in because of that – I came from a corner shop." Yve Ngoo, who moved to Tyneside as a 2 year old child of a white mother and Cameroonian father, likewise made reference to an aspect of class already explored when expressing what makes her feel proud to be a Geordie (the perceived aura of classlessness, attributable in part to the historic prevalence of working-class culture): "I would say it's a culmination of living in an area which has quite a level socio-economic landscape ... There's people who think they've got money, they try and buy themselves out of the Geordie culture, but on the whole there's a kind of commonality with people. I think that's something that we do – that solidarity is there."

With these observations in mind, Renton's rejection of 'the patronising assumptions of most writers who approach these subjects, treating 'middle-class' people ... as if they or we were the exemplars of all liberal anti-racist virtue', is readily seconded here. As is the assertion of Piara Powar, a former director of British football's anti-racism organisation Kick It Out: 'this idea that the middle classes aren't racist' is 'just a stereotype'.[3] Ged Grebby, founder of anti-racism charity Show Racism the Red Card, reinforced Powar's belief when we met at the organisation's North Tyneside headquarters, insisting: "We tend to say that racism is across the board; it's across class, it's across geography. We would argue that the working class haven't been overtly any more racist than the ruling class."

Dissecting what he called a media 'demonisation of the white working class' following the murder of Stephen Lawrence in London, and the subsequent inquiry, Michael Collins contrasted the experience of immigration of 'certain white middle-class columnists of the left' with those whose neighbourhoods the immigrants moved into, observing that: 'the modern-day white working class had a more varied, more honest, more intimate experience, having known non-whites as lovers, muggers, husbands, killers, wives, victims, neighbours, rapists, friends, foes, attackers, carers.'[4] Dave Renton made a similar point from a North-East perspective, 'England has always placed her new migrants in the ghettoes of existing poverty ... [including] the migrants to Newcastle's West End in the 1960s ... Thus, while working-class people have been by no means immune from racism, they have also been the first to meet new neighbours, to share their schools, to meet fellow employees, and to work beside them peacefully.'[5]

Therefore when considering a Your Homes Newcastle report published in August 2010, which revealed that 42 of the 100 asylum seekers interviewed had experienced a racist incident in the previous twelve months, with Benwell, Walker and Byker cited as areas to avoid, the most appropriate link to establish is surely that of racism and poverty, not racism and the working class *per se*.[6] Helen Rae, the *Evening Chronicle*'s health reporter, suggested in 2009 that about '40% of the residents of Newcastle live in the most deprived areas of England,' making *Guardian* journalist Seumas Milne's nationwide observation particularly pertinent: 'No one should be surprised if demoralised and powerless people reach for the nearest scapegoat – and it's no coincidence that some of the worst racism is found in the most economically deprived areas.'[7]

When I referred to Michael Collins's beliefs about how 'the vision of a multicultural utopia needed its common enemy, and increasingly it was the tribe that played a major role in previous utopian fantasies', and 'the way that the implementation of anti-racist policies is beginning to owe a debt to McCarthyism, with working-class whites exclusively cast in the role of villain', Ged Grebby similarly rejected the cynically simplistic 'white working class = racist' equation, holding up trade unionism as an example.[8] "Most of the things that we rely on, the positive things – if you look at our campaign it's based on trade unions. We would say the trade unions are the opposite to racism because everything a trade union stands for; unity, solidarity, an injury to one's an injury to all, is the opposite of being racist and dividing people, setting them against each other. The idea that you can leave somebody in isolation and target them."

Renton expands on this theme, hinting that the decline of organised labour may have a direct correlation with racist conflict: 'While it has long been possible to see trade unionism as a sort of barometer for the success of working-class politics, we could almost treat racism as the same process in reverse, as the product of trade union demoralisation, and a decline of class sentiment'.[9] Nevertheless, Yve certainly seemed to imply a positive class dynamic when affirming: "I don't think we're inherently racist [on Tyneside]. I don't think we have the historical structure to be inherently racist. It's very much been an all in the same boat kind of mentality, until quite recently." But when asked whether she thought the concept of Geordies is inextricably linked with the white working class, her response was equally assured: "Of course it is. If Cheryl Cole was black she wouldn't be lauded as this fabulous Geordie example of womanhood and feistiness."

In 2004 Beatrix Campell maintained that in the North-East region: 'Compared with Leeds or Manchester, what you've got is breathtaking whiteness. I've never got over that and I don't like it.'[10] Asked to put a local spin on the national statistic suggesting 90% of Britons do not think you have to be white to be truly British (the validity of which Renton challenges), Narinder Kaur estimated that up to 60% of Geordies would consider that you *do* have to be white to be properly Geordie. Yve meanwhile agreed that historically at least the concept of Geordie could be interpreted as exclusive in an ethnic or racial sense, also suggesting that unlike in Liverpool: "Black people are still not really embedded [on Tyneside] yet."

Michael Collins has identified a historic dynamic in England whereby 'many of the urban white working class saw themselves more as part of an ethnic group united by colour and culture, than as a class united by their work', while acknowledging nonetheless that 'In certain white northern towns it was possible to maintain the notion of a working class dominated by the local industries'.[11] The latter sentiment could certainly be applied to Tyneside in the recent past, but it would be extremely naïve to imagine that a sense of identity so often referred to as *fierce* and *tribal* has not, for some,

Cullercoats fishwomen. Hilary Fawcett maintains that historically, 'there has been a strong differentiation in terms of gendered identity in the North-East based on the traditional sexual division of labour and persisting even into the post-industrial present.'

ABOVE: An all-women window-cleaning team and conductresses at Wingrove depot, Fenham. Elaine Knox has claimed: 'One half of the region's population has been omitted from its history'. RIGHT: Swan Hunter apprentices and munitions workers at Armstrong Whitworth.

© Sue Clayton

ABOVE: Author Catherine
Cookson and film director
Sue Clayton. Rob Colls
believes that Cookson made
'a conscious decision to leave
the North-East and forget it
… As a woman, the region's
masculine identity was not
open to her in the way it was
open to the men.' Clayton
encountered problems with
her Geordie accent whilst at
Cambridge University.

ABOVE: The Northern Pride festival has become a fixture of Tyneside's calendar in recent years, and in 2014 the event extended to three days for the first time. OPPOSITE PAGE, FROM TOP: The North-East's first openly gay council leader, Nick Forbes, has recollected being bullied at his school in County Durham. Newcastle Panthers, the region's first gay-friendly football team, was formed in 2008, whereas Gay Men Tyneside has been established for 22 years. Anti-homophobia street art by IDa4 (aka Chris Fleming) appeared in the heart of Newcastle's gay scene during the 2014 Winter Olympics in Sochi, Russia.

Although there has been historic inward migration to the North-East, the numbers have generally been lower than many other parts of England. ABOVE: Photograph taken on Tyneside by Hungarian immigrant Laszlo Torday, date unknown; Lord Mayor of Newcastle reception, 1979.

ABOVE: A new Gurdwara, inspired by the Golden Temple in Amritsar, India, opened in Newcastle's West End in 2013. RIGHT: Narinder Kaur caused controversy in 2007 by declaring she would never bring her children up in Newcastle whilst presenting an *Inside Out (North East)* documentary exploring race relations in the city.

© Steve Meddle/REX

Newcastle's Chinatown Arch. Incoming immigrants including Irish and Chinese have made their mark on the area.

Show Racism the Red Card

LEFT: Chi Onwurah, Labour MP for Newcastle Central, has spoken of experiencing racism whilst growing up in the city. ABOVE: John Akinropo was elected as the first Young Mayor of North Tyneside only three years after arriving from Nigeria. BELOW: Shola Ameobi (right) and brother Sammy are active supporters of North Shields-based Show Racism the Red Card, founded in 1996.

LEFT: New Conservative Club, Pilgrim Street. There was a time (1912 to be precise) when Tyneside Conservatives felt confident enough to build grand gathering places for like-minded people. BELOW: Burt Hall takes its name from Thomas Burt, who has been described as the first working-class MP, in whose footsteps Sharon Hodgson (below right), Labour MP for Washington and Sunderland West, has followed.

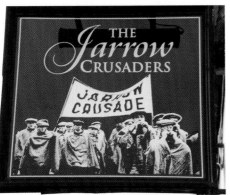

The Spirit of Jarrow bronze statue and nearby pub sign in Jarrow, South Tyneside.

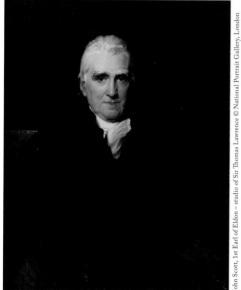

Reactionary Lord Chancellor John Scott (above left) and Whig Prime Minister Charles Grey (above right) both have prime locations in Newcastle city centre named after them. LEFT: Grey Street, 1860. BELOW: Eldon Square, 1840.

Grey's Monument, Newcastle.

Joseph Cowen by Lock and Whitfield © National Portrait Gallery, London

ABOVE: Joseph Cowen 'promulgated his egalitarian mission by all the means at his disposal,' and 'made Newcastle politics in his own image: heretical, independent-minded, community-centred, *progressive*', according to Joan Hugman. Crowds gather for the unveiling of Cowen's monument in the city in 1906.

ABOVE: Newcastle Civic Centre was opened in 1968 by King Olav V of Norway and parts of it are clad in Norwegian Otta slate. BELOW: *Swans in Flight* by David Wynne is situated in the quadrangle, and symbolises the city's political and cultural links with the Scandinavian and Nordic countries.

Newcastle's Coat of Arms and motto – Fortiter Defendit Triumphans – can be found at numerous locations throughout the city. FROM ABOVE LEFT: The Newcastle Arms pub on St Andrew's Street; the building that hosts Sabatini restaurant on the Quayside; St Nicholas Cathedral; Newcastle Royal Grammar School; iron grilles on the Fish Market (now Neptune House), Quayside.

also had an ethnic dimension. Insularity and parochialism are perceived as cultural characteristics of the North-East, and it was therefore unsurprising when Sir John Hall, asked to identify Geordie traits or qualities, opined: "They're too introvert. They're too basically narrow in their views ... I think it's one of the problems of the area ... Generally speaking, I think we look too much inward on ourselves and sometimes I think maybe in a sense the word Geordie draws us in and is a hindrance."

Although not specifically speaking about ethnicity when making these observations, coming from the man who coined the phrase Geordie Nation, his sentiments are surely relevant (when I asked him about this term he actually seemed quite underwhelmed by it, saying: "Yeah, well it's like a brand ... I coined that in respect of the football club and all the fans that supported Newcastle. Because in effect if you're going to market Newcastle ... any business has to have a brand"). Relevant because the sense of separatism, geographic isolation and insularity – the island-within-an-island mentality – appealed to by that rallying call, may well have been, and in parts still be, a factor in the reluctance of some Geordies to embrace diversity and other cultures, observed earlier by Graeme Danby. In the same year Narinder's documentary aired and Renton's book was published, cult American film director John Waters avowed: 'You can't be a racist if you travel a lot. Racists are people who stay in one place,' and although a crass generalisation on one level, the germ of truth it contains may be pertinent when considering race, racism and notions of Geordie identity in relation to Akenside Syndrome.[12]

Peter Murray, a Labour Party activist in Jarrow, suggested to Renton 'that the region probably is more racist than other English areas, not from malice, so much as ignorance', identifying poverty, economic immobility and geographic insularity as probable factors: 'We're a very poor area. People don't have the money to travel abroad. I know people who all their life have never been outside South Tyneside.'[13] Danby said that in the past the region was "very insular because we had ship-building, we had engineering, we had mining," and made a similar point when relating how his grandma spent most of her life in Consett, County Durham, never once going to Newcastle in her 96 years, adding that he also knew people "in Blyth who've never been to Newcastle."

A generational aspect was also evident when Sky Sports boxing commentator Glenn McCrory, brought up in Durham like Danby, told me: "The farthest my mum will go is to Durham on a Saturday," and said both his parents "just have that insular little world that I think a lot of people in this region do." Going back further, Renton alludes to Catherine Cookson's literary depictions of North-East culture: 'their narrowness, for there were those who couldn't see beyond the confines of the county of Durham', and, narrower still, suggests she was referring to 'the strong sense of local identity that could distinguish between the people of South and North Shields … and set people apart as enemies.' When we further consider Cookson's description: 'Little beyond Shields and Jarrow to many a Shields man was an enemy' alongside Peter Murray's modern-day perspective, it seems there are clear implications for those of non-white ethnicity.[14]

It was difficulties faced by former Newcastle United striker Andy Cole after moving to Crook, County Durham in the 1990s that provoked Harry Pearson's contemplation on whether the North-East is more racist than other parts of the country. Ged Grebby also cited a geographical element to instances of racism within the North-East comparable to Pete McDonough's in the previous chapter: "If you look at County Durham it's a lot worse and that's due to the lack of mix. Wherever the mix between races and between different peoples is poor, in terms of it's an all-white community, you're going to get more prejudice because basically you can start pretending these people are alien and people haven't got the personal contact to refute that."

Nonetheless, both Andy Cole and Ruel Fox spoke out about their families experiencing racism on Tyneside – then Newcastle United chairman Sir John Hall endorsing an anti-racism campaign launched in 1995 – and Renton meticulously charts how in the timescale he examined, until recent years, the North-East lagged behind many other parts of England in terms of Commonwealth and other inward migration. Responding to the question of whether Tyneside has been slow to embrace multiculturalism, Narinder Kaur supported Grebby's theory: "Yes, definitely, but it's not their fault. Because they've not had it. If you've got it in front of you, you have to start accepting it."

Narinder has previously talked of how, as one of only a few people of non-white ethnicity in her North Tyneside neighbourhood, her 'whole life has been one of struggling to be accepted by the wider community,' and claimed to have 'suffered the effects of racism at George Stephenson High School … It was appalling and it was every day.'[15] She also believes being called 'Paki' while growing up played a pivotal underlying role in her motivation to go on *Big Brother*: "People ask me [why I went on *Big Brother*] and I'll say because I was called 'Paki' all my life and I thought I want to do something where they'll actually remember my name, not just 'Paki'." So did she have a sense growing up in West Moor that her peers in the wider community accepted her as a fellow Geordie? "Probably not, because then I wouldn't have wanted to run away from Newcastle as fast as the wind would take me. And that's what I wanted to do. Because I thought 'I've not been accepted here.'"

Narinder left Tyneside when she was 19 to study Law at Derby University, and the Akenside Syndrome arc similarities to Tony at the same stage of their lives are strong. Referring to sociologist Martin Barker's belief that post World War Two racism and racist language adopted a more cultural as opposed to biological form, Dave Renton explains how in this paradigm: 'racial identity was perceived in terms of rigid cultural differences, concerning food, language, music or other tastes', and to some extent Narinder could identify with the reflections of film-maker Tina Gharavi, an Iranian-born former South Shields resident currently living in Paris.[16] Gharavi has claimed that migrants to Britain often 'experience a cultural schizophrenia as they oscillate between two cultures … one culture in the home and a different one outside. This dual identity is very problematic.'[17] Wilkinson and Pickett meanwhile refer to studies in London that 'have shown a higher incidence of schizophrenia among ethnic minorities living in neighbourhoods with fewer people like themselves,' and *schizophrenia* – particularly the cultural variety – and *dual identity* are terms very much in tune with the condition of Akenside Syndrome.[18]

Recalling a sense of there being "a secret life at home," Narinder said she felt embarrassed about the Indian food her family ate: "I remember if my friends were coming round I'd be like: 'Mum, quickly hide it.' Because they'd be like: 'What you eating? Eeeh, Narinder's eating Paki food – what is it?' They didn't mean it in a horrible way [but back then] they saw it as 'foreign'. Like 'Whooaa!' It was *too* different." However, from another perspective she felt self-identifying as a strong, feisty Geordie woman was both empowering and character-forming, something she remains proud of to this day. "I think if I'd grown up anywhere else I would not have been that woman. And people say: 'Oh God, you're an Asian girl but you're so feisty.' And that's not the Asian identity, that's the Geordie identity. It put it in me. It is a region of very strong women and that for me is what I take from being proud of being a Geordie."

This feeling of gender solidarity adopted a less appealing dimension, however, when Narinder elaborated further on whether she felt accepted growing up in West Moor. A long pause ensued as she considered an appropriate response, before finally stating: "The girls were always very good – it was always the boys [who racially taunted and bullied her]." Contemplating how almost all the physical attacks endured by campaigner Peter Tatchell have been at the hands of men, Elizabeth Day reported him believing 'that most instances of hatred and oppression stem from a warped sense of machismo'.[19] And while a sense of proportion is necessary when relating this belief to what we're exploring here, having already encountered problematic issues around notions of Geordie identity including misogyny, machismo, male Geordie aggression and limited historical thought processes regarding masculinity on Tyneside, as Narinder reiterated: "It was always the blokes that were racist, it was never the girls. I never had a girl who was racist. It was just the blokes, boys. I've never had a problem with a Geordie woman, *ever*", it seems the potential link is worthy of consideration.

One of the primary reasons she felt embarrassed about Indian food and the associated smells as a child, was a perception of pressure to conform to the norms of local culture – "I thought 'My God, I have to make out I'm the same as them'" – and this prompts questions about the accent pillar of Geordie identity in the lives of non-white Tynesiders. At which point it should be acknowledged that the infinite complexities of the debate around multiculturalism are, as with the finer points of feminism, beyond the parameters of this project. Nonetheless, while for some on the left the thought of inward migrants being compelled to attain a reasonable level of English, never mind adopt the accent of a particular region, is an affront to the incomers cultural and linguistic heritage, for others when this occurs it is deemed praiseworthy. Talking about factors that have helped integration in *The English*, Jeremy Paxman approves that the 'vigour of English regional accents and identities means that in one generation it is impossible to tell on the telephone the colour of a Mancunian, Liverpudlian or Brummie's skin.'[20]

Similar approval emanates from Stuart Maconie's appraisal of his time spent in Newcastle's West End: 'The accent becomes even more outlandish and wonderful than the original Geordie here, the why-ayes and howays now seasoned with spicy dollops of Farsi, Kurdish and Urdu.'[21] For Narinder shared linguistic commonality was essential to integration whilst growing up on Tyneside: "You had to have the accent. If you didn't have the accent you were definitely not going to fit in. I managed to scrape through by the skin of my teeth because the accent helped. You've got to have the accent."

Although still believing she has a Geordie accent, her years living in other parts of the country have had an effect: "I mean it goes sometimes because I've lived away." Deploring those in the media who suggest Cheryl Cole should get rid of or tone down her accent, she nonetheless felt: "I had to get rid of my own a bit, not because it was common because I liked having it; it was because people literally didn't know what I was saying." She also added, echoing contributors to the chapter on Geordie women: "I can adapt it. I'm not like 'Ah, I've got to keep it.' I'm not really that bothered about it."

Yve considers her Geordie accent and turn of phrase to be characteristics she feels proud of, but as she is of a similar generation to Narinder, a younger perspective was also sought. Olamide John Akinropo was born in Nigeria and moved with his family to Tyneside in 2006, aged 13. Three years later as a student at Burnside Business and Enterprise College, Wallsend, he was elected by his peers to be the first Young Mayor of North Tyneside. We met at Wallsend Town Hall a year into his 18-month term of office, and I asked whether he considered himself to have a Geordie accent: "I've got that tendency in my voice and probably speak Geordie. Because when I talk, my mates, they'll go: 'You're becoming a full Geordie now.'" This tendency was something that Yve had also observed amongst recent arrivals to the area: "Look at all the little kids who have been born here in the last couple of years from immigrant and asylum seeker families – they're broad Geordie. So cute."

Asked if developing a Geordie twang had been a help or a hindrance, John replied, "I think it makes you feel more part of the community," but now studying in Liverpool, he may have encountered reactions similar to those experienced, perhaps unwittingly, by former Newcastle United footballer Shola Ameobi. Like John, Ameobi moved to Newcastle with his Nigerian parents in the 1980s, and there is a specific football commentator who on various occasions has made reference to the fact that he has a broad Geordie accent. Each time he alludes to this it is in awed, almost unnerved tones; as if contemplating some previously undiscovered anthropological oddity. Recognising this phenomenon closer to home in the past, Yve remembered how even when attending Stonehills North East Media Training Centre in Pelaw, Gateshead, people would say to her: "You're dead Geordie, you. I wasn't expecting that. You're black."

Narinder likewise recalled how when she first left Newcastle for Derby: "everyone used to say 'An Asian Geordie? Never seen it, never heard of it," with her accent in particular provoking disbelief and incredulity; "They can't get their head round it: 'Oh my God – you're Asian and you've got a Geordie accent. Oh my God – an Asian Geordie. Oh my God – I can't believe you're a Geordie.' They'd be shocked." Having examined the historic sense of insularity within the region, here we witness a combination of the at times cringe-worthy ignorance about Newcastle from outside the area, with an overwhelming ethnic perception of Geordies as being uniformly white. The introduction to an article by Newcastle MP Chi Onwurah, entitled *Why all identity begins at home*, clearly indicates a familiarity with this:

> "'Where are you from?"
> "Newcastle."
> "No, where are you from?"
> "Newcastle."
> "But where do you really come from?
> "Newcastle, you f**cking idiot, do you want me to sing you the Blaydon Races?"

> Well that last comment never actually made it to my lips but it often passed through my head when faced with those for whom my appearance did not shout of the city I grew up in.'[22]

Having brought Shola Ameobi on to the field of play, it seems like an appropriate juncture to turn our attention to the football pillar of Geordie identity in relation to race. Regarding the game's twin potential to unite and divide, in the late 1970s and early 1980s when I first started regularly attending matches at St James' Park, the latter was painfully evident in racial terms. Viv Anderson, the first black player to represent England, allegedly dreaded playing at Newcastle's ground, and the vulgar, dehumanising racial abuse that rained down from the terraces at times was truly sickening. The racist National Front were a propaganda-plying presence outside St James' Park before home games, and at a match in 1984 an infamous incident occurred in which West Ham player Bobby Barnes, now Deputy Chief Executive of the Professional Footballers Association, endured a shocking barrage of crude racism, including monkey chants and a banana thrown on the pitch at him, which led then Newcastle manager Jack Charlton to plead for action against such repugnant scenes, and prompted questions in the House of Commons.

Narinder's reaction to football-related questions was in alignment with most contributors to the Gay chapter, as she insisted: "I hate it. *Hate* it. I would never go to a football match. Football wasn't on my agenda [growing up] ... I wasn't part of that world." However, whereas she prioritised gender over racism-related issues for this lack of interest – "I wouldn't go because as a woman I'd be so bored" – as a young boy arriving in Newcastle not long before Narinder left for university, the exact opposite was true of Ameobi. He grew up with an intense love for the game which eventually led him to Tyneside Sunday League football. An active supporter of Show Racism the Red Card, in November 2010, aged 29, and having been on Newcastle United's books for over a decade, he spoke out for the first time about the racism he experienced growing up in Fenham.

Fortifying the impression of Sunday League football evoked by Pete McDonough, Ameobi recalled: 'Most Sunday afternoons you would get someone targeting me in a racist way. I just loved football so I just got on with it. I've never let it affect me because I know it's ignorance at the end of the day.'[23] Further unburdening himself about what David Morton described as 'a shocking catalogue of racist abuse while growing up in Newcastle's West End ... which scarred his childhood,' he revealed how as a youngster: 'I'd be walking or playing in the streets and there would be a bunch of guys and I'd see them in the street looking at me and speaking between themselves

... They'd shout stuff and racist remarks. I was quite scared of them. There were a number of times where I would be chased through the streets. They never caught me, but I wouldn't like to think about what they would have done if they had.'[24]

As with Shane's recollection of prejudice and intolerance of difference on Tyneside, it's important to point out Ameobi's relatively young age, and by extension the fact that the incidents he recounted are not of the dim and distant past. In February 2014 Dipu Ahad, a Labour councillor for the Elswick ward in Newcastle, tweeted that he had been called a 'Paki' many times in his life, and in May 2014 the *Chronicle* reported a worrying increase in people admitting to being racially prejudiced in the North-East.

But when it comes to overt racism at English football grounds the past really is a foreign country – ironically so – and they did things differently there. Ged Grebby remembered the 1970s and 1980s as a time when, at St James' Park, "the anti-racists had to keep their mouths shut because it was the majority of people laughing along". In 1992, with the help of influential Tyneside figure Malcolm Dix and others, Sir John Hall took control of Newcastle United. A combination of his vision for the club, allied to the all-seater stadium requirements imposed by The Taylor Report (published in 1990 by lifelong Newcastle fan Lord Justice Taylor, whose portrait hangs in the hall of his alma mater, Newcastle's Royal Grammar School), changed the match-day experience out of all recognition.

In 1996 Show Racism the Red Card joined the fray. Whereas Grebby saw football as a hindrance to racial integration and harmony in the 1980s, he feels his organisation has played a significant role in reversing the trend: "We turned it into the opposite. There's less racism now in St James' Park than there is in everyday life, or even in everyday football. You've got more chance of being racially abused playing in a Sunday League as an Asian player than you would if you were a professional." On returning to Tyneside in late 2008 for an 18-month stay, I was cheered by the number of non-white people wearing Newcastle United merchandise, claiming their right to a share of this potent symbol. And according to Grebby more Asian and black people are attending games both home and away: "Overwhelmingly I think things have improved in terms of the racial mix, and in terms of anti-racism – it's improving all the time. I wouldn't want to go back to those days of pretending that these people have got any right over Geordie identity."

Football's perennial potential to enthral and appal trundles on, exemplified by the pitch invasion by around 400 Newcastle fans in a pre-season friendly game at Darlington in July 2011. Scenes described by Lee Ryder in the *Chronicle* as 'shameful images of football thuggery reminiscent of yesteryear ... [on] a truly shameful night,' which according to Alan Pardew 'brought shame on everyone connected with Newcastle United,' were actually provoked by an ostensibly good-natured and affectionate chant sung about Shola Ameobi's younger brother Sammy.[25] It was the occasion of Sammy – ten years younger than Shola – making his first-team debut for Newcastle two months earlier that prompted the elder brother to reflect on how he perceived things had changed in Newcastle since his arrival: 'It was tough when we first arrived. But things have changed. There's big differences in Newcastle, all for the better. People are accepted for who they are now. It means Sammy sees things from a different angle to me; it's great for him to have been able to grow up in the north-east the way it is now.'[26]

The positive perception of change lauded by Shola is undoubtedly true on some levels, but as Dave Renton notes, the problems of 'constructing any sort of objective distinctions' when probing 'the shifting fabric of human relationships' are considerable.[27] In November 2011 two 17 year-old boys were arrested by Northumbria Police for racially taunting Sammy Ameobi via Twitter using the word 'nigger', whereas in 2012 Facebook was twice the chosen platform for racist abuse against Shola himself (a 43 year old man from Washington, Tyne and Wear, being arrested for the second incident). And certainly based on my own research and personal experience, a very mixed picture regarding racism and racist attitudes on Tyneside takes shape.

Shola Ameobi is an affluent footballer whose Jesmond home once featured on MTV show *Cribs*, and while Yve's comments about the host of black players who have passed through St James' Park in recent times are not applicable to him, they are telling nonetheless: "They're never really exposed to racism apart from the odd chant on the pitch, and they're not the kind of people who would live next door to these people in Byker, these racists in Byker." Around the time of writing this chapter I noted in various Tyneside media outlets; reports of a British black man who allegedly suffered racial abuse from two male teenagers and was punched in the face at Byker metro station, an Asian shopkeeper in Jarrow who was bitten on the arm and whose children were subjected to racist remarks, and six males aged 16 to 25 from South Shields and Jarrow who were charged for threatening behaviour and racist abuse toward an Asian woman on the metro, after allegedly returning from an English Defence League meeting in Newcastle.[28]

· In February 2011 the BBC Tyne website reported on an unnamed Tyneside council estate said to be riven with racist intimidation toward ethnic minorities, including incidents such as racist graffiti on front doors, smoke bombs through letterboxes, bricks through windows and in one instance death threats. The same article revealed that Northumbria Police received over 1000 reports of racial incidents in 2010, and in July 2011 the website highlighted an incident near Narinder's old school, George Stephenson High in Killingworth, in which the police were 'seeking a dog walker after a couple were racially abused and subjected to a sustained assault.'[29] Isolated incidents that say more about the underlying ideology and newsgathering motivations of said outlets? More proof of the poverty and racism nexus? Or an ominous indicator of a rotten core of racism that informs some people's sense of themselves as Geordies? Take your pick. Add as many different facts, statistics and interpretations as you like – it's ultimately all about perception, especially when it comes to an individual's experience of Akenside Syndrome.

After three years of living on Tyneside during which time his schoolmates had been largely welcoming, John Akinropo chose to interpret the fact that, up to that point, the only serious incident of racism he had experienced was when "a couple of drunk lads" called him a "black cunt" while walking down the street in Wallsend, as signifying that racism wasn't prevalent. Acknowledging there will always be "that minority group of people that do feel like they still have to be racist" in the area as well as anywhere else, he suggested there "probably isn't that much racism as people might think in Tyneside … in recent years it's really probably gone down; the level of racism has reduced."

Reinforcing Akinropo's and Shola Ameobi's impression of recent improvement, under a sub-heading entitled 'Perceptions of Racism in Newcastle' in the Racist Incidents Report 2010, of the 80 asylum seeker responses recorded, almost 54% perceived Newcastle to be better than other places regarding racism as opposed to 10% who thought it worse. Positive paraphrased responses included; 'Newcastle has improved since arriving in 2003', 'Better than when I first came to Newcastle', 'After 5 years the city is much better than it was years ago', and 'Newcastle better than Sunderland, further south is better, but Newcastle is the best in the North'.[30]

Another incoming perspective was offered by Muan'a Kabala Mbikay to Dave Renton, which is of interest concerning the North-East's perceived insularity and historic reluctance to embrace different cultures: 'For a long time Newcastle has been a closed place. Sometimes it's really difficult ... Most people don't seem to have sufficient information about different cultures. People don't realise, they could learn something by meeting new people ... You know, this is globalisation. There's no way that Newcastle can escape.'[31] The flip side of this is that racism and intolerance of difference are universal human traits observable across the globe. Chi Onwurah, educated at Kenton Comprehensive School, noted this prior to becoming the North-East's first black woman MP in Ted Short's former Newcastle Central constituency at the 2010 General Election: 'yes, I experienced some racism [growing up in Newcastle], but I've had the same experiences in many other places, including Nigeria.'[32]

Similar sentiments were a common theme of the angry responses to Narinder's documentary. A campaign slogan from the inception of Show Racism the Red Card has been 'Geordies are Black and White', and Ged Grebby asserted: "I think like anywhere we've got problems with racism; like anywhere I think it's a minority." As for local attempts to minimise racism, he reflected: "It doesn't jump out from the region; it jumps out from the point of view of a problem generally. It's not just in this area. I wouldn't say it was specifically linked to the North-East in any way." It was in this broader national context – expanded on by Renton who, pre-empting the rise of Ukip, detected how 'signs of a different and more hostile spirit ... have grown in recent years, as the North East has become integrated into a general, national or European pattern of hostility and distrust towards migrants' – that Grebby observed: "The big rise in racism both regionally and nationally is Islamophobia."[33]

Though acknowledging that it wasn't a scientific survey, judged on local school visits made by his organisation, he estimated: "One in three young people are using racist terminology like 'Paki' or 'Chinky'", adding that in some classes up to two-thirds made negative associations with the word *Muslim*. Yve, who like Narinder and Chi Onwurah endured racism at school, also insisted, "Things have changed dramatically. The racism I encountered at school was based on skin colour, ignorance and old coloni- alist ideals and attitudes; the racism today is built on Islamophobia, it's built on economic and social fears, worries, lack of integration, language. It's more than skin colour, it's more than racial, it's cultural now."

Nonetheless, analysing Narinder's claim that she used to still get 'the odd kid saying 'There's that Paki off *Big Brother*' when returning to Newcastle, Yve seemed to imply that ignorance and lack of education remained a major factor: "You know when it's done in malice, you know when it's done through just not knowing the vocabulary and the words to use. They were hardly going to go: 'Oh look, there's that south-east Asian woman from [e.g.] Kerala who was on *Big Brother*. Anybody who's Asian is a 'Paki'. And that's the mentality still." Narinder is, of course, neither an immigrant, a Muslim nor from Pakistan; she was born in England into a Sikh family and is happy to identify herself as a British Asian Geordie, but the ignorant and the racist tend not to make such distinctions. And it seems clear that her profound experience of Akenside Syndrome was ostensibly caused by the colour of her skin and the experience of being called 'Paki' whilst growing up on Tyneside.

Asked if any of the taunts she endured related to her perceived 'English- ness', she categorically dismissed the suggestion. "No, it was never about my Englishness. No. No. Because I made myself to be so wanting to be white. It was all about *colour*, not Englishness. I remember wanting to get bleach – that's what I wanted to do. I won't forget that. I remember thinking, 'Shall I get some bleach and put it all over and make myself white?'" This poignant childhood yearning to fit in was also experienced by journalist Anushka Asthana growing up in Manchester, where, she has recollected: 'I really struggled to be comfortable with my identity … I didn't understand if I was Mancunian, British, Punjabi or Indian', also recalling, 'I tried rubbing talcum powder into my face' and how despite her mother's attempts to comfort her, 'I still wanted to be white.'

However, Asthana's belief that 'it was only in accepting that I was Indian that I finally felt comfortable being British', enables us to speculate on potential coexisting causes beyond the simply racial when analysing Narinder's acute Akenside Syndrome.[34] She talked of growing up within 'a strict Asian background' which included a 'very strong masculine element,' and her constant referral to being proud of and having a powerful identification with strong Geordie women suggests, in my estimation, an unconscious desire to escape the patriarchal confines of her parents' Sikh generation, as well as the exclusively male racism of some boys at her school. Her reference to boys and 'the odd kid' is arguably significant too. Though she did not feel accepted when progressing to Tynemouth Sixth Form College either, there were no taunts of 'Paki', and some perspective can be garnered from Chi Onwurah's take on her own experience of bullying and teasing: 'You get that sometimes, especially from kids because that's what they do.'[35]

Following Narinder's documentary a contributor to the *Inside Out* message board suggested: 'Sadly, I believe racism will ALWAYS exist in children and schools, you can be picked on and bullied at school for having the smallest difference to the rest of the class.'[36] Eddy Amoo, one of the mixed race brothers behind The Real Thing (*You To Me Are Everything/ Can't Get By Without You*), grew up in and around Liverpool 8, scene of the 'Toxteth Riots' in 1981, and has similarly talked of how, looking back on taunts he received growing up such as 'nig-nog': 'I think I realised that this was not racism so much as that kids are cruel. The boys thought it was cool, or funny, the thing to do.'[37] None of which is to undermine, belittle, play down or minimise the racist taunts Narinder suffered as a child, but rather to illustrate that the acute Akenside Syndrome sufferer can sometimes find it hard to achieve a sense of perspective regarding what they consider to be at the heart of their ambivalent feelings towards Tyneside.

While other contributory factors often play a part, the perceived primary cause can cauterise, enmeshing itself into the psyche of the individual, particularly if they leave the area at the stage of their life that Narinder did – an optimum moment for those more likely to experience Akenside Syndrome. And while some may interpret her youngest sibling status as informing the attention-seeking tendencies true of all reality TV contestants (she acknowledges she could be seen as over-sensitive and related how none of her siblings remember the racism being as bad as she does), her status as the only child from a working-class family to attend university is of more relevance here. By accident rather than design all contributors to the Women chapter were graduates, and Keith Armstrong's appraisal concerning Jack Common is worthy of note: 'if your consciousness is raised through learning and experience making you something of an intellectual, an element of alienation can also come into play'.[38]

When an individual leaves home at the traditional late teenager stage to attend university, they are in effect beginning their journey as an independent adult far away from where they grew up. Like Dorothy in Oz the new location can assume a romanticised dreamlike quality, and while not questioning Narinder's claim that she encountered much less racism in more multicultural cities like Derby and Leicester, the fact that her experience of these cities was from an exclusively adult perspective needs to be factored into the equation. Subjective recollections of Derby and Leicester, though no doubt reflecting her own experience, paint a picture too good to be true for everybody in those localities, and she accepted that her concluding *Inside Out* pronouncement on racism in Newcastle swung too far the other way: "I think where I was wrong was you can't label a whole region racist. You can't."

Yet during our conversation, balanced, perceptive and intelligent observations made by Narinder regarding race on Tyneside were occasionally punctuated by generalising flashes of anger and emotion; powerful contradictory feelings symptomatic of Akenside Syndrome never seemed far from the surface. Her reconsidered perspective on racism across Tyneside was that "it's getting *better* but it's not as good as it should be by this stage." And responding to Mobin's perception of a 'disturbing minority of extremely ignorant and stupid people' regarding attitudes to non-white people, she maintained: "I don't know about 'disturbing' – yeah, there is a minority. In my day it was more of a majority. These days it's becoming a minority."

Crucial to this perceived improvement, she felt, is the spirit of reinvention that has animated Newcastle and surrounding areas in recent times: "I think these days Newcastle's not as racist because they're becoming more trendy. It's almost like Newcastle's now becoming fashionable and trendy and 'racist' doesn't work in that." Despite this, and the fact that she hadn't personally encountered any racism since moving to Newcastle when we spoke, past experiences made her wary: "It's coming. I'm scared; I hope it doesn't. I hope I'm so wrong."

We must move on now from the traditional sociological staples of gender, sexual orientation and race, to more eclectic groupings. And I suspect those who have known Akenside Syndrome will nod in empathy as we depart, reading Narinder's twist on a Geordie rite of passage: "When I get the train and we go over the Tyne Bridge I think, 'Ahh, Newcastle.' I see the Tyne Bridge and I see the Angel of the North if I'm on the A1 and I think, 'Ahh, Newcastle.' And I feel relaxed and I feel comfortable and I think I'm home. My family's here. Then I do have that: 'Oooh – I don't really belong here. I shouldn't really be here. Best leave soon.'" She is now living back in Leicester.

Apart from a few leafy enclaves of prosperity, cities like Manchester, Bradford and Newcastle became the sort of places where you could have pinned a red rosette to a donkey and seen it elected.

Jeremy Paxman, *The English*

Once Aa met a Tory,/doon in Jarra toon,/man, he looked sae lonely,/ had nee marras roond! ... Even the posh end of Jarrow votes Labour.

Extract from *Coda* by Paul Younger in *Geordies*

Thousands, perhaps millions, of Conservatives think that by putting a blue sticker in their window at election time they are demonstrating that they are a cut above their neighbours ... for some voters, support for the Conservatives is the equivalent of a positional good – desirable not because of its intrinsic value but because of what it demonstrates about the owner's place in society.

Roy Hattersley, former Deputy Leader of the Labour Party, *Too posh for compassion, The Guardian* 17th July 2006

Bob Errington, a retired teacher [from Gateshead], described himself as a "misfit" because he voted Tory. "Gateshead is socialist. When was the last time they had a Conservative MP? People just follow the routine. They just don't think. They just vote as per their parents ... Their parents voted Labour so that's what they do. It's in their roots. They think of the Jarrow March even though that is history now and the region has changed."

BBC website article by Brian Wheeler that appeared during the 2008 Conservative Party spring conference held at Sage Gateshead

Without being stereotypical and generalising, you should be able to go round parts of Gosforth, and Whickham, and Low Fell, and others, and you should be able to throw a stone and hit a dozen Tories at the drop of a hat.

Jon Jo MacNamara, Conservative councillor for Cullercoats (2006-2010)

POLITICS

Black and White and Red all over?

I F THE HISTORIC ENMITY MANY TYNESIDERS HAVE HELD TOWARD THE Conservative Party lingers on to this day, I'm not altogether sure that conjuring up an image of stoning Tories is a wise move. But although Newcastle has been described as 'the Geordie Republic of Labourland', the political nuances of Tyneside tend to get lost in generalisation.[1] South Shields may be 'the oldest constituency in the country that has never returned a Tory member of parliament' since the Great Reform Act of 1832, but Tynemouth – only a few minutes away on the Shields ferry – was held by the Conservatives for 47 years between 1950 and 1997.[2]

Fergus Montgomery, South Shields-born and Jarrow-educated, served as Conservative MP for Newcastle upon Tyne East from 1959-1964; Piers Merchant represented Newcastle Central for a term in the 1980s; North Tyneside Council had an elected Conservative Mayor from 2003-2005 and 2009-2013, and as late as 1978 Newcastle City Council had 33 Conservative councillors compared to 40 for Labour. Yet at time of writing there isn't a single Conservative councillor in Newcastle or Gateshead, and only one on South Tyneside. Small wonder that the Tory in *Jarra toon looked sae lonely* and Bob Errington described himself as a misfit – both were feeling blue because they were experiencing politically provoked symptoms of Akenside Syndrome.

On BBC3's *Geordie Finishing School for Girls* in 2011, Simon Donald explained the intricacies of Geordie language to four former public schoolgirls from down South, and he left them with a closing top tip which is pivotal in understanding the toxicity of the Tory brand on Tyneside. 'The people of Newcastle are very friendly when it comes to everything,' he advised, before cautioning: 'basically snobbery is one thing that they don't like.'[3] Paxman discusses the historic evolution of 'a fatal association ... between political affiliation and social aspiration', and, understood in this context, voting Tory is perceived by the individual as comparable to consciously losing a regional accent.[4]

It's an addition to their social plumage, an act of self-improvement and a signifier of superiority, exemplified by the Tory-supporting, elocu-tion-lesson-taking Geordie Charles Jennings met in Newcastle's Turkish baths. Conservative philosopher Roger Scruton has described how histori-cally in England: 'Everywhere the middle classes strove to ape the manners of their 'betters', adopting the customs, vocabulary and accent that seemed to them to be proper to the gentry', and it's not difficult to understand why such overt social snobbery, most typically associated with Tories, is consciously rejected in many parts of Tyneside where a different kind of aspiration has held sway – the aspiration to some notion of classlessness, collective advance-ment and egalitarianism.[5]

Asked whether he had experienced any prejudice or snobbery in politics because of his accent or class background, former Tory MP Derek Conway, chairman of Gateshead Conservatives in the 1970s and early 1980s, said: "I think that is inevitable. My intonation has always been northern and snobbery does still exist. When I was short-listed for the Kensington & Chelsea by-election one local councillor asked if I thought the people of Chelsea would wish to be represented in Parliament by someone from a council house and secondary modern school." Conway orchestrated David Davis's campaign for leadership of the Conservative Party against David Cameron in 2005, to which there was a clear class dynamic, and responding to criticism of Conway's alleged *modus operandi* from certain Tory elements, Davis dismissed it as 'snobbery from the nastiest people in Parliament'.[6]

Another Tory MP from a working-class background – speaker of the House of Commons John Bercow, allegedly loathed by some fellow Conservatives – has similarly categorised his opponents as either bigots or snobs. Believing bigotry to be curable, he nonetheless regretted: 'As I'm aware, there's no known cure for snobbery. I feel rather sorry that those people, usually of no very great distinction, who think that because of the school they went to, the house they live in, or the person they married, or the money they've got, that they're better than you.'[7]

Clearly it won't do to caricature all Tories this way; even a partisan observer like Roy Hattersley acknowledges alternative motivating factors such as philosophical commitment to a belief in property, patriotism and private enterprise. Conway was also keen to point out: "People can be socially aspirational in Labour politics! I'm a Conservative because I believe the power of the individual and the motivation of the family unit is more effective than the power of centralised State control. I am not bothered about what class I am perceived to be in, life's too short."

Be that as it may, the Conservative Party's ideological commitment to social inequality and anti-egalitarianism inevitably leads to some form of social grading which cultivates snobbery. Supporters of social hierarchy expect people to know their place within it, and as former *Sunday Telegraph* editor Peregrine Worsthorne has observed: 'The Tory Party can never prosper by espousing egalitarianism, a role alien to its history and genius, indeed to its very *raison d'être*.'[8] David Cannadine likewise notes: 'many conservatives still believe freedom must mean freedom to be unequal, and thus for hierarchy to continue. Hence their belief that liberty and equality are not compatible. Liberty, freedom and hierarchy, yes; liberty, freedom and equality no.'[9]

According to research published by NatCen in September 2013, 23% of people on Tyneside identify as Conservative supporters, and whether or not they consider themselves either of these admittedly crude types of Tory voter – committed ideologue or social snob – it's easy to imagine their frustration with what David Byrne, a former Labour councillor in Gateshead, referred to in *Geordies* as the region's 'overwhelmingly collectivist and socialist objectives'.[10] Although his political allegiance is obvious, he is clearly not incapable of objective analysis. Just before the 2010 General Election he wrote in *The Journal* praising former Conservative Prime Minister Harold Macmillan for doing 'the North East a great deal of good in the early 1960s,' and insisted that the 'people of the North East have been useful idiots for New "Labour" for 13 wasted years. Time for a change perhaps.'[11]

Coalition government may have announced change nationally but the Conservatives and Liberal Democrats were trounced on Tyneside in 2010; a defeat compounded at subsequent local elections, leaving the area's political landscape largely unchanged. Feeling that you cannot comfortably be who you want to be, or express yourself in the way you would like within the culture you inhabit, can be central to the Akenside Syndrome condition. And while 'the elimination of Conservatism as a serious political force in Tyne and Wear politics' may be a source of satisfaction for those of us who credit ourselves with progressive political principles, the image of social ostracism conveyed in Younger's ditty, and the description of himself as a misfit by Bob Errington, sit uneasily within a culture said to pride itself on warmth and inclusiveness.[12]

When I tracked Errington down to his home in Gateshead he declined to be interviewed; a North Tyneside councillor agreed to meet me only to have her daughter 'ring in sick' on her behalf on the day; e-mails and letters to various Newcastle Conservatives were met with tumbleweed-inducing silence. Mary Toward, then PA to the now former Conservative MEP for North East England, Martin Callanan (who as the last Conservative councillor in Gateshead was perhaps best known for his vehement opposition to the Angel of the North), informed me he would be too busy to participate. It all felt a bit weird, as if those approached sensed I was a Stasi-like figure to be viewed with suspicion.

Fortunately Toward did agree to be interviewed and I asked whether she ever felt wary telling people on Tyneside of her political allegiance. "No, but I know lots of people who are. They don't want the next door neighbour to know they're a Tory," she responded, confirming that she believed this to be a common phenomenon across Tyneside. Referring to Errington's avowal, she lamented: "It's sad that he feels he's a misfit, because this is a democracy." Mike Summersby joined the Conservative Party in 1977 and left twenty years later, having represented the South Gosforth ward on Newcastle City Council for twelve of those years. One of the last

Tories purged from Tyneside's urban core, I wondered if he felt Errington's sentiments could be viewed as indicative of politically provoked Akenside Syndrome: "I can understand what he's saying. After all, in these days when more and more people are being drawn to an awareness of diversity; multifaith, multiculturalism and so on, what a terrible society it is when someone has to say something like that. And it's really rather sad that. I think it does fit exactly into your definition of Akenside Syndrome."

Sir John Hall, who switched political allegiance from Labour to the Conservatives, declared: "If you step outside anything, *any* dominant structure, party, grouping – you're always viewed with suspicion. But you should not be afraid to say what you feel." Toward, active in Gateshead for the Conservatives over many years, who contested Newcastle's Newburn ward at the 2012 local elections (coming fifth behind Labour, Liberal Democrats, Newcastle First and an independent before finishing last in Castle ward in 2014), felt the on-going stigma attached to Tories impacted on the party's ability to secure representatives: "Even to try and field candidates in every ward for local elections – most times it's really hard because people don't want to be seen as a Conservative." Meanwhile Mike Summersby went further: "I think there is a stigma in some areas. And I think that's one of the social deficits of ingrained political thinking, whether it's on the left or the right. I think if people can't openly declare their politics without necessarily going into political discussion, then there's something wrong."

Derek Conway's over-arching explanation for Tyneside's continuing emphatic rejection of the Tories was simply that "old habits die hard." Like Conway, Labour MP Sharon Hodgson was brought up in Gateshead, and before the 2010 General Election (when boundary changes saw her switch from the now defunct Gateshead East and Washington West seat to Washington and Sunderland West) she offered her own take on the matter: "A lot of it will be historical and memories are long." Reflecting on the respective political trajectories of herself and Conway, she remarked: "I suppose his journey travelled within the Conservative Party is probably a lot further than my journey within the Labour Party. Because the Labour Party was set up by working people to get representation in politics. And so I'm just fulfilling what the Labour Party was originally set up for." This fusion between working-class identity and political identity is important when considering both David Cannadine's contention that British politicians have, historically: 'conceived their task to be that of imposing their visions *of* the people *on* the people', and the influential role notions of class can play in certain individuals' experience of Akenside Syndrome.[13]

Burt Hall on Northumberland Road in Newcastle was built in 1895 for the Northumberland Miners' Association, and was named in honour of Thomas Burt, variously described as the first working miner, one of the first working men, or one of the first working-class members of parliament. Now part of Northumbria University, this architectural homage to the MP for Morpeth from 1874 to 1918 stands as a concrete (or rather brick, terracotta, ashlar dressings and Lakeland slate roof) reminder of the hard-fought process Hodgson described.[14] As she pointed out, "Let's face it, before Labour all MPs were upper class to upper middle class. It was only aristocracy and very wealthy people who could become MPs." And yet admirable though the achievements of pioneers such as Burt were, when Dave Renton refers to North-East workers being 'socialised into beliefs' in the past, it suggests a sense of pre-ordained political identity imposed upon rather than arrived at. A compulsion that like other facets of Geordie identity already examined may provoke feelings of restriction and alienation in some Tynesiders.[15]

That memories are long regarding antipathy toward the Conservative Party is assured, and Younger and Errington evoking Jarrow and the iconic crusade for jobs comes as no surprise. Moffat and Rosie relate how on 11th November 1936, 'the Tory Prime Minister Stanley Baldwin declared that it would have been 'cowardice' on his part to receive the Jarrow marchers, listen to their plea or accept their petition', and as symbols of a Conservative deaf ear to Tyneside go, they don't come any more powerful.[16] Considering that 'much inter-war Tory propaganda was devoted to stigmatising and demonising the working class, or at least the trades union and industrialised section of it', Baldwin's cowardly, calculated snub is at least contextually understandable.[17]

However, Moffat and Rosie also speak of 'huge sympathy' shown toward the marchers as, 'All the way down England, they were welcomed, fed and accommodated, often by local councils run by Conservatives.'[18] But such sympathy was not universal, with the eldest daughter of Alfred Roberts, an independent councillor for Grantham where the march passed through, remembering: 'He did not think that what they were doing was right'.[19] This anecdote is subtly significant in the emasculation of Tyneside Toryism to political pariah status, because Alfred's younger daughter, Margaret Roberts, later became known as Margaret Thatcher.

It's impossible to overstate the role played by the late Margaret Thatcher and her political credo in the evisceration of representative Tories on Tyneside. As previously noted, in 1978 – the year before she entered Downing Street as Prime Minister – there were 33 Conservative councillors on Newcastle City Council compared to Labour's 40. By the time of her defenestration in 1990 the ratio was 4 to 63. Natasha Vall cites unemployment figures for Newcastle in Thatcher's first three years in office rising from 8% to 18%, still being at 16% for men in 1991, the year after she was ousted from power.[20] When a local reporter suggested she should be talking to the one in five who were unemployed during her visit to Press Productions Systems in Wallsend in 1985, she notoriously rebuked him by slighting detractors in the region as 'moaning minnies'. Thatcher biographer John Campbell insists that the 'defiant humour' of 1997 film *The Full Monty*, 'did not disguise the bitter sense of rejection felt by whole communities while the rest of the country prospered' due to the geographical imbalance of Thatcher's policies, and in *Auf Wiedersehen, Pet* and *Billy Elliot* we can discern a North-East cultural response also.[21]

The revisionism which saw Labour Prime Ministers Gordon Brown and Tony Blair eagerly embrace status-boosting photo opportunities with Thatcher has not gained much traction on Tyneside. Contemplating another Geordie in Newcastle's Turkish baths lauding her, Charles Jennings was perplexed: 'The thought of Thatcher getting any kind of approval up here sounded wrong.'[22] And when the conclusions of two commentators whom most would adjudge reasonably balanced are taken into account, it's easy to see why her ideologically extreme form of Conservatism fatally clashed with the popular social, cultural and political self-image of many Geordies. David Cannadine draws attention to 'her belief in the permanence of social inequality and the importance of social subordination', whereas John Campbell claims: 'She explicitly abandoned [her father's] dedication to serving the whole community,' whilst exploiting an image of him as a homely corner shop owner as 'a smokescreen for the increasingly fractured society her policies were deliberately creating'. He goes on to insist that she 'explicitly jettisoned the traditional Tory ideal of 'one nation'.'[23]

Sharon Hodgson was 13 in 1979 and remembers her mother crying on the night of Thatcher's victory, citing this and how "everybody around me was losing their job and you just saw the North-East crumble around you" as galvanising factors in her political awakening. She recollected feeling the way Thatcher treated the region "was just so callous. That there was no other explanation for some of the things her government did to the North-East and to everybody around me, than to think that it was cruel and vindictive and spiteful because we all voted Labour. And no matter what she did, we wouldn't vote for her. So it was like she would smite us." Speaking before Thatcher died in 2013, Hodgson identified a specifically regionalised repulsion: "People who grew up here feel a different level of dislike for her, bordering on hatred, to other parts of the country. Even among Labour people it's slipped over into a more extreme dislike than any other Labour people I've met."

Someone who definitely doesn't recoil at the mere mention of Margaret Thatcher is Sir John Hall. He used to be a Labour person – 'I was born into the Labour Party and my father took me to hear its great speakers – Bevin, Bevan and Attlee. I owe everything in my life to the Labour government of 1945' – but underwent a Damascene conversion in the Thatcher era. A time during which enterprise zone subsidies and tax inducements enabled him to oversee the opening of Gateshead's Metro Centre in 1986; the project that made both his name and fortune.[24] Once described as 'Margaret Thatcher's favourite businessman', and reported referring to himself as 'a capitalist with a social conscience' and a 'great Thatcherite', it was interesting to hear him reflect on his *volte-face*: "I found I could follow the teachings of Margaret Thatcher," before later adding, "I'm not a hardened Conservative ... I don't support everything they do. But I'm a private sector person and I believe in private enterprise."[25] It seemed to me that even the region's most prominent Conservative supporter was a little reluctant to define himself as Tory blue in tooth and claw.

Hall professed to never having experienced Akenside Syndrome, as did Derek Conway, while Mike Summersby self-diagnosed occasional political ambivalence but nothing pronounced or problematic, albeit insisting: "It's not that I don't think it exists. Of course it does – I'm sure it does." Frustrated letters from Tories to local newspapers support his supposition. In *The Journal* Stephen Warrick from Newcastle, describing himself as 'a working-class Geordie and a committed Conservative (in the One Nation tradition of Conservatism),' affirmed that 'Margaret Thatcher … changed our country for the better', bemoaning: 'As I look around Newcastle and see all of the low-income estates which have seen no progress whatsoever in their outcomes or their circumstances, I really wonder how deluded Leftists really have to be to still believe Labour is for the "common man".'[26] In more fulminatory form in the *Evening Chronicle*, a Heaton resident ranted: 'you very rarely see any hard working Geordies nowadays … Working class, you must be joking. Thank God Mrs Thatcher did come on the scene because we'd be in a heck of a state more than what we are now.'[27]

Thatcher famously denounced class-based notions of collective identity as 'a communist concept. It groups people as bundles, and sets them against one another', and, according to David Cannadine, she 'went a long way towards achieving her ambition of banishing the language of class from public discussion and political debate about the structure and nature of British society.'[28] But many on Tyneside would agree with Owen Jones's assessment that this was no more than a political sleight of hand – 'Thatcher had not the slightest ambition to get rid of social classes, she just didn't want us to perceive that we belonged to one' – and besides, expunging it from the personal psychology of individuals, or the regional and national consciousness, is an altogether different matter.[29] As former Thatcher aide Ferdinand Mount pointed out, simply not talking about it does not mean that class division and inequality have gone away.

For Mike Summersby the claim that Newcastle enjoys a high level of cultural class convergence was not unreasonable but limited: "I think the cultural institutions in the city tend to support that overall conclusion. But I think undoubtedly there are pockets of division all over the place where class does emerge as an issue." Jon Jo MacNamara elaborated on the point: "I suppose we identify with being Geordies first and foremost before we identify with class, but I still think that we then scratch the surface and we go back to class. I still think it's there. Although we mask it by pride in identity of where we are from, yes." The latter observation reminded me of

A Walton's claim that 'our mask of fierce regional identity hides a mass head in the sand mentality', exposing, it could be argued, the idea of Tyneside as classless to be a self-defeating false consciousness.

Former Labour Home Secretary Charles Clarke once remarked that all MPs are upper-middle class, and amidst all the complexities surrounding the issue (in 2013 the BBC's Great British Class Survey claimed there were now seven definable classes) I wondered where on the class panorama our MPs brought up in Gateshead would place themselves. Derek Conway's analysis was this: "If class is defined by how you live your life rather than spending capacity, then I lead a middle-class lifestyle. Preferring books to TV soap-series, classical music to pop music, independent holidays to package tours, private schools to State, supper parties to restaurants. These preferences would define me as middle-class."

For Sharon Hodgson the question provoked a tension similar to that explored by John Prescott in his documentary, *Prescott: The Class System and Me*. "This is the real dilemma I certainly have," she mused. "I come from a very working-class background and I still consider myself to be working-class. In my head I am working-class. And we probably live a comfortable middle-class lifestyle." At which point we must consider a disquieting assertion by Prescott's ghost-writer, Hunter Davies: 'It's hard to see anyone from his background, or with his character, rising as high in politics ever again', with which Conway concurred; "a working class persona is not an asset in becoming a senior politician in any party."[30]

Thomas Burt would have a heavy heart hearing such sentiments, and it's imperative to explore the ramifications of this damning verdict on our society and democracy in relation to what some still regard as the primary signifier of class status in England, and, of course, the second pillar of Geordie identity: accent. Does the insistence of Peter Arnold – former Liberal Democrat leader of Newcastle City Council and chairman of The Northumbrian Language Society – that it is 'absolutely deplorable that people should change their accent to satisfy those who think you need a posh accent to get ahead. It's simply not true … It's complete nonsense', hold true from a parliamentary perspective?[31]

Well, not according to Mike Summersby: "I'm sure for all the wrong reasons a heavy localised accent does motivate generally against a person reaching the top of the professional tree, and certainly in politics." Jonathan Freedland asserts that in Britain, 'the cockney of Jonathan Ross or the Geordie of Peter Beardsley ... is fine for an entertainer ... But imagine the chairman of the Conservative Party talking like Danny Baker. It hardly seems likely.'[32] And added to Kate Fox's appraisal that the English 'reliance on linguistic signals, and the irrelevance of wealth and occupation as class indicators ... reminds us that our culture is not a meritocracy', we once again witness the glib cliché *accent doesn't matter anymore* being systematically dismantled.[33]

Perhaps Margaret Thatcher's vocal tendencies exacerbated loathing of her on Tyneside. A contemporary at Oxford remembered a reunion in the 1950s at which she 'had lost the Midlands accent that her fellow students had known. Now she sounded more like Princess Elizabeth, who was not yet Queen', and according to Judith Holder she subsequently: 'played by the Establishment rules for getting on in politics and ended up sounding more like a southerner than many southerners.' Holder also recalls the incident at Prime Minister's Questions in 1983 when Thatcher baited Denis Healey using a Lincolnshire dialect word 'frit' (frightened), and how the media 'pounced on that inadvertent exposure of her northern roots like a pack of bloodthirsty foxhounds.'[34]

Geoffrey Wheatcroft, author of *The Strange Death of Tory England*, also referred to the 'frit' incident when regretting the way in which: 'Modern politicians are packaged and homogenized, their rough edges smoothed off and their origins toned down, all at a great loss of personal authenticity.'[35] Derek Conway agreed that Wheatcroft's observation was "broadly right" and believed his own accent had changed "a bit but not hugely. I still retain my guttural "a" and have a b*a*ath not a b*a*rth, a l*aa*ff and not a l*a*rf! I think this is an issue across the professions, not just politics. Few CEOs of major PLCs have broad regional accents, not many professors either!" And when it came to the nationwide perception of Geordie accents, he opined, "It is widely taken to represent a low level of educational attainment or intellectual capacity."

Echoing Conway regarding a lack of regional accents in the higher echelons of other industries also, Sharon Hodgson insisted: "Until the reality changes of people with an accent having high-powered jobs, being intelligent, then people will think of people with an accent as being working-class, manual labour, blue-collar jobs, maybe not highly educated." With a hint of self-reproach, she said, "I've stopped myself doing it now – making the assumption that if you hear somebody with a strong accent they'll be less educated," before advocating Geordie accent assertion: "The more people who get out there and can be successful and be intelligent and retain the accent, the less people will [make the aforementioned associations]."

In her maiden speech to the House of Commons in 2005, Hodgson read the first verse of dialect-heavy North-East folklore song *The Lambton Worm*, prompting the *Chronicle* to report a 'shocked veteran Conservative backbencher [remarking:] "How on earth can Hansard be expected to deal with that sort of regional rubbish?"'[36] She wanted to jolt the House, make a statement over and above the actual words, "That I'm not afraid of who I am or where I've come from," but the subtle forces of linguistic homogenisation soon came to the fore. Interviewed for a political website not long after becoming an MP, the subsequent article included dialect words she had allegedly used, such as 'me' for 'my'. "I was really annoyed and frustrated. I felt he'd deliberately done that to humiliate me," she recalled. Moreover, after an early television appearance a speech coach persistently contacted her constituency office offering her services: "I wouldn't see her. I thought no, I'm *not* going to start going down that road of thinking 'Oh, I can't speak like that' … I speak like probably 90% of my constituents.

"There's a difference between having an accent and using slang, and I try never to use slang," she continued. "And I discourage the kids. But I'll never tone the accent down and try to use different vowel sounds. I think it sounds false when somebody changes the vowel sounds and I just *won't*. I *resist*." Hodgson reflected that the speech coach "probably really felt that she could help, but I thought I don't want to start going down that road. Because I would become so conscious about the way I speak. The whole point of me going on this journey was to be a role model, and if I start changing then I won't sound like other people from round here." Nonetheless, when asked if a person with a strong *English* regional accent such as Geordie could achieve high office in today's Labour Party, or indeed any political party, a note of hesitancy marked her response: "As a passionate advocate for the North-East I would optimistically say yes. Realistically, I would say hopefully."

Praiseworthy though Hodgson reaching parliament against the odds is, as with all Labour MPs in the area it owes something to the hegemony of the Labour Party. Her seamless switch from one constituency to another exemplifies why The Electoral Reform Society labelled the North-East comfortably the most boring political region before the 2010 General Election. Such political predictability has meant that Geordies with Conservative parliamentary aspirations have generally had to gravitate southwards. After contesting seats in Durham and Newcastle without success, Derek Conway came to a "practical realisation" regarding the need for migration: "I thought it unlikely I would get a winnable seat as they were in such short supply and the areas that had them were dominated by the "county set" who would not approve of someone from my background … I would have preferred to represent the area of my birth and upbringing."

All of which led me to more or less assume that a Labour MP such as Sharon Hodgson would not be able to identify with the concept of Akenside Syndrome. I was wrong. Ruminating over whether she'd experienced such feelings, she concluded: "I'd be lying if I said totally no. Not in the last twenty years. But there was a time when I was about sixteen, seventeen, and I would say I felt it then. The area where I was living was a really deprived part of Gateshead and everybody around me just felt they were on a trajectory and living a very different life. I was in a one-parent family; Mam was on benefits, I was encouraged to leave school." She eventually found work, took driving lessons and bought a car, recalling, "For that period, between about [the age of] sixteen and twenty-two, I felt I had [Akenside Syndrome]. Because the community around me; the girls got pregnant and got flats and were all pushing buggies. And I'd come out of the house and sometimes there would be little crowds and I would feel so odd. I was a bit odd because I was working and I had aspirations, and they chose a different path. My aspiration was to have a better life than the life I'd had."

Alongside the pertinent image of Thatcherite decay, discomfort with notions of communal conformity and expectation can be inferred, and comparison can be made with Sting's memory of feeling resentful about what he felt he was being led to aspire to. Whether such observations accurately portray the culture of Tyneside at any given epoch is less important to us here than the person experiencing Akenside Syndrome believing it to be so – that it is their perception. Although in no way stigmatising the whole community or suggesting everyone in her former neighbourhood made her ill at ease, Hodgson nonetheless remembered feeling, "that they thought I was odd. I think there was probably odd comments ... there would be things like 'Who does she think she is?' and 'Ah, she's a bit...' And I just would feel that people thought that I thought I was better than them."

To understand Hodgson's sense of Akenside alienation more fully we need to extend our exploration of politically imbued architecture and monuments in Newcastle. The statue of Whig Prime Minister Earl Grey (like current PM David Cameron educated at Eton and Oxbridge) surveys the nationally acclaimed street named in his honour from atop Grey's Monument. Architectural irony has the overseer of the Great Reform Act 1832 in close proximity to Eldon Square, named after reactionary Lord Chancellor John Scott who vehemently opposed it.[37] Scott, later Lord Eldon, was educated at Newcastle's Royal Grammar School followed by Oxford, opposed the abolition of slavery and catholic emancipation (as well as pretty much anything else considered liberal and progressive), and has been described as 'an instinctive and hardline conservative ... one of the most hated and feared men in England ... [and] also something of a snob.'[38] Ouch. Definitely not in keeping with Tyneside's modern-day perception of itself.

Stroll with me down Grey Street. Hang a right along Mosley Street and a short walk up Collingwood Street on to Westgate Road – nod at the monument to Tory-supporting George Stephenson if so inclined – brings us to the statue of Joseph Cowen; Liberal MP, radical, republican, *Newcastle Chronicle* proprietor, a Geordie associated with bricks even more than Dennis, Oz and Neville from *Auf Wiedersehen, Pet*. According to Joan Hugman, Cowen 'promulgated his egalitarian mission by all the means at his disposal,' and 'made Newcastle politics in his own image: heretical, independent-minded, community-centred, *progressive*.'[39] Now we're getting close. But it's to the political heart of Newcastle that we must go in order to appreciate the legal implications of Hodgson's experience.

Work began in 1958 on Newcastle Civic Centre and it has been described as an 'impressive municipal government building of Scandinavian style'.[40] Opened in 1968 by King Olav V of Norway, parts of it are clad in Norwegian Otta slate, and every Christmas a tree donated by the people of Bergen – one of Newcastle's twin cities along with Malmo in Sweden – stands outside the building. In the quadrangle a bronze sculpture in water by David Wynne takes pride of place. Named *Swans in Flight*, the five swans depicted symbolise Newcastle's close political and cultural links with the Scandinavian countries.[41] Considering all of this, we must contemplate whether a Geordie version of the Law of Jante is a factor in some people's experience of Akenside Syndrome.

Derived from Aksel Sandemose's 1933 novel *A fugitive crosses his tracks*, the Law of Jante is 'used colloquially as a sociological term to negatively describe an attitude towards individuality and success common in Sweden and the rest of the Nordic countries,' and refers to 'a mentality that de-emphasizes individual effort and places all emphasis on the collective, while discouraging those who stand out as achievers.' The ten Law of Jante rules are as follows: **1.** You're not to think you are anything special. **2.** You're not to think *you* are as good as *us*. **3.** You're not to think *you* are smarter than *us*. **4.** You're not to convince yourself that *you* are better than *us*. **5.** You're not to think *you* know more than *us*. **6.** You're not to think *you* are more important than *us*. **7.** You're not to think *you* are good at anything. **8.** You're not to laugh at *us*. **9.** You're not to think anyone cares about *you*. **10.** You're not to think *you* can teach *us* anything.

However, as befits a set of rules advocating the collective over the individual, they are 'usually referred to as a homogenous unit: *You are not to think you're anyone special or that you're better than us*' – a sentiment which ties in precisely with what Sharon Hodgson described. The historic existence of a 'village' or 'small town' atmosphere on Tyneside, and how such environments can feel claustrophobic and restrictive for some has been investigated elsewhere. And I suspect many Geordies who have suffered from Akenside Syndrome would recognise the social code of the small Danish town of Jante depicted in Sandemose's novel, whereby: 'the Janters who transgress this unwritten 'law' are regarded with suspicion and some hostility, as it goes against the town's communal desire to preserve harmony, social stability and uniformity.'[42] Similar to an earlier observation by Sir John Hall, it's clear that the 'darker side of egalitarianism' can elicit estrangement indicative of Akenside Syndrome. Let's vote with our feet and move on, because a chapter is a long time in Tyneside politics.

I don't think Newcastle will ever be a "classless" society – you don't see many parents dropping sons off at the Royal Grammar [School] and going on to shop in the Shields Road! I think the divide is more material than snob-based.

Derek Conway rejecting the notion that Newcastle can be described as classless

The Tories no longer feel like friends. They feel like former friends who are starting to disown us.

Dr Bernard Trafford, current Head Master of Newcastle Royal Grammar School, quoted in *The Guardian* (8th October 2011) reacting to David Cameron's reference to *"the apartheid between our private and state schools"*

The RGS was always a curious beast; a public school in the centre of Newcastle.

Nick Brownlee; author, former *Chronicle* journalist and Old Novocastrian

It's in the nature of English public schools to look down on the towns that give them space … Letchworth was a place of utter disdain, a hideous troll nowhereville inhabited by ghastly common oiks. None of us lived in houses like that, or knew people who did; we didn't dress like them, eat like them or sound like them … All public schools, without exception, have this barely concealed distaste for their hosts … I still remember the absolute sense of entitlement.

A.A. Gill reminiscing about his schooldays in *The Angry Island*

In a few schools up and down the country, teaching is a simple matter because the pupils have a reasonably foreseeable future which can be contemplated cheerfully. They have waiting for them the same assured position in adult society that their parents had. The teacher must prepare them for that position by the appropriate character-conditioning, initiation into the peculiar code of behaviour which is the mark of their kind, and a laying-on of the gold leaf of culture to make them look worthy of the job already picked for them … [A parent wishing to "load the dice" in his children's favour] begins to decorate his offspring with some of the recognized tokens of luck, old school ties, refined manners and accents

An ironic educational rumination by Willie Kiddar in *Kiddar's Luck*

RGS

Class dismissed?

I T'S HARDLY SURPRISING BERNARD TRAFFORD (OLD GREGORIAN) SEEMED to get a bit miffed with David Cameron (Old Etonian) and the Conservatives following his apartheid jibe. Research published by The Smith Institute after the 2010 General Election suggested that while only 7% of the population was privately educated, a whopping 54% of Conservative MPs elected went to private schools, as did 41% of Liberal Democrats (for Labour it was said to be 12%).[1] According to The Sutton Trust, 62% of ministers at Cameron's first Cabinet meeting attended independent schools; an improvement on Margaret Thatcher's 1979 figure of 91%, and John Major's 71% in 1992, but almost double the still vastly over-representative 32% of Tony Blair (1997) and Gordon Brown (2007).[2] Furthermore, on Prize Day in 1903, the same year that the Governors and Trustees of Newcastle's Royal Grammar School (RGS) purchased land for the school's present Jesmond site, the then chairman 'concluded his speech with a quotation from a fellow alderman that 'the future grammar school would be the Eton of the North of England'.'[3]

We've seen how a belief in the power of the individual and private enterprise can inform the political identity of Conservatives, and in this sense the

Tory and private school ethos are closely entwined. Education campaigner Fiona Millar has said: 'Belief in an elite education system runs like a deep blue vein through the Conservative party', and in *Royal Grammar School, Newcastle upon Tyne: A History of the School in its Community* – published in 1986 – contributors with close links to RGS spoke of its 'liberal and individualistic tradition', and of how 'respect for individuality has been generally preferred to repression'.[4] Indeed, former Head Master Alister Cox's declaration: 'Determinedly we espouse the virtues of disciplined orderliness *and* untrammelled individuality, the philosophies of competitive thrust *and* compassionate concern,' could almost be read as a manifesto for so-called 'compassionate Conservatism'.

Cox also pointedly observed: 'If a future Labour Government were to outlaw the Royal Grammar School along with other fee-paying schools, there would be consternation in the most unlikely sectors of Newcastle and its area. Senior Socialist councillors, a succession of whom have visited the School as Lord Mayor on their first day of office, would certainly question the wisdom of such a step in relation to a school whose corporate presence and institutional stature they had personally savoured.'[5] Presumably that was a cautionary nod in the direction of then Labour leader of Newcastle City Council, Jeremy Beecham, now Lord Beecham, a prominent former RGS student (known as Old Novocastrians or Old Novos for short), but Cox needn't have worried. Nine years later the soon-to-be next Labour Prime Minister, privately educated at Fettes in Edinburgh (often referred to as 'the Eton of Scotland'), was playing headers keepy-uppy with Newcastle United manager Kevin Keegan, and would later reflect in his autobiography on how he was very non-political in his view of politics, how the private Durham Choir School he also attended was hated by local proletarians, and how in his innermost heart he knew he wouldn't send his own kids to many inner-city secondary schools.

Politics and private schools are uneasy bedfellows then, and the advent of Blairism blurred boundaries further. The tension felt by some individuals within a collectivist environment has emerged as a significant factor in their experience of Akenside Syndrome; and an elitist institution which champions untrammelled individuality appears to be fundamentally at odds with 'a region whose people believe in inclusive collectivism,' where David

Byrne also suggests it 'is easy to identify the overwhelmingly collectivist and socialist objectives of the people'.[6] His use of the word *overwhelmingly* is worth noting, as in a speech made before he became Prime Minister, Tony Blair used a similar word in relation to socialism, but in a different context: 'The historic problem of old socialism was the tendency to subsume the individual, rights, duties and all, within ideas of the 'public good', that at its worst came simply to mean the state.'[7]

Joseph Cowen, a passionate advocate of egalitarian principles, nonetheless believed socialism 'would reduce man to a cypher or to a machine … his free will would disappear', and Jack Common's biographer Keith Armstrong, very much a free thinking socialist and activist himself, has made a similar point to Blair: 'in my own experience, I have seen certain self-professed 'socialists' only too ready to stifle the individual voice in favour of the mass, whereas the situation is actually complex and any real 'socialism' can only spring from the interface between the individual and the collective and the balance between the two.'[8]

Feeling overwhelmed, subsumed, stifled and a perception of free will being impeded – basically feeling that you can't be who you want to be or do what you want to do in the environment you inhabit – are all classic indicators of Akenside Syndrome. With regard to private schools on Tyneside, explored here by focussing on the area's oldest and most symbolic institution of its kind, there's clearly a wealth of topics to engage with. To get us in the mood, I cordially invite you to join me in singing a few lines from the now redundant RGS School Song:

Fortiter defendit, fortiter defendit, fortiter defendit triumphans
Fortiter defendit, fortiter defendit, fortiter defendit triumphans

Many a name on the scroll of fame, Is the heritage of our land,
Collingwood and Armstrong, Eldon and Bourne, Akenside, Stowell and Brand,

Penned by Senior English Master J.B. Brodie, the song was first sung in public in 1914, and the chorus is derived from Newcastle's city motto: *Triumphing by Brave Defence.* Fortiter ye not, as you notice among the Old Novocastrians celebrated in the lyrics a certain Mark Akenside.

Bernard Trafford was appointed Head Master at RGS in 2008 after 18 years in the same role at Wolverhampton Grammar School, and we met almost a year into his tenure at the official Head's residence, a stone's throw away from the school in Jesmond (Tories hit with said stone unconfirmed). He has wide knowledge of the independent school sector and hearing A.A. Gill's comments prompted him to ruefully reflect on his own schooldays at Downside School in Somerset: "Yes, we did use words like 'oik' when I was a boy. Isn't that awful?" However, of the private day schools he has led, he affirmed: "My experience, longer in Wolverhampton, but I think it's still true here, is that people have friendships right across class boundaries within the school," with Gill's sentiments being more applicable, "I hope, from a generation ago. It's not true here; it's not [true] in the day sector." Although wary of projecting such attitudes exclusively on to boarding schools, he nonetheless noted: "Boarding, I suppose, is a bit more cut off from its local community because of what it is."

As independent day and boarding schools are fee-paying institutions within the private sector, they differ by degree not principle (Master of Wellington College Anthony Seldon has insisted: "'Public schools" are the posh end of the market of independent or private schools, all of which are funded by private sources'), but Trafford's differentiation was one most contributors wished to emphasise.[9] Nick Brownlee, whose 2008 book *Bait* was not a social history of working-class Geordie men's lunch-boxes, but the first instalment of his Jake & Jouma crime fiction series, felt it was a crucial distinction: "Because RGS was a day school, I think that made a big difference. Had it been a boarding school, it would have been a different matter. But I think the fact that at 4 o'clock everybody went home to wherever they lived, that kind of kept you grounded in where you were. People had lives outside school. So you weren't cloistered inasmuch as you would have been had you been at an expensive school like Sedburgh or something like that. So I don't think there were any of [the attitudes described by Gill].

"Obviously there was the Jesmond Triangle where you had all the girls' schools [private institutions Central High and Church High which in 2014 merged to become Newcastle High School for Girls] and the RGS," he continued. "They were who you tended to knock around with. I think the only people we used to look down on were people from Dame

Allan's. Because they weren't quite as good as us. If you couldn't make it to RGS, then you went to Dame Allan's or King's [other private schools in Newcastle and Tynemouth respectively]." This reminded me of a post on the short-lived *RGS is better than Dame Allens* [sic] Facebook group created in 2006. One group member commented: 'It would be difficult to put into words the gulf between the 2 establishments, without getting abusive toward the Dame Allans' [sic] cattle! I fucking hate that school and everything about it. I like no-one from there and find it impossible to say anything positive about their existences. We exclipse [sic] them in every department; sport, academia, banter, class, attractiveness, ability, and most of all social status.' Charming.

Giles (pseudonym requested by the contributor), who used to commute from Northumberland, reacted to Gill's comments in a similar fashion to Brownlee, an RGS contemporary: "I never met any of the locals, if you know what I mean. When we were in our formative years, starting to go to pubs, people from the RGS all went to the local Jesmond pubs and it was full of RGS, Central High, Church High and not many locals. You never saw any state school kids generally. I don't have a recognition of [Gill's sentiments] or anything like that; you do feel different but I never felt superior to anybody."

Brownlee, who attended RGS from 1977-1986, and in October 2012 was guest speaker at the Old Novocastrians Association Dinner, also observed: "As far as comprehensive schools, there wasn't really much consideration of it. We didn't really have much to do with them." And going back a generation, Peter Stark, an influential figure in the cultural regeneration of Gateshead Quays who attended RGS between 1956-1965, responded to being asked whether he could recall a 'them and us' mentality between school peers and state-educated Tyneside children by simply stating: "We didn't see them." So while it is perfectly reasonable to draw attention to the more cut-off environment of boarding schools, attending a private day school can certainly involve insularity and a sense of social separatism.

Former RGS teacher Brian Mains has talked of 'perceptions of social status' as being a 'great cultural value', and to better understand the Facebook contributor's evident self-satisfaction from a national perspective, the thoughts of author and critic Bidisha are worth considering.[10] Analysing comments made by fellow alumni of private day school Haberdashers' Aske's on *Mumsnet*, suggesting David and Victoria Beckham were 'too working class' to send their offspring there, she asserted: 'Haberdashers', like all institutions of its type, confers a sense of entitlement. Arrogance fills the gap where experience should be; blind confidence, reinforced over centuries of privilege, enables ex-pupils to make demeaning comments. These graduates will soon rule the world, exulting in their own prejudices, consorting only with those of the same type, keeping inequality firmly in place.'[11]

Whereas in earlier chapters we witnessed how feelings of social exclusion within the dynamics of Tyneside culture can provoke Akenside Syndrome, here we are investigating whether educational social exclusivity has similar potential. Keen to engage with modern-day perspectives beyond the pubescent immaturities of a 'just for fun' Facebook group, I talked individually to three RGS sixth formers, all of whom have since completed undergraduate degrees.

Coming from a privately-educated Newcastle background, did Gill's overview – including the avowal that: 'On the other side it's a solemn resentment that occasionally boils over into violence' – resonate with Rahul?[12] "For me personally, to a small degree. Because occasionally you're going to get people shouting at you because you're in a suit, stuff like that. When I walk from Longbenton metro, [the kids hanging round there] give me dodgy looks. One of them shouts." Nick Brownlee also recalled getting the bus from nearby Four Lane Ends whilst at RGS, and being "mocked by the local hooligans at the comprehensive school who called me a snob". Rahul went on: "But overall not really, because most people I know don't judge me because I'm at a private school. They'll judge a lot of private school lads because of the way they act. Because generally the attitude around here *is* quite arrogant. Because it's so competitive it's quite 'up your own arse' and they just tend to look down on people. Quite a lot of the time you'll find there's this little private school circle – you won't find many state schools inside it."

For Jamie however, the day school status of RGS allowed him to cultivate and maintain friendships beyond fellow students, negating any resonance with Gill's bleak outlook: "No, definitely not. Because I know loads of people who go to state schools and I associate with them. They know that I go to RGS – they're fine with that. Some of the people I know who go to state school I'm more than happy to spend time with rather than people who go to this school." Recalling that he too used to occasionally get shouted at on public transport in Newcastle, he felt this had abated towards RGS students in lower year groups, believing that "the prejudice in society against private schools is on the decline."

Oxbridge-bound Chris, meanwhile, seemed genuinely scornful: "I just don't like those comments at all. I don't really like people who think that they can only be friends with people in their private school and who are of their class. I still keep in touch with all my mates who've gone to state school through football. I play Sunday League with them all. That's a good way to keep in touch with them." Elaborating, he insisted: "You can't just not talk to them because of their class. You've got to base it on [the individual] as a person. But there are people in this school who would just not talk to them because they view them as plebs, as Gill said."

Perceiving a tangible division between RGS pupils and their state-educated counterparts generally, Chris felt the tendency to stereotype was dual flow rather than one-way traffic: "From state schools to us I think there definitely is a divide, because they just look at us as 'poshies'. They just kind of generalise everyone as being rich and posh. If you look at it from the RGS out, there are more people who would happily get along with state school people than there is state school happy to get along with private school people, I would say. But then there are certain members of this school who think they're too good to talk to people like that and stuff, so…" His evaluation chimed with the observations of Jo Chipchase, who contended: "I think a lot of inverse snobbery exists on Tyneside. I experienced accusations of being 'posh' throughout my teenage years because I went to a private school – Dame Allan's – and my dad drove a company car."

'The division between those who enrol in the state system and those who are educated at fee-paying schools', according to David Cannadine, 'is widely thought to perpetuate and intensify the view that Britain is not one but two nations, characterised by what many believe to be social apartheid', and we can certainly discern signs of a perceived two nation Tyneside in this respect.[13] Cannadine's employment of the emotive phrase 'social apartheid' illustrates how David Cameron was treading a well-worn path. Andrew Adonis and Stephen Pollard have referred to 'a 'two nation' education system' which contributes to a 'public perception of a class system, in the sense of deep structural barriers and inequalities reflecting and intensifying social segregation', while renowned geneticist Professor Steve Jones denounced private schools as a 'cancer on the education system' in 2009.[14] Even from within its own ranks, Anthony Seldon has spoken of the independent sector 'perpetuating the apartheid which has so dogged education and national life in Britain since the Second World War', asserted the need to combat 'a triumphalism of separateness,' and controversially insisted in 2012 that 'British independent schools in the 21st century have lost their moral purpose.'[15]

In 2008 Bernard Trafford alluded to Seldon when writing in *The Guardian*, 'Few of us in the independent sector recognise the apartheid epithet', and I asked what he thought of such comparisons.[16] "I've lived with it so much," he said. "I do, lots of us, if you've got a reasonable social conscience, feel guilty about this. And we're made to, you know? That we're not in the mainstream or something. Must be doing something wrong. Something a bit dirty. It's often that suggestion; you do have to be a bit apologetic in a certain amount of company, or at least low profile." Educational debate is often factional and fractious of course; yet cross-fertilisation occasionally occurs whereby the view of a conservative commentator such as *Daily Mail* columnist Stephen Glover – 'there can be a narrowness of outlook associated with private education and privilege and wealth' – can be seen to complement that of Owen Jones: 'Separating children on the basis of their parents' bank balances denies children the opportunity to mix with others from a whole range of backgrounds, fostering divisions at the earliest age.'[17]

Peter Lowdon, an undergraduate at Edinburgh University when I talked to him, now studying for a PhD in Zurich, was born in Newcastle, raised in Jesmond, and attended Heaton Manor Comprehensive – the nearest state high school to RGS. He expressed similar views when contemplating how attendance there benefited him, having declined the opportunity to try and get in to RGS offered by his parents: "I think it improves your social skills and just social awareness. I think in a school like the RGS you're only really mixing with people whose parents are from the same kind of wealth bracket. I mean, of course you get a few people who get in on scholarships, but pretty much you're mixing with the same kind of people. You can get a very, very good education there but I don't think you get a social education."

Putting aside the broader ideological debate surrounding education, it is self-evident that at schools like RGS, after satisfying academic selection criteria, over 90% of pupils are only able to attend due to their parents' ability to pay the fees. For some, the image of Trafford's profile on a blown up pound coin adorning the cover of RGS publication *The Grammar* in 2009 would speak volumes. Nonetheless, he rejected Lowdon's appraisal: "It's commonly said. I don't think it's true that they don't get social skills and so on; I think that's quite untrue. In terms of the broad range, yeah, they won't have the same range of social issues probably, and the whole breadth of that. And that's why we try to make sure they get outside school and come up against things."

Warming to the theme, he recalled: "From school and Oxford, I did know people that it was embarrassing to go into a pub with. Why do you go into a pub and say [exaggerated upper-class accent] 'Oh, I say!'? And people do. On the other hand, you can go into a pub and see some people from other social classes who are equally crass … So there will be people who go to RGS who are insensitive like that and perhaps arrogant because they've had a lot of choices, but there will be insensitive, odd and arrogant people at Heaton Manor as well." He also insisted on the importance of families developing the social skills of their offspring, an aspect mentioned by Giles too: "I think you can get a social education going to the RGS – it often depends on your parents. It's where you live and things like that. You could go to Heaton Manor and not get a good social education." However, although believing Lowdon's observation to be too general, Giles conceded that he had made "some relevant points. I think it's important to mix with people from different social groups, and let's face facts – you're not going to meet too many at RGS."

Peter Stark agreed with Lowdon: "I think that's true. That was true for me and I would imagine it's true now. I didn't get the range of ease. There were social skills that I didn't get. I mean apart from anything else it was a single sex school.[18] And I didn't get that connectedness or rootedness, or, if it had been a properly comprehensive school, a sympathy or an understanding with a range of abilities." Confirming Stark's expectation of a modern-day relevance to Lowdon's analysis, Jamie declared: "To be honest, I'd agree with it on the most part." Although adjudging himself to be "fine on the social education", he contended: "I look at people in this school and – it's not that

I worry for them because you get some incredibly intelligent people here. But it's one thing being intelligent on paper, but some people they just don't really have life skills. And I consider that just as important as the brains really. But yeah, that statement is correct. There is a large proportion of people here who don't have a social education. But to assume that everyone doesn't have a social education, that would be wrong."

Rahul believed Lowdon's summary was "90% true … It's a very true statement in all fairness, because most of the people I seem to see just fall into their own little group." Describing Newcastle society generally as "all these circles bound together and everyone's just so friendly to each other," he further appraised that whereas "all these groups just merge into one big circle, in RGS it's sort of out of this circle. RGS will know who Dame Allan's is, they'll know who Central High is, they'll know who Church High is – the state schools are just left out of this circle. He's right, it is bad social education because it's not only that they aren't in this massive circle – they don't *want* to be in it. They think they're a bit higher, a bit more elite. There is just this elitism feeling which keeps them out of the circle and keeps them within their own little bracket as [Lowdon] put it. You could say it's because it's people from the same wealth bracket, which it is in broad terms, but it's not. It's just because of who they are; they go to RGS, they don't go to a state school, therefore they're outside of the circle and they want to be outside the circle, because they believe they're above everyone else."

Completing the triumvirate of recent RGS students, Chris weighed up Lowdon's comments by reflecting: "Generally I would say that's possibly true, because I've seen people in here who I don't think they'd fit in or they wouldn't be able to hold a conversation with your average Joe out on the street. No, you don't get a [social education]. You get a very good education but you don't really get taught all the life skills maybe you need. And you kind of have to pick up on them yourself, like you would have got in a state school. I don't know if it hardens you up or what. Maybe it gets you more used to different types of people and how to talk to them and not feel intimidated when you're around certain people. Whereas some people will get on the metro and as soon as a bunch of chavs get on they'll feel a bit intimidated … I'd say it hasn't really affected me, but it's affected other people in this school."

Analysis of Chris's observations so far lends support to conclusions drawn by researchers at The Joseph Rowntree Foundation when investigating how early class attitudes can be formed, as reported by James Meikle: 'Those growing up on [council] estates regard rich children as "posh" … [whereas] private school children spoke of chavs being at one end of the social spectrum and of rich at the other, with themselves in the middle.'[19] I'm not sure whether Mark Akenside employed 18th century pejorative terms for people perceived to be of lower social status than himself, such as troll, oik or chav, but aged sixteen he wrote these lines in a poem entitled *The Poet: a Rhapsody*, in which he laments having: *To live remote from grandeur, learning, wit;/ Immured amongst the ignoble, vulgar herd,/Of lowest intellect; whose stupid souls/ But half inform their bodies; brains of lead/And tongues of thunder…*[20]

And certainly when Gordon Hogg researched a timescale of RGS history including the years Akenside attended, he concluded the 'bulk of Newcastle's pupils came from the 'middling sort'' and that the school itself was 'largely the preserve of the 'middling' class'.[21] Though there has been a recent, not entirely convincing attempt to rehabilitate Akenside's character for posterity, what he *is* often accused of is conceit, snobbery, arrogance, turncoat tendencies (gliding effortlessly from republican to royalist, lifelong Whig to Tory to secure personal advancement), and of treating poor patients he attended very harshly: 'he was cruel, almost barbarous, to the patients, particularly to females. Owing to an early love-disappointment, he had contracted a disgust and aversion to the sex, and chose to express it in a callous and cowardly harshness to those under his charge.'[22]

Akenside left Newcastle to study Theology at Edinburgh as a late teenager – the optimum age for those who fall prey to the condition named after him – returning to Tyneside for three years before departing for good. He never married, leaving 'all his effects to his warm and constant friend Mr [Samuel] Dyson', whose patronage sustained him throughout his adult life.[23] And although some believe the story apocryphal and motivated by spite, it is alleged his lifelong limp was inflicted by an accident involving his father's butcher's cleaver, a godsend for those who wished to disparage his social pedigree. True or not, as an ambitious social climber who went from Newcastle butcher's son to metropolitan doctor to royalty, it is unsurprising allegations that this 'middling sort' Old Novocastrian was 'touchy and sensitive about his humble origins', and 'ashamed of his native place', have stuck.

Margaret Wilkinson relates how former RGS Head Master Samuel Logan, a driving force behind the school's relocation to its current Jesmond site, shared 'his clerk's conviction that the School had been 'originally intended for the benefit of the middle and higher middle class population of the town',' and also cites disgruntled early twentieth century Board of Education inspector, Mr Piggott, describing Newcastle as 'the most snobbish [town] of its size in the whole of England'.[24] Therefore the potential for a sense of dislocation amongst RGS (and other privately educated) students within the broader 'working-class' Tyneside environment seems obvious.

Peter Stark affirmed, "RGS was a middle-class Geordie school when I was there," yet did not necessarily feel traditionally middle class people had always felt at home, welcomed or that they 'belonged' on Tyneside during his lifetime: "No, I don't think so. I think at school – at Chillie [Chillingham] Road and then at Ravenswood – I was aware that my parents aspired to more for me than most of the other kids in the school. And then going to RGS I was very conscious that I was taking another step away from something." However, of the school itself, he remembered it being "profoundly identified with the city it was in" and could recall no overt sense of alienation from the broader Tyneside culture. Jo Chipcase, a Dame Allan's Old Girl (Allanian), remembered an incident when a group of girls from Benfield Comprehensive School tried to roadblock her "for a possible attack of some sort" as she was riding her bike, and said: "Although I was never bullied, there was definitely a certain attitude – amongst some of my peers at least – towards the perceived 'middle classes' in Walkerville, where we lived until 1990."

Although rejecting the tendentious tendency of commentators to defend or attack private schools using the term 'middle class', when added to the "cultural confusion about can you be middle class and have a strong regional identity?" question posed by Charlotte – privately educated in Jesmond – the fact that attending a private school often instils or reinforces a specific sense of middle-class identity demands consideration. Some of the Old Novocastrians I spoke to felt attending RGS in itself denoted middle-class status. Nick Brownlee exemplified this: "I was in Jesmond when I was at school, so I'm pretty middle class … you had to be really to go to the RGS," while Giles asserted, "Very few people who go to the RGS could probably say they were working class, I would have thought, because you've got to pay to get there. And even a scholarship – I can't imagine there are too many scholarships."

"Middle class without a shadow of a doubt. I'm at this school – I'm going to be middle class," was Rahul's forthright assessment of his class status, adding: "I consider myself to be middle class because I've been to a private school and I've grown up with a fair bit of money. The school I'm at and the people I'm around – that has a big effect on you, your environment, and it's sort of made me middle class … all the kids I knock around with here, they're quite rich." Based on what he'd studied in politics lessons at RGS, Jamie said he would be classified as middle class too, but reflected: "I'd probably say I'm in the middle between working class and middle class, because I wouldn't want to consider myself too middle class. I'd still want to think there's a bit of graft in me." Meanwhile Chris identified himself as "probably middle class" citing one reason: "The thing that mostly picks me out is nothing really at home or anything; just going to the RGS – that's the only thing."

Rejecting the proposition that Newcastle could be considered a more 'American', money-based society of social stratification, Rahul asserted: "It's more of a class-based system. It's who you are you'll get more judged for. Like the way you talk, the way you act, what you wear, what you do – that's what gets you judged." So did Nick Brownlee believe traditionally middle class people felt at home, welcomed and that they belonged in the city? "I would say recently, yes. I think the middle classes are something which has come into Newcastle in the last ten, fifteen years; the Jesmondites, the Gosforthites. Before that there was always a bit of a gap between the rich and the poor in Newcastle – I always thought it anyway. You were either thought to be a wealthy snob who lived in Gosforth or you lived in a council estate in Four Lane Ends or whatever."

In response to the same question, Chris suggested: "Maybe not, really. Because there are lots of lower class people in [Newcastle/Tyneside] and they [the middle classes] maybe look on them badly, and maybe they feel more suited to somewhere a bit more down South." Asked whether working-class

Tynesiders accept their middle-class peers as genuine and authentic Geordies, he was equally doubtful: "I would say probably not, to be honest. Because maybe they see them as having more money and not having to go through the same type of life as they do." A perception of class division on Tyneside – both past and present – with the potential to cause Akenside Syndrome quite clearly exists, and regarding the theory that Newcastle is a largely classless conurbation where civic pride over-rides class distinction, Giles implied the two claims need to be looked at separately: "I don't think there's a classless society in Newcastle but I agree that people generally are proud to be from Newcastle, wherever, however they've been brought up."

Peter Stark avowed that historically, "The North-Eastern identity could accommodate you right the way through what would normally be a class differentiation – as long as you are identifying as a Geordie it over-rides the class differences," albeit adding: "Of course that could be seen as a false consciousness or whatever." And like all contributors who had attended RGS, Nick Brownlee self-identified as middle class yet felt happy, proud and confident calling himself a Geordie, with even Northumberland man Giles happy to be associated with Newcastle. So when it came to Charlotte's cultural confusion there was sympathy but limited identification. "I'm sorry she would say that. At the RGS you felt an important part of the city," said Brownlee. Rahul could "sort of identify with it but I think it's more [applicable to the] upper middle class," Jamie saw her point of view but thought "generally it's down to the individual," and Chris was able to "kind of pick up on that, but I wouldn't say it's true in every case because I call myself middle class and I would definitely say I have a strong regional identity to the North-East."

Bernard Trafford disagreed with a claim made by Bill Lancaster in *An Agenda for Regional History*, that the motivation behind Tyneside's middle and professional classes sending their children to private schools was a desire to keep the area's popular culture at arm's length. "I've lived with that for so long," he countered. "The suggestion that our parents are always just trying to avoid their kids mixing with the riff-raff and so on. And I guess there must be a proportion who are like that. There is a snobbish element everywhere that will buy something [for a sense of distinction] and those aren't my kind of people, I don't think. So that's a label – that idea about

people just taking their kids away from the riff-raff and popular culture ...
There's an element of truth but not too much, I would say."

But what about Jack Common's assessment, delivered via Willie Kiddar,
that parents send their children to private schools in the full knowledge they
will be socially and educationally conditioned in a way which, in keeping
with the traditional tenor of the class system, enhances their life chances
in a wholly un-meritocratic fashion? Loss of a regional accent, as Kiddar's
narrative sardonically implies, is a fundamental component of this social
conditioning. It's an appropriate time then, to revisit Andrew Taylor's
thoughts regarding the rise and growth of public schools in the 19th century,
and the role this played in establishing Received Pronunciation: 'Instead of
speaking with an accent which revealed their geographical background, they
began to speak with an accent that revealed their social class ... The whole
point of RP is its geographical anonymity.'[25]

Kate Fox contends that 'the two main factors affecting social mobility
in England are still education and marriage', whilst Roger Scruton has
explained how historically the 'instruments of social exclusion were princi-
pally three: land, education and accent.'[26] On a regional level, Brian Mains
has highlighted a quintessential example of the toxic interaction between
class, accent and education from the 19th century Taunton Commission,
regarding reluctance among the higher echelons of Northumberland society
to send their sons to schools in the county, including RGS: 'It is true that the
strong accent or "burr", which might be caught from provincial schoolfellows,
is also of the nature of a deterrent'.[27]

Here we have an unadorned portrayal of North-East accent akin to
contagious disease, polluting the prospects of the socially aspiring and
endangering their desire for vocal-based distinction. I asked Bernard Trafford whether, in the modern-day, attendance at a school like RGS inevitably
leads to a loss or mellowing of regional accent (where one can be said to have
pre-existed) – whether a process of verbal homogenisation occurs. "That's
interesting," he ruminated, "Well yes, I don't think I could disagree with
that thesis. I've always thought it was when they went off to university they
lost it. That was how I felt at Wolverhampton. That some came back quite
posh, especially if they were at posh universities. You would say: 'Oh, well
you've changed. And you're going to be very successful.'" Did he believe

then, contrary to Peter Arnold's assertion, that such verbal homogenisation is beneficial to his students' future life prospects? "It probably is. I wish it wasn't."

Peter Stark, who lost his Geordie accent at RGS and lists not maintaining "the ability to be bilingual" as one of his top ten regrets in life, offered empirical evidence: "If I hadn't had access to a more standardised English, there are at least two jobs in my early career that I wouldn't have got at that time. There's no shadow of doubt." He recalled making "a conscious decision to lose my accent which happened during school," also remembering that "the predominant feel of the accent around the school was definitely Geordie, albeit middle-class Geordie." Given his own accent loss, did he feel some Tynesiders would consider those with a weak or no accent as not being authentic or 'proper' Geordies? "I honestly don't think you can think of yourself as a Geordie if you haven't got access to the accent, the dialect. Or if it doesn't inflect your speech in some way. It seems to me to be so fundamental a part of the definition of what we're talking about," was his unambiguous response.

Akenside Syndrome feeds on the unequivocal, the absolute, and considering accent strength is relative and always in the ear of the listener, often shaped by their prejudices and preconceptions, Stark's summation reminded me of another Facebook group created by an Allanian called Frances Watkinson. Called *I am from Newcastle and no I don't have a Geordie accent*, at its peak it boasted over 4000 members and featured in a *Journal* article (19/04/08) whose headline read: *Website nets the 'Fraudie' Geordies*. Provoked into creating it by people questioning her lack of an accent at university in Cardiff, Frances posted a potential t-shirt slogan response to such queries, including the line: 'No, I don't have a Geordie accent; You don't need to point it out', and the group was laden with lamentations of Geordies displaying accent-related symptoms of Akenside Syndrome, a number of whom had been privately educated on Tyneside.

Nowadays living in Cumbria, there was no such accent-related soul-searching from Nick Brownlee: "I try and keep my accent without getting the Cumbrian inflection." Of his time at RGS, he noted: "I think everybody had an accent but there was – I always used to call it – a 'Darras Hall' accent … very sort of [affected 'posh' Geordie] 'Hello, how are you doing? I'm from

Gosforth, you know.' And the Geordie is there but I think it was specifically modulated for the public schools around Jesmond. You go to dos and you hear these fellas speaking and they still have this same sort of strange accent, and they all live in Morpeth and Matfen." Overall though, he felt "everybody spoke like I do. There was nobody very posh and there was nobody who was a pit yakker. Everybody just had quite a nice North-East inflection to their accent I thought … 80% spoke as I do."

Giles, having recently heard his former schoolmate on the radio, approved: "Nick Brownlee's got a nice accent – it's well-expressed," also observing, "There's nothing better than an intelligent Geordie accent. It sounds very dignified." However, the potential contradictions of subjectively recalled memories came to the fore when he assessed how many fellow RGS students he believed had Geordie accents at school. Despite attending at more or less the same time as Brownlee, he insisted there were: "Not many; very few," and asked whether those who had a distinct Geordie accent were very much in the minority, affirmed: "Definitely, I would say, yeah."

This was more in keeping with the expectations of one of Bernard Trafford's daughters when hearing of his move to RGS. Having studied English Language to postgraduate level, Trafford recalled her instinctive evaluation being: 'You won't hear many local accents at that school, Dad.' Had she been proved right? Could he perceive any significant vocal difference between students in Newcastle and Wolverhampton? "The vowel sounds are different," he attested. "An awful lot of kids have no accent, or no regional accent, but the vowel sounds are still slightly different. I mean there's still quite a lot of local accent in the school, but not as much as in Wolverhampton where it was even more prevalent. I would say, yes, up the wealthy end of Wolverhampton there was probably a bit more local accent even amongst the very rich and successful than there is here, where it's a bit lost perhaps."

This was endorsed by Rahul, who felt he had undergone a process of verbal homogenisation whilst at RGS: "I had a stronger accent when I was younger but since I've been coming here it's kind of died down. It's got a lot less Geordie. Because I suppose, once again, it's the environment. Only one in fifteen kids in the Year, I'd say, has a Geordie accent. Most of the people – well they don't really have an accent but they just have straightforward normal [i.e. 'neutral'] accents." Estimating the percentage who he felt didn't have a Geordie accent to be a very specific 89-91%, Rahul also insisted that some RGS students, particularly older year groups in his experience, would "call you a charv because you're talking with a Geordie accent."

He recalled an incident during which one of his elder brother's friends mocked his accent when he was younger, telling him: 'Ah, you talk like a bit of a charv, you. You're never going to get into university if you go into an interview like that. You'd better get a proper accent.' However, he felt an initial impulse to impress the girls at Central High – "They're all very middle class. Not many of them had a Geordie accent and I was just trying not to be myself really. I had this whole new accent, this whole new persona" – and environmental erosion were bigger factors in his own accent degradation: "It's going to inevitably fade out because of the environment you're in – 91% of the people you're hanging around with don't speak with a Geordie accent."

Pondering the process of private school accent homogenisation, Bernard Trafford said, "Perhaps it's more of the little kids that speak with more of an accent than the sixth formers," and Jamie proffered personal evidence in support of this proposition. "My accent's definitely changed," he acknowl-edged. "Every time I watch videos of when I was younger, my accent is completely different." Did he still consider himself to have a Geordie accent at all? "I wouldn't say myself that I do. But when I go to other places people say that I've got a Geordie accent. But when I'm here [in Newcastle] people are like; 'Whereabouts are you from?' Because basically with your accent, it's moulded by the people who are around you. And I'm spending more time around well-spoken people."

So whereas Peter Stark was keen to assert that RGS did not drum his accent out of him, by which he meant there weren't elocution lessons or other overt pressures, Rahul and Jamie were cognizant of and comfortable with the educational environment erosion of theirs. But Chris bucked the trend when considering this rupture from the accent pillar of Geordie identity. Marking his place on the accent spectrum, he said it was: "More [Geordie] than other people in this school, but [lighter] compared to other people in the region." And, though interviewed separately from Rahul, he estimated the RGS accent divide at an almost exact same ratio: "There's a lot fewer with

Geordie accents. There are lots of people here from Northumberland, right out in the sticks. And they, I don't think, have the accent … [The split is] probably 90% to 10% [in favour of those without accents]. It's quite high."

Consciously rejecting the tendency towards verbal conformity and geographic anonymity, he felt consistent contact with friends outside of school who had stronger accents countered vocal descent into RP neutrality: "I'd rather sound different to everyone as well. I'd rather sound like I was from the North-East, not sound like somebody who could be from anywhere. I feel proud to have an accent." It all sounded very admirable, but I couldn't help wondering whether exposure to the heightened social dynamics of Oxbridge would provoke a vocal reaction more inclined toward the Claytonian rather than the Waddellesque.

Having examined a brace of pillars with clear potential for provoking private school alienation from the broader Tyneside culture, before blowing the final whistle on this chapter there is no intention of missing a sitter of a chance to notch up the hat-trick. In 1892 Newcastle East End and Newcastle West End football clubs merged to become Newcastle United, whose permanent home was to be St James' Park. Perhaps not coincidentally, in the same year our erstwhile friend Mr Logan, RGS Head Master, issued what Margaret Wilkinson describes as a 'stern dictum' – 'No Association Football is to be played in this School in any form whatever'.[28] Back of the net! Almost a century later one of Logan's successors, Alister Cox, would refer to 'the great diversification of sport' available at the school, without irony or apparent awareness of an elephant in the room which could not have been more obvious had he been attending a party hosted by Babar and family, with special guests Nellie and Dumbo.[29]

Remarkably, Daniel Finkelstein's observation of football being boycotted by the educated middle class was evident in Newcastle until James Miller, Bernard Trafford's predecessor, introduced it for sixth formers at RGS in the early 2000s. Nick Brownlee, who attended the school during Alister Cox's reign, remembered that football "was positively frowned upon. I played rugby for the first team but I was football-mad and all my mates were. And we petitioned to have a football team and were told in no uncertain terms: 'No, you can't have a football team – it's a rugby school.' Football was hugely popular at school – we just weren't allowed to have a team! I think it was always the situation that the RGS is a rugby school, and maybe that's because of the middle-class upbringings of the school."

Before getting on to the subject of football at RGS with Bernard Trafford, I asked if he could discern any subtle differences between the general cultures of Wolverhampton and Newcastle. "Yes, it's palpable," he replied. Acknowledging a strong identification with their football team by the people of Wolverhampton, he nonetheless noted: "And I thought that was a town really identifying with football – and then I came here! And it is extraordinary ... fanatical belief." With this in mind I wondered why he felt RGS, located within a mile of St James' Park, had resisted football for so long. And while citing a probable desire by successive sports masters to retain the school's strong rugby reputation, he also suspected another motivating factor: "I fear snobbery because the gentlemen's game is rugby in terms of winter. So I think that was about being a posh school when people cared about that. It was a class thing, I would say. Gentlemen play rugby and oafs and louts play football. Which of course is such rubbish, but there was that. That's sheer prejudice."

Jamie, who played for the RGS first team alongside his captain Chris, offered a student perspective on how the introduction of football was received: "RGS has a massive tradition related to rugby, so quite a few people were against it, in the same way that people would be against the introduction of girls in the school. But personally I was ecstatic about it. I realised I was sick of playing rugby. There was a mixed reaction but on the whole I thought people thought it was good. Sort of the school broadening its horizons; because just a traditional rugby school, a traditional all-boys school – it's just a relic of the past, isn't it?" With Old Novo Fraser Forster being part of England's 2014 World Cup squad in Brazil, Jamie's views reflected a consensus that after more than a century of dubiously motivated RGS own-goals, from Mr Logan's anti-football diktat onwards, James Miller had scored a raker into the top corner.

When asked if the football-supporting, beer-drinking, working-class, accent-based version of Geordie identity may have promoted a privately-educated strain of Akenside Syndrome down the years, above and beyond the Old Novocastrian it is named after, Peter Stark wasn't enamoured with the framing of the question. "I think inevitably the answer to that has to be yes," he agreed. "But I think it's probably inherent in your question that the answer has to be yes." A loaded question? "I think it's a very loaded question – if you're saying does an education that separates you from the vast majority of the population produce a sense of difference, then it does. And is that a case for a *truly* comprehensive education? Yes, I think it is. Is it a case for the end of the kind of privileged private education that we're talking about? Yes, I think it probably is. Does it mean that a doctor and a lecturer and a priest and a dentist can't feel authentically, comfortably and happily integrated as a Geordie? No, I don't think it does for a minute."

But having gone to Leeds as an undergraduate in the 1960s, and establishing his reputation as an arts administrator further south, he recalled experiencing Akenside Syndrome acutely before returning to the North-East as Director of Northern Arts in 1984. "A large part of it had been a feeling that I'd lost the accent. That I was inauthentic in my own place. And I do want to say that it was nothing to do with the school having got rid of the accent; it was to do with me having made the choice and it was generational rather than class or school." Referencing RGS contemporaries including Jeremy Beecham "proudly speaking a soft Geordie, but very distinctly Geordie as Jeremy still does," he regretted: "I didn't. I was the guy who needed somehow to find some other tool to redefine myself."

When it came to people higher up the socio-economic scale readily identifying as Geordies, there was certainly support for this – and Alister Cox's claim that those with RGS connections, 'feel ourselves to be central both in location and in sentiment and in these senses to 'belong' to the city of Newcastle' – as only Rahul cited a recent identification with Akenside Syndrome.[30] "The only reason that I've ever questioned whether I fitted in is because of the colour of my skin, really," he reflected. "My parents aren't from here. I've got a Geordie accent but – it's hard to say because everyone's talking about their history and their roots. What do I say about my history and my roots? Obviously the odd person's going to shout 'Paki' at me or whatever – that's going to happen anywhere really, isn't it? It's not because of Newcastle specifically. But overall I've really felt like a part of Newcastle – I've always been really proud to be a Geordie."

Akenside Syndrome ranges from the relatively mild and harmless to the profound and detrimental, but there has been an inclination to seek out the latter and employ phrases such as *suffer from* or *fall prey to*. Broadening understanding of its potential causes and effects, Peter Stark and Bernard Trafford took a different line. Having fully reconciled feelings of ambivalence towards his hometown, Stark insisted: "Akenside Syndrome doesn't bother me. I don't see it as a negative. I see it as an inevitable part of being a genuine part of a strong regional culture, but not the dominant part. And being a bit of it that is more connected – has the chance to be more connected – to the rest of the world than most." So whilst experiencing Akenside Syndrome may feel wretched and disorientating at the time, it can be worked through and perhaps viewed retrospectively as enriching. It can be seen as a phase of personal growth which, if successfully navigated, raises self-awareness and cultivates a more rounded personality.

When I read the symptoms connected with Akenside Syndrome to Bernard Trafford, and asked whether RGS students would historically fall into the high-risk category, his response correlated with Keith Armstrong's views on educational and intellectual enlightenment. "Well actually yes they probably have got a high risk and they should have," he declared. "Because I think that's about education and questioning. And I think there's that argument that all the great artists, writers, whatever, were slight misfits. You know, they don't quite fit in." This reminded me of Russian novelist Yevgeni Zamyatin, who lived in Jesmond in 1916 at around the time *Kiddar's Luck* is set, and held the Jesmondians he observed in contempt, satirising them as repressed bourgeois conformists in his novellas *A Fisher of Men* and *Islanders*.

Zamyatin's most acclaimed novel *WE* is widely thought to have influenced George Orwell's *Nineteen Eighty-Four*, and as we leave RGS contemplating the private schools of Jesmond, alongside Newcastle's fabled aura of classlessness and spirit of egalitarianism, a compulsion to paraphrase Jack Common's friend Orwell takes hold: *All Geordies are equal but some are more equal than others*. But our time in Jesmond is not yet done, as two of Newcastle's most renowned artists of recent times are Jesmondians, and they aren't exactly known for their repressed outlook on Tyneside life. Let's take the short walk from Eskdale Terrace to Lily Crescent, looking out for boys with flatulent tendencies and unfeasibly large testicles along the way.

If the future generations look back on the literature of the age, they'll more usefully look back to *Viz* than they would, for instance, the novels of Peter Ackroyd or Julian Barnes … because *Viz* has got a genuine vitality of its own which comes from the society which it represents.

Auberon Waugh, quoted by William Cook in *25 Years of Viz*

Geordie has been put firmly on the national map by popular TV dramas and films and perhaps more than anything else by the earthy humour of *Viz* magazine … the natural humour of [Newcastle], a great scatological urban humour, sharp and earthy. Not for nothing is this the place that created and has nurtured *Viz* magazine.

Simon Elmes, *Talking for Britain: A Journey through the Nation's Dialects*

If the region's greatest and funniest writer [Jack Common] found Jesmond alien and un-Geordie, it is a measure of the erosion of cultural class barriers that *Viz*, the quintessential expression of local irreverence to English conformity, is largely the product of Jesmond middle-class youth. This dominance of regional over class identity is expressed in many facets of everyday Newcastle.

Bill Lancaster, *Newcastle – Capital of What?* in *Geordies*

… a bowler-hatted bloke gushing like a water-closet, as he shot out a mixture of pork pie and beer and clutched the back of his neck after each vomit.

Jack Common describing a Bigg Market scene in *Kiddar's Luck*

Dead drunk, some tumble on the floor/And swim in what they'd drunk before/ Hiccup cries one/'reach me your hand/The house turns round, I cannot stand'./ So now the drunken, senseless crew/Break pipes, spill drinks, piss, shit and spew.

The Collier's Wedding by Edward Chicken, an 18th century parish clerk at St John's Church on Newcastle's Westgate Road

I was surprised; so much drunkenness, cursing and swearing (even from the mouths of little children) do I never remember to have seen and heard before, in so small a compass of time.

John Wesley, founder of Methodism, writing about Tynesiders in 1742

THE BIG HARD *VIZ* ONE

Donalds Ducked?

I DIDN'T ASK BERNARD TRAFFORD WHAT TYPE OF ART SPRANG TO HIS mind when contemplating artists as social misfits, but had I done so it seems reasonable to assume that Johnny Fartpants, Buster Gonad and his Unfeasibly Large Testicles, Vibrating Bum-Faced Goats, Tina's Tits, Norman's Knob, Lord Shite and Nanny No-Dumps, Terry Fuckwitt and The Bottom Inspectors would not have been the first examples he reached for. Then again, who knows? William Cook noted how Trafford's fellow Old Gregorian Auberon Waugh made comparisons between *Viz* and the work of Rabelais and William Hogarth, and saw echoes of Orwell in The Bottom Inspectors; while in *Pies and Prejudice* Stuart Maconie quotes the *Daily Telegraph* praising *Viz* for possessing the "iconoclastic Toryism of [Jonathan] Swift'."[1] All of which may lead us to existentially empathise with a Fuckwittian perspective on life: 'EVERY DAY I LOOK AROUND ME AT THIS WORLD IN WHICH WE LIVE... AND I THINK TO MYSELF: "BUGGER ME! I HAVEN'T GOT THE FOGGIEST NOTION WHAT THE FUCK IS GOING ON".'[2]

The shock experienced by John Wesley whilst visiting Tyneside, the bawdy lyrics of Edward Chicken, and Jack Common's snapshot of Bigg

Market over-indulgence, form a historical thread of Newcastle culture woven into the modern day fabric of the city by the extraordinary success of *Viz*. It begs a variation of the age-old question: is *Viz* an example of art imitating Geordie life, or is *Viz*-like behaviour by certain Geordies life imitating art? The playing out of culturally conditioned roles reflected in and perpetuated by artistic output. We've already observed Donna Air saying that people from outside the region 'have the stereotype of these big, lardy *Viz* characters,' and when it comes to perceptions of Geordies there can be no doubting the seismic impact the magazine had from the mid-1980s onwards.

As well as Auberon Waugh's eulogising and Simon Elmes's evident approval, in *Up North* Charles Jennings guiltily confesses to buying *Viz* – 'for the cultural critique, you understand' – and praises its 'brilliantly realised, scabrous sociopathy', whereas Stuart Maconie refers to it as a 'receptacle of Geordie culture … which has done its fair share of propagating an image of the city that has made millions snigger but presumably had the north-east development corporation choking on their skinny macchiatos.'[3] According to William Cook, *Viz* 'completely reinvented the Great British sense of humour', and the fact that critics including Beatrix Campbell and Peregrine Worsthorne have felt compelled to pass comment further demonstrates how it penetrated the national consciousness.[4]

From the mid-1980s to the early 1990s and beyond, alongside the second series of *Auf Wiedersehen, Pet* (in which loutish Oz remained the most memorable character), the rise of Gazza and the advent of children's TV series *Byker Grove*, *Viz* could be found at the epicentre of a nationwide Geordie zeitgeist (not to be confused with *shitegeist*, an entry in *Roger's Profanisaurus*) which in some ways has come to define modern-day Geordies ever since. I can still vividly recall the exact classroom and lesson at West Denton High School where a fellow student first showed me a copy of *Viz* in the 1980s. For many years from that moment on, I would be most displeased if Santa did not leave a healthy *Viz*ian deposit from his large sack in my stocking at Christmas, be it a *Porky Chopper*, a *Big Bell End* or a *Rusty Sheriff's Badge*. Like many across the nation I thought *Viz* was the *Dog's Bollocks*, and had the poor quality t-shirt emblazoned with Roger Mellie on the front to prove it.

Yet for all the acclaim this Newcastle born and bred 'venerable British institution' receives, we've encountered pronouncements from its creator, Chris Donald, indicative of Akenside Syndrome.[5] I met him at The Forth pub on Newcastle's Pink Lane and his response to my standard opening question – *Do you consider yourself to be a Geordie?* – seems like a good point of departure from which to try and understand why this may be: "Yes, well I do now but when I was a kid I was very uncomfortable with it because at the school I was at – Heaton Comprehensive – there was half the lads came from Heaton and half the lads came from Jesmond, and the Jesmond ones were considered to be the posh ones. And my dad used to say… he didn't use the word Geordie but 'You're not to talk slang. You're not to use slang.' He wanted me to talk properly.

"And so at school I was considered not to be a Geordie," he continued. "And then we went on holiday; I'd be down in Oxfordshire staying at my Aunty's and people would stop me in the street and say 'Ah, you're a Geordie, are you?' And I got very confused because I didn't know if I was or not." In this opening gambit we can detect themes of marginalisation at school, class division, accent-related social aspiration, and identity confusion provoked by competing notions of what constitutes being a Geordie from both within and without Tyneside. In short there's a veritable *smorgasbord* of Akenside Syndrome appetisers that the Fat Slags, even with the help of Fat Sod and Fatty Balatty, would struggle to digest at one sitting.

Reflecting on Bill Lancaster's suggestion that *Viz* originating from middle-class Jesmond could be seen as 'a measure of the erosion of cultural class barriers' in Newcastle, and that it is in 'a curious sense … a classless city', Chris was sceptical: "I would tend to disagree with him probably – there are other places that are more classless than Newcastle. Places where everybody has moved in within a shorter period. Like places with a lot of immigration. When you're living in a city where you've been brought up, you're always going to be aware of your class. And a lot of people – working-class people – are very proud of being working class, even though they're not really [working class] anymore."[6]

He was equally doubtful about there being more social empathy between different classes on Tyneside than in other places – "I don't think so, no. It's not something that strikes me as obvious. I don't know if it's imagined but it just seems to be more of a gap here" – but conceded that regional identity could be seen as prevailing over class identity to some extent. "Oh yeah, definitely. I think it's down to the fact it's such an insular city. It's not siege mentality but it's very much the fact that there's no other conurbation nearby. That's the fact that makes us have a more clear regional identity than other places. So yeah, the regional identity I suppose does over-ride the class barriers a bit. Not perhaps as much as some people think."

When Chris recalled the Jesmond of his youth being so culturally different from working-class areas of Newcastle in *A Picture of Tyneside*, he was speaking from personal experience of both sides of the divide, as his father Jimmy grew up in Shieldfield, whereas his mother Kay was a Jesmond girl. In his autobiography *Him off the Viz*, Chris's younger brother Simon refers to Jimmy as 'one of the aspirational working class,' who 'bagged himself the ultimate goal for a working-class social climber – a middle-class wife.' But while he has talked of how their paternal grandmother's 'Geordie working-class sense of humour was a joy', Chris remembered that "the two families just didn't get on at all well", and recalled questioning his own class status as a child in conversation with elder brother Steve, who sadly passed away in 2008.[7] "I had this argument with my brother when I was a kid. He'd say 'We're middle class' and I'd say 'Well we're not middle class, we're working class – Dad's from Shieldfield' ... but because we had a house in Jesmond you couldn't deny it, I'm afraid. We're middle class. So that's just the way it was."

In Chris's formative years, the pre-Thatcherite 1960s and 1970s, class identities and conflicts were more clearly delineated, and I wondered if growing up with a sense of himself as middle class in a city so overwhelmingly identified as working class caused any discomfort. "Yes," he affirmed. "You were meant to feel uncomfortable being middle class. I mean you weren't supposed to but you did. It was a bit like *The Likely Lads* and you were like Bob Ferris [Rodney Bewes] and the other kids at school would be like Terry Collier [James Bolam]. It felt like you were doing the wrong thing by being middle class, and being middle class wasn't particularly acceptable. It wasn't something that people aspired to. Or there was a definite divide between the people that aspired to it and the people who definitely didn't aspire to it." Dick Clement and Ian La Frenais did indeed dramatize this divide in their sitcom *Whatever Happened to the Likely Lads?*, which aired in the early 1970s, with Bob chiding Terry in one episode for being like Andy Capp before his time and held back by his class barrier, and Terry retaliating by saying he loves Andy Capp and is proud of his class, and mocking Bob for flirting with the 'lower lower middle middle' class.

Andy Capp also cropped up when I asked Chris whether he felt another of Bill Lancaster's assertions – that historically some have found Geordie culture 'embarrassingly working-class' – rang true: "There's an element of that. My dad certainly did, I think, as he was aspiring to be middle class … I think he was embarrassed by the whole working-class thing. He didn't like pubs. And he didn't like smoking. And he didn't like people who spoke slang and all the rest of it. It's almost a bit cartoony. It's sort of cartoon Geordies. Like the Andy Capp thing – it is a bit embarrassing. But at the same time I'm not one who's trying to distance myself from it completely, the way some people do."

When I met Simon at the Tyneside Cinema, he recollected how their dad "used to be infuriated by [*The Likely Lads* and *Whatever Happened to the Likely Lads?*] because he thought it was all stereotyping of the Geordies," and also recognised the prevalence of Terry Collier-like disdain whilst growing up in Newcastle: "There used to be a very distinct feeling amongst working-class people that if you were middle class you weren't a proper Geordie." The link between class and Akenside Syndrome has been strongly forged by now, and the class tension explored by Clement and La Frenais, also observed by Chris in the Donalds' extended families, was to replicate itself to some extent within himself and Simon; both developing different class identities without wholly identifying with either side of the ultimately mythical, but psychologically and tribally powerful working/middle class dichotomy.

Kate Fox maintains that 'a great deal of everyday English humour is preoccupied with class issues', and when it came to the scattergun approach of *Viz* towards its targets, the brothers' ambivalent class loyalties enabled them to cultivate 'the comic's classless appeal.'[8] Melvyn Bragg has suggested that Chris – who has said conflict between the working class and middle class was a source of inspiration for his cartoons – was 'a lower middle-class Geordie lampooning his fellow working-class Geordies', but as elder brother Steve pointed out to William Cook: 'You can't make comedy out of something that you completely identify with, because you can't separate yourself from it.'[9]

Nevertheless, whereas it seems Chris felt more drawn, or compelled, to the kind of middle-class identity aspired to by their father, Simon was more inclined toward the predominant working-class culture he saw around him. Kay was diagnosed with multiple sclerosis in the mid-1960s, and this led to a pronounced dissonance between the family's Jesmond location and their actual financial status, which, as Simon described, "Put a cat amongst the pigeons of the middle-class dream that they had. They'd been living the English suburban dream, if you will. The little house in the right neighbourhood; they had all the nice curtains and all the rest of it. Dad took a less well-paid job in order to be able to care for her part-time. And that changed everything because they couldn't live the middle-class dream out anymore. And also it made my mam question a lot of what that was all about. We lived in a middle-class house in a middle-class neighbourhood, but we were poor. And we had free school uniforms and free school dinners and we didn't have any carpets and we didn't have a TV set.

"We lived out this very strange existence where when I went to secondary school I encountered a lot more working-class kids than middle-class kids, because at the Heaton School the Jesmond kids formed the minority and I guess – I don't know – through half of my roots being working class, I found myself quite naturally getting on very well with those lads. I think quite early on in my secondary school education I started to feel I belonged more with the working-class people than I did with the middle-class people. And I think it was because of that thing that we had no money. I think that I just felt more comfortable amongst them, because the middle-class kids tended to probably be a bit more snobby about that than the working-class kids. Although we did get called 'Posh Tramps'. But I think it actually gave me a really good vision on life. I think it's interesting to see that some commentators see *Viz* as being a middle-class product. Others see it as being a working-class product. But everyone sees it as their own."

Asked if being called a Posh Tramp and the broader confusion surrounding his class status had had any lasting psychological impact, Simon said: "No, I don't think the class thing did. I think my mam's illness had a lasting effect on us all. Certainly if it hadn't been for that I think I would probably have just grown up a middle-class kid and had a pretty different perspective. I look back and I think if my mam hadn't been ill I probably would have grown up in that sort of terrible cotton wool world."

Chris meanwhile reflected on whether *Viz*, like *Spender* and *Billy Elliot*, could be interpreted as an example of Akenside Syndrome manifesting itself through artistic output: "Certainly if I hadn't been in the slightly uncomfortable class situation – being stuck on the fence between one thing and another – I'm sure that there wouldn't have been a comic." Elaborating on this feeling of not fully fitting in with or belonging to one class or another, he employed an analogy that will chime with many Geordies, artistically inclined or otherwise, who have experienced Akenside Syndrome: "I feel a bit like a bagatelle. That's what I am – a bagatelle ball what hasn't settled and has never settled in a slot. Sort of just keep bouncing around and it never actually settled in a way. So yeah, it could be ambivalence that keeps you bouncing."

One of the factors that propelled Chris's bagatelle ball into a state of perpetual restless motion was clearly his experience at Heaton Comprehensive School. His recollection – "It was very much the case when I was at school that if you were staying on at school there was something the matter with you. It was just a thing that posh kids did" – complements Jack Common's evocation of attitudes toward Heaton schooling in *Kiddar's Luck*: 'Most of us didn't want better jobs. We despised people who came home clean from their work and had in consequence a somewhat unreal and unaffirmed look, lacking the used coarseness of full men.'[10] Common was born in 1903, and Margaret Wilkinson quotes from the Report on Secondary and Higher Education in Newcastle upon Tyne presented to the city council in 1905, which highlighted 'some of the regional prejudices hampering secondary schooling', including 'a half contempt for subjects which at first sight look unpractical or detached from the work-a-day duties of life'.[11]

Further illustration there of underlying anti-education attitudes on Tyneside, which may still contribute toward what a modern-day council official described as 'the historic gap between Newcastle and the rest of the country' in terms of educational attainment.[12] As for class division in a Heaton school context, this was clearly an issue for Chris. Discussing school bullying in his former *Sunday Sun* column, he recalled a drawing pin being stuck in his knee, a live worm hidden in his school dinner, and a pickled rat's arse catapulted into his face whilst at Heaton Comprehensive; also telling of being dangled over the edge of a bridge – his haversack thrown in the river – when walking home through Jesmond Dene.[13] In *Rude Kids* he further asserted: 'There were plenty of real bullies at Heaton, or 'hards' as they preferred to be known ... You had to watch your eye-line very carefully if you were in the presence of potential aggressors. Any look adjudged to be 'funny' could be punishable by a severe kicking.'[14]

Being bullied and the feelings of social exclusion it can engender increase an individual's likelihood of Akenside Syndrome alienation, and I wondered whether this had provoked or exacerbated ambivalence towards his Tyneside roots. "It was just to do with it being a badly run school and there being such a wide social divide within the school as well," he reasoned. "There was a lot of class-based bullying. We used to be like herds of gazelle when we used to walk home through Jesmond Dene, because there would be kids hanging round and you'd all group together and walk past them as fast as you could. And these bullies would be waiting to pick someone off if they got separated from the pack – like in the bloody Kenyan plains or whatever."

Despite describing himself and Jim Brownlow, his schoolmate and co-founder of *Viz*, as 'loners, slightly too weird to fit into the social main-stream' at school (also telling William Cook they 'would occasionally get called homs and poofs because we were two blokes who were hanging around together'), Chris wasn't minded to read too much into the bullying he endured: "Other people had far worse bullying, I'm sure. So I wouldn't say it was a particular problem for me. For my big brother it was. He had a terrible time of it."[15]

There appears to have been a descending trajectory of bullying experi-enced by the Donald brothers, with Simon also recalling in his autobiography how Steve's Asperger's Syndrome 'led to him being the focus of attention of a number of bullies, becoming known as 'Professor Posh'.' Regarding his own experience, Simon wrote: 'For a kid like me, with a gentle suburban upbringing, being thrust into the cauldron of Heaton School was traumatic', referring to himself as 'an innocent Jesmond softy' during his early months there, and relating how he 'encountered class hatred for the first time' on his first day from a teacher who mocked him as 'a posh lad' in front of his classmates.[16]

What's interesting about this anecdote for our purposes is Simon's subsequent psychological reaction: 'this incident did make me realise what it was like to be alienated. It made me determined that in my life I wouldn't make snap judgements about people or follow the divisive class boundaries that this teacher was trying to use to alienate me from my own friends.'[17] Consciously or otherwise, he seems to have avoided the extremes of bullying experienced by his elder siblings via a process of assimilation and affiliation. "I don't think I suffered anything like my brother [Chris] did with bullies," he reminisced. "But I think that's probably because I was more friendly with the bullies than he was. I think Chris was a bit – and still is a bit – well, he's a bit more middle class than I am. I think I gelled much more with the working-class kids who tended to be the bullies. I can't say I wasn't bullied at all, but then I think *everybody* is bullied to some extent at school. It's a question of how you deal with it that takes you through to what you become in life."

To which we might add that how an individual reacts to being bullied as a child can have a profound impact on whether or not they develop Akenside Syndrome, and, if they do, to what extent this will continue to be problematic for them in their adult lives. Kate Fox has identified 'a universal human coping mechanism' whereby 'in all cultures, people who are perceived to be threatening tend to be the subject of ... defensive jokes,' and bearing in mind that Simon has talked of 'extreme violence [being] a trait of our writing that would continue through the early years of *Viz*', I suggested maybe their experience of bullying and violence played a part in the creative impulse and energy that flowed onto its pages.[18]

"Ah, absolutely," he agreed. "I think Chris will always say that he created Biffa Bacon from his observation of bullying on a train once [Skinheed, Norman the Doorman and Big Vern were other pugilistically predisposed early Chris creations]. But that was the catalyst – that was the thing that made him create the cartoon strip. I think the references in the cartoon strip come from a whole life of witnessing violence. The early 1970s, the mid-1970s were a pretty violent time generally – being beaten up was part of growing up then. I think a lot of what we did, the more violent characters,

I think that is a direct reaction against what had happened to us, especially the likes of Biffa Bacon. It happens in a lot of Sid the Sexist stuff that I did, and it happens with Mr Logic. When Mr Logic is misunderstood he usually ends up getting beaten up. It's a social observation really; that's one of the things that tends to happen – the characters who are misunderstood usually end up getting beaten senseless by the thugs."

Bullying can take many forms beyond crude physical brutality, of course, and Andrew Taylor has pointed out one of England's favourites: 'Bullies have always enjoyed using language to beat their victims over the head – but nowadays, it isn't only the toffs who beat up the oiks.'[19] As Chris recalled, the eldest Donald sibling bore the brunt of this type of bullying too: "My big brother Steve used to get picked on for having a posh accent. But that was my dad. He was the first kid and my dad taught him to talk posh really, because that was what my dad wanted. He wanted to have kids from Jesmond who spoke properly. He didn't want us speaking like all his mates in Shieldfield had. Or the people who he frowned upon in Shieldfield."

Paradoxically perhaps, in *Comic Dialect* Tom Hadaway asserted that 'language is power, and having our dialect tolerated as merely amusing is one way of rendering us powerless – one way of denying us a share', whilst simultaneously praising Chris and *Viz* for recognising that 'dialect is not merely sometimes, but always and forever about defiance.'[20] The thing is, interpretation is always and forever in the power – or the humour reflex – of the receiver, not the creator, and according to William Cook: 'For outsiders, the Tyneside patois was all part of the appeal.'

Chris acknowledged this in *25 Years of Viz* – 'Only ten or twenty per cent of it was written in the vernacular, but they obviously found that funny' – and considering Cook transcribed his use of 'me' for 'my' literally, proclaiming: '*Viz* spoke with a Geordie accent,' there was an obvious question to ask.[21] Does Chris think that he speaks with a Geordie accent? "No, I haven't got a Geordie accent and I've even been uncomfortable as recently as within the last month. I found myself uncomfortable saying the word *hotel* in the pub where I live," he laughed. "I know people who are just as middle class as me who have tried to put on a Geordie accent and they've got words horribly wrong. I'm just happy talking in my natural voice but then if I answer the phone my kids will say: 'Dad, you're doing your Geordie voice.' And it's because I'll be talking to someone from the pool league, and I don't do it deliberately but I do [do it]. Yeah, you vary your accent. I suppose everybody does. But no, I'm very conscious of the fact that I haven't got a Geordie accent, and if I'm with people who have got Geordie accents I'm scared that I'll get caught out trying to sound like a Geordie. And I don't want to be caught out trying to. It's a funny business actually, that. I've never been totally comfortable talking."

When further asked whether he had encountered prejudice on Tyneside because of not having a strong accent, Chris was adamant: "Yeah. Oh yeah, you do. You definitely do," and the equation of Geordie with the broadly accented, heavy dialect-using working class (and the linguistic faction-alism and intolerance this can breed) was obviously a major factor. But the seeds of on-going discomfort with the way he speaks seem to have been originally sown by his father's accent-related social aspiration. He called to mind how Jimmy "would have a Geordie accent and if I went to work with him where he was out selling things to people, he could put that on at the drop of a hat. He could just switch it on, his accent, and be like his Geordie self again. But then if he was talking to his posh friends he had his telephone voice and all that. And so I was aware of him having sort of a dual personality."

Jimmy's well-intended but perhaps ultimately misguided attempt to influence his sons' accents seems to have had a lasting impact on Chris, and when I speculated on this, he reflected: "Well I just think that, no, you shouldn't force people to talk [a certain way] – I mean you can stop them from swearing and stuff; there's certain words, I suppose. You could try and regulate what words people use to a certain extent but you can't try and influence their accents. I don't think that's fair." The historic importance of accent with regard to fitting in and feeling that you belong on Tyneside also cropped up when Chris contemplated feeling half Geordie and half not whilst growing up, and whether Simon's adoption of a more working-class persona had enabled him to evade accent-related angst: "I mean our accents – living in the same house he developed a different accent to me. And I was aware of that. And people used to comment on it. But it's psychological. I don't think he deliberately put it on but it's just the circles he moved in perhaps, to a certain extent."

In a battle rap against fellow North-East comedian Seymour Mace at the 2013 Edinburgh Festival, Simon was flayed by the lyric, 'You pretend you're working class, like you worked down the pit/But your posh Geordie accent gives away you're full of shit', yet when I asked whether he considered himself to have a Geordie accent, a familiar pattern regarding perception emerged. "It's a curious one because when I meet people from the rest of the country some of them will say 'Wow! Love the Geordie accent!' or 'Wow! Where you from? Where's this marvellous accent from?' And you get other people who say 'Where are you from?' And you say Newcastle [and they respond]: 'Oh! You haven't got an accent [in a somewhat disdainful tone].'" The latter reaction epitomising a common scenario explained by Peter Lowdon, in which some people from beyond Tyneside "assume that you have a *Byker Grove* pidgin Geordie accent that's like: 'Whey aye, man. Aye, let's gan doon the Grove.'"

Simon elaborated on the evolution of his accent, remembering: "When we were growing up my dad, who came from Shieldfield, he absolutely drummed into us when we were kids, in a very old-fashioned way, that we must *not* have an accent. He'd obviously trained himself out of his own and then tried very hard to make us speak what he would say was Queen's English, I suppose. But what we found when we went to school was that that doesn't go down too well! So I guess when you mix with more working-class kids you find yourself speaking more like them. So I'm a bit of a bizarre mixture between the two. And it depends who you're with." As for experiencing prejudice because of how his accent may be perceived on Tyneside, one particular anecdote sprang to mind: "My mate Big Pete from Blyth once actually accused me of rounding my vowel sounds. He thought that I was trying to be posh. And I said, 'No, Pete. You've kind of got it the wrong way round. I have always been posh and if anything I would be going in the other direction.'" He chuckled, "I guess it only goes to show that I must have gone sufficiently in the other direction that he could only see the chinks on certain days like."

An understandable temptation would be to dismiss the type of accent and class tension recounted by the Donalds as a relic of the past, a cultural snapshot of the era in which they grew up not applicable to the present day, yet within months of speaking to them I noted an article in the *Evening*

Chronicle in which their old school was praised, having 'been awarded accreditation by Newcastle City Council's anti-bullying team RESPONSE in recognition of its hard work to tackle the issue.' Commended as 'the only secondary school in Newcastle to have formal accreditation', it's difficult not to imagine that this was because the issue remained an ongoing problem.[22]

To obtain a Noughties perspective I asked Peter Lowdon, whose schooling trajectory was exactly the same as that of Chris and Simon, whether his own lighter Geordie accent had ever been an issue at Heaton Manor. "Oh, of course," he asserted. "I mean you get the charvs who are like: 'Here man, poshy.' I got it, my friends got it, anyone who didn't have the strongest Geordie accent got it. It was obviously an issue for them. It wasn't an issue for us but, yeah, there was definitely a lot of it going on. I think it's been going on since Heaton Manor was opened, I would imagine. Always people looking at other people's accents and trying to [enforce] this one-upmanship; there is a lot of conflict, people do divide themselves up." Nick Forbes lives in Heaton, as it happens. His anti-bullying mission may be a little more complex than imagined.

There is an inevitable element of compare and contrast between the Donald brothers here, with the intention of exploring how certain aspects of Geordie identity may have affected them, how this in turn might have influenced their feelings about Newcastle, and to what extent such feelings subconsciously transposed themselves into *Viz*, the comic that has presented a particular potty-mouthed portrayal of Geordies to the nation for over thirty years. And a relevant difference between the siblings in relation to Akenside Syndrome has been remarked upon by William Cook: 'It's far too flip to label them as extrovert and introvert, but Simon is younger and more outgoing while Chris is older and more introspective, and this clash of personalities helped to give *Viz* its spark.'[23]

Inviting Chris to comment on this disparity of temperament in a broader context, I asked whether to some extent the loud and aggressive aspect of Newcastle's culture, wherein lairiness is celebrated, is not really conducive to the introverted character. "Yes. That's an interesting point. Yeah, that's true. It's not like an ideal place to be, for want of a better word, a Smiths fan – withdrawn, introverted people. Yeah, I'm sure [living in Newcastle and fitting into that aspect of the culture] would be easier for Simon. He's definitely the extrovert and I'm an introvert, there's no doubt about that," he acknowledged, later adding: "If Morrissey had been born in Newcastle I think he'd have probably killed himself when he was twelve."

His brother responded by correcting my suggestion that Newcastle's city centre culture celebrates lairiness to a certain extent: "Not to a certain extent – I think to a fuckin' limitless extent!" Speaking just before selling his house in Jesmond ahead of a move to London, Simon, who variously describes himself as 'naturally being an exhibitionist', 'attention seeking' and 'gifted with an ability to speak endlessly' in his autobiography, reinforced Chris's observation, recognising the compatibility between his extroversion and urban living: "I like the city life. I like people. I like the anonymity that you can have in a city as well; I think in a city you can choose to just disappear."[24]

Of his own move out of Newcastle in the early 1990s, Chris recollected a series of steps that led him to leave his hometown if not by accident, then not quite by coherent design either: "I've occasionally regretted it, and there's times recently when I've thought when our kids have all finished school I'll come back." To Jesmond perhaps, where the *Viz* journey first began in 1979? Here again class-related issues from his youth seemed to be a factor: "I've got this thing about being from Jesmond. It was just the fact that you were from Jesmond. I think I've got a particular problem about having come from Jesmond! Just as a tag being from Jesmond has always been a bit of a problem.

"I wouldn't live in Jesmond anymore because I drove through it today and somebody honked his bloody horn at me. Some bastard in an open-topped BMW. And I just thought: 'You wankers – this used to be a nice place.' It's gone horrible, Jesmond. It's just gone to pot. So many students and such a strange kind of student as well – they all seem to be rugby players. Acorn Road's full of all these stupid boutiques selling fucking candles. It's nonsense." Brotherly harmony descended on this issue, with Simon regretting in *Him off the Viz* that whereas the Jesmond of his youth was well-to-do but had a mixed-class element, 'Those streets where I grew up are nowadays sadly predominantly occupied by loudmouthed middle-class student arseholes.'[25]

I asked Chris whether he had ever suffered from Akenside Syndrome. "I would say before *Viz*, yes," he confirmed. "Because of the reasons I've talked about. About being uncomfortable out of your class and everything before *Viz*. And then suddenly *Viz* came along. *Viz* did a funny thing because it was started off originally for students and what I would term intellectual people." Remembering how many of those he hung around with in the run-up to launching the comic were not from Newcastle, he reflected, "They were all outsiders really. I was very aware of not being happy in the Geordie [environment such as] the Bigg Market. I would go and seek the company of these other people – *Viz* was popular with them first. Then suddenly it became popular with what we would call working-class people. And I remember it vividly." Working for the DHSS at the time, colleagues started pestering him to see *Viz*: "And I thought 'Oh God, they've accepted me. Even though I'm from Jesmond they've accepted me as a Geordie. And I go out to the Bigg Market with them and now they want to see my student magazine, and when they see it they're going to think I'm a twat.'"

The reverse was true and he recalled how, as the *Viz* sensation snow-balled, "It became accepted locally. Eventually the local press accepted it and then they all got a bit proud of it. And we used to get publicity all the time and suddenly Newcastle was proud of *Viz* and it was a national success story. I was then happy. Well, I was more happy then because I'm accepted as the *Viz* bloke. But if it hadn't been for *Viz* I'd probably still be pottering around not knowing whether I was coming or going, whether I was a Geordie or not. I'm the last person you want to ask [about having Akenside Syndrome] because of the fact that *Viz* has given me that acceptability and status – I'm sort of happy now."

On the surface it exemplifies how the cultural output of an ill-at-ease creative person can ironically gain them acceptance from the community from which they have felt estranged. But our mission here is to scratch the surface of Geordie identity, and to understand the myriad ways in which Akenside Syndrome can affect those who have experienced it. Chris's slightly qualified response – 'sort of happy' – made me contemplate that those affected on the acute end of the scale are never likely to be fully 'cured' of the condition; though it may mellow and can be managed in various ways. The most obvious being to physically remove yourself from the perceived source of alienation.

He was still living in the northern-most periphery of the Newcastle city region when we spoke, and this led me to consider a scenario of him brooding over a return to live in the city itself. An image of a bagatelle ball took shape, one side adorned with a *Viz*-like cartoon of Chris's face, content and happy, and the other displaying the same face but contorted with angst. The bagatelle table depicts a map of Newcastle with a hole in each neighbourhood. Biffa Bacon is holding up an ASBO warning in Cowgate; coming to rest in the city centre around the Bigg Market involves the ball nestling in the crotch of Sid the Sexist; while Student Grant is protesting against tuition fees next to the Jesmond slot. Chris's ball just kept bouncing until a recent, soon-to-be permanent move to Gosforth.

John Forster, who like Mark Akenside was born in Newcastle the son of a butcher and attended RGS, coined the phrase 'the attraction of repulsion' to describe his close friend Charles Dickens's ambiguous relationship with London. I inquired if the same could be said of Chris's relationship with Newcastle too: "I'm not repulsed by it but I'm schizophrenic [about it]; one minute I'll think Newcastle's great and the next minute I'll think it's awful. I wonder whether rather than just being somewhere in the middle, I actually fluctuate between the two constantly.

"I wouldn't say I was repulsed by Newcastle but then again I would say when we were writing a cartoon about the Fat Slags eating chips and that in the Bigg Market, when you're actually in the process of writing it you are thinking: 'Oh, it's funny but it's also repulsive.' And it's the disgustingness of it a lot of the time which is what makes it funny. It's so vulgar and it's that vulgarity that attracts you to it. You do find it vulgar so yeah, there is something to that. But I think perhaps I fluctuate from wanting to be part of it to thinking 'that's disgusting' and wanting to take the mickey out of it or say 'that's terrible'." Referring to the attraction of repulsion with regard to himself, Simon was emphatic: "*Absolutely*. I think that's absolutely right. I feel a great affinity, a great closeness with Newcastle and its people, obviously because I am one of them. But there is a horrible dark side to it, I think like there is to any city. I think that that is something which both repulses me and draws me in, because that's obviously what a lot of our work has been about – that darkness is what has inspired so much of my work."

Nevertheless, Akenside Syndrome ambivalence was not something Simon recognised having experienced, but he knew a bloke who had: "I personally haven't but my best mate has gone to live in Italy. He grew up, similar background to me, and he had troubles with vandalism or burglary. And he ended up blaming it all on Tyneside. As if Tyneside is the only place that's like that. And I think he's ended up with a real love-hate [relationship with Tyneside] and tending much more towards the hate now. I've never had a problem really with Tyneside because it's always been good to me. Tyneside's never turned on me and I hope it never does. And I can't see why it would because I've always taken the piss but in an affectionate way. Affectionately, but quite cruelly at times!" However, while Akenside Syndrome symptoms are broadly similar, differing mainly by degree, the underlying causes can be many and varied. And the circumstances behind Simon's short-lived move to London – he's now back in Newcastle also – are worth considering to better understand the condition.

In his autobiography he recalls a week in the late 1980s spent with the *Viz* team at London's celebrity hang-out, The Groucho Club. Things happened every day which made him think: 'You've made it, you've escaped!' and there are parallels with the theme of escaping Tyneside mentioned by Robson Green, that also feature in the autobiographies of Jimmy Nail and Sting.[26] On the whole, people who feel they've escaped from something or somewhere, real or imagined, tend not to want to go back, except perhaps as an occasional visitor. And while Jo Chipchase didn't feel escaping from the North-East formed part of her own psychological make-up, she spoke of how a hypothetical return to live in Newcastle "would be a step backwards … I've never considered it. The geographic location and 'a step back to my youth' don't really appeal … I would see this as throwing in the towel and making a slightly uncomfortable return to my childhood roots: to somewhere long departed." Or to paraphrase Eric Burdon and The Animals, she didn't want to be sent back to Walkerville.

Simon evoked the idea of emotionally-linked flight from Newcastle again when pondering the reasons for his move to London. Referring to the untimely death of his eldest brother and the break-up of a long-term relationship, he wrote: 'I also wanted to escape from what had happened with Steve, and indeed with Julie.'[27] Moving away from a place where you've experienced emotional trauma, be it the loss of a loved one, a failed relationship, an unhappy childhood etc. is a natural enough human instinct, but in the words of Stephen King's most colloquially expressive character,

Dolores Claiborne: 'runnin won't solve your problems if you've been hurt bad enough – wherever you run, you take your head n your heart with you, after all'.[28] Paul Gascoigne learnt something similar during his brief spell in China: 'What I began to learn was that I couldn't escape from myself, even all those thousands of miles away.'[29] As time goes by the place can come to represent the trauma and distinguishing between the two becomes increasingly difficult; a permanent return viewed fearfully and equated with psychological and emotional regression.

Chris left *Viz* in 1999 and Simon followed in 2003. Meanwhile in 2001 *Newcastle upon Tyne: A Modern History* was published, with the blurb claiming that after the death throes of heavy industry: 'Newcastle does not look the same and its people don't think as they did ... the city seeks a new identity'.[30] The Millennium Bridge spanning the Tyne opened to the public in 2001 also, and in keeping with the spirit of the times Newcastle City Council commissioned a New Year's Eve extravaganza to be held outside the Civic Centre – *The Bus of Fools*.

A Tyneside take on the Spanish tradition of *Fallas*, those attending witnessed the burning of effigies of *Viz* characters including the three most synonymous with Newcastle; Sid the Sexist, Biffa Bacon and the Fat Slags, all of whom were on a bus driven by the Grim Reaper.[31] A kind of bonfire of the Geordie profanities, if you like. Given that Millie Tant was on board too, it wasn't surprising that Chris wondered, "considering the name of it and everything, whether it was some sort of symbolic cleansing, trying to get rid of them as it were."

The Bus of Fools event was granted additional funding from the Northern Arts Lottery Fund, and 2002 saw the inaugural exhibition at the Baltic Centre for Contemporary Arts on the Gateshead side of the Millennium Bridge. The cultural regeneration of Tyneside's urban core was gathering pace, with The Sage concert hall joining the Baltic on Gateshead Quays in 2004. By 2005 Chris Donald was getting twitchy, presenting *A Picture of Tyneside* on BBC3 in which he sensed a fault-line running through the old and new Tyneside. Not a great lover of the arts, he created a new character, Art Carbuncle, described in an *Observer* article (entitled *Now true Geordies mock the Tyne's 'art revolution'*) as someone 'who sees artistic statements in the everyday trappings of working-class life.' Alan Plater was also quoted saying: 'I think Tyneside needs Chris Donald as much as it needs ... Baltic, and there should be room for both.'[32] And that sounds like a cue to leave the artistic world which produced Sherlock Homo, Shitty Dick and Billy's Bollocks, and meet our final group, some of whom may be inclined to take their art more seriously; asking ourselves as we exit page right – what good are the artists on Tyneside?

You'll sail the seas … 'cos you're not the type to bide in the bottleneck …
You'll roam afore you'll settle down … you're no sardine … In Norway the
sardines come in from the ocean in billions and billions … Swimming up the
fjords … On they come. They don't know why and they don't want to know
why … And they go bang into the nets like a hundred locomotives … Then
they put 'em in barrels and send 'em over here to be laid out in the tin coffins,
head to tail and tail to head. All they know is the shoal … All they care about
is to eat at eating time and spawn at spawning time. So into the net they run
and end up in a little tin box … Don't be a sardine. Navigate yourself.

Advice given to thirteen year old Arthur Haggerston by the lodger, Harry,
in Sid Chaplin's 1961 novel set in Newcastle, *The Day of the Sardine*

Artists are wanderers, exiles, rootless men. Norman Cornish is immobile,
static, except for the daily journey between home and work, from
daylight to darkness and back again … He is at odds with his world, but
in a curiously ambivalent manner; a mixture of love and revulsion

Sid Chaplin reviewing the art of late North-East painter and
former pitman Norman Cornish in *The Guardian* 1960

[Jack Common had] a desire to leave the community he was brought up
in, whilst, at the same time, retaining a great love of the city of his birth

Keith Armstrong, *Common Words and the Wandering Star*

[The other people walking in Jesmond Dene] made a kind of slow march of it
which imposed the collective step on my own. When I became aware of this,
or irritated by it, I'd weave and dart my way ahead for a minute or so…

Willie Kiddar in Jack Common's *Kiddar's Luck*

The sad part about this play, Melvyn, is that most people feel they have
to go. Billy Elliot had to go. Lee Hall had to go. You had to go. Do you have
to go or do you stay? This is the core point of *Pitmen Painters*.

Rob Colls on *The South Bank Show* featuring Lee Hall

A PORTRAIT OF
THE ARTIST AS A
YOUNG GEORDIE

Should I stay or should I go?

P ISS ARTISTS ARE THE GROUP MOST COMMONLY ASSOCIATED WITH
Newcastle but there are Tyneside artists of a different stripe including
writers, actors and musicians, on whom we shall now focus. Mark
Akenside, like Jack Common, Jimmy Nail, Sting and Brian Johnson, opted
to leave Newcastle, never to return. And as an aspiring poet – sarcasti-
cally caricatured as 'the greatest poet of the age' in *Peregrine Pickle* – he
is an appropriate symbol for the group most susceptible to suffering from
the syndrome named after him.[1] Indeed, fellow poet Keith Armstrong's
description of Jack Common having a 'desire to leave' Newcastle whilst
'retaining a great love of the city', and Sid Chaplin's assertion that Norman
Cornish 'is at odds with his world, but in a curiously ambivalent manner;
a mixture of love and revulsion', quintessentially epitomise the artistic strain
of Akenside Syndrome.[2]

The dedication to Common and Chaplin as well as the people of the
North-East at the start of *Geordies* – two artistic individuals alongside the
collective mass – inadvertently illustrates one of the root causes of the condition. Perhaps felt more intensely by those of an artistic bent, Common
explores the theme in his essays, as Armstrong points out: 'the relationship

between the individual and society; the tension between a collective approach and an individualistic one; and a search for a balance between the two.'[3] In an attempt to strike this balance, or evade the disorientation caused by staying in a place where they feel it is unachievable, many artists, as Rob Colls explained to Melvyn Bragg, feel they have to go. And it's easy to imagine indecision bugging them prior to their departure, as they brood over the fact that if they go there may be Akenside Syndrome trouble, but if they stay it will be double. For as John Carey points out in *What Good are the Arts?* – ambiguity is all well and good in art, but in life it can be distressing.

A popular way for the Geordie artist to portray his sense of difference and dislocation from the Tyneside mass is by utilising the image of a young man resisting the uniform conformity of a crowd. Striving for self-definition we earlier witnessed Gordon Burn ploughing a lone furrow against the departing droves at St James' Park, and a teenage Mark Akenside 'Immured amongst the ignoble, vulgar herd'.[4] For Sid Chaplin, swimming with the shoal is imbued with imagery of restriction, entrapment and death; his protagonist Arthur Haggerston failing to heed Harry's entreaty to navigate himself, to be an individual, as he ends the novel working in a sardine factory on the banks of the Tyne: 'There I go. Stiff and straight and swimming in the gravy, but that's no consolation when the lid's clamped down.' Haggerston describes himself as 'a Manor character brought up to pay his way, take his turn and stand by a pal' but is left languishing, his wanderlust unfulfilled, concluding that his gang of friends 'are just tired cardboard figures who talk but have nothing to say to me ... To the Manor lot I'm the crazy one ... odd boy out.'[5]

Having earlier been urged by another surrogate father-figure, Flack, to 'Read books ... Get learnin'. Be a somebody', Haggerston's fish-can-filling fate is a cautionary tale against unfulfilled potential.[6] How much autobiographical feeling went into the character from Chaplin is open to debate (though my inference is quite a lot; his son Michael telling me, "As a young man [Sid] felt a great sort of ambivalence about the culture that he came from. That on the one hand he sort of gloried in aspects of it, but there were other aspects of it that completely appalled him"), whereas it is generally acknowledged that in the figure of Willie Kiddar the reader enjoys a vivid representation of the young Jack Common, albeit through the politicised prism of his adult self.

Kiddar considers himself one of those 'queer characters for whom words were more than words', and melancholically marvels at the 'far-distant and miraculous folk who actually wrote books'; his own literary ambitions checked as he contemplates his heritage, which he fears will lead to, 'the routine of the factory or some similar industrial hour-glass regularly turning the sands of uncelebrated and nearly-unconsequenced labour.'[7] Mark Akenside also wrote of the poetically inclined: 'What shall he do for life? he cannot work/With manual labour', and Arthur Haggerston is ensnared in the nets of exactly such stultifying routine, calling it 'work-misery' and bemoaning: 'Every morning I rolled out of bed with a feeling of being trapped.'[8]

Common illustrates Kiddar's resistance to the unremitting momentum of the mass in the Jesmond Dene scene, where he is irritated by the imposition of 'the collective step' and attempts to navigate his own individual path. Increasing the impression of a young Geordie artist inhibited by the collectivist environment that envelops him, as with Haggerston there is a sense of alienation from his friends: 'I was becoming uncomfortably aware that there were attractions upon me that pulled in unknown directions and threatened to take me out of the orbit my fellow corner-lads so naturally swung into ... I think it was becoming apparent to them that I had a life of my own that they wouldn't want to share, particularly not now when they were near entering upon an early manhood that they most decidedly wanted to be orthodox.'[9]

Located on Lower Grainger Street in Newcastle is Sean Henry's bronze sculpture *Man with Potential Selves*, comprising three representations of the same figure in different poses; standing, walking and apparently floating. It chimes a latter-day echo of Kiddar's sage advice: 'The younger you are the more important it is that you should consort with your unrealized selves. Friends prevent that by their presence. They can't help insisting that you play the part they know as you and which is all the miserly economy of communication has so far allowed you to publish to them.'[10]

Lee Hall was born in 1966, two years before Common died, yet there are striking correlations between the two in terms of authorial Akenside alienation. Talking to Melvyn Bragg on *The South Bank Show* Hall recalled how, having left Cambridge University, there was a 'divide that I'd been having in myself ... was I a middle class Cambridge person and an academic, or was I like my mates in Newcastle that rather eschewed all that stuff.'[11] Here again we see education playing a crucial role in alienating an individual from his working-class roots, and a hint of what Wilkinson and Pickett describe in *The Spirit Level*, whereby in some working-class communities and cultures, 'Talking about abstract ideas, books and culture, is seen as posh and pretentious.'[12] Hall's identity confusion would find expression in some of his most acclaimed work including *Billy Elliot*, as he made clear to pupils at his former school in the East End of Newcastle: 'There were many similarities between our lives. I didn't always fit in with the crowd because I liked films and writing, and Billy wanted to be a ballet dancer'.[13]

Expressing Yourself, a song from *Billy Elliot – The Musical,* includes lines encouraging individuality, suggesting those who want to dance should dance and those who want to mine should mine, and the image of the lone ballet dancer silhouetted against a backdrop of miners is the leitmotif which best expresses Hall's desire to be different, to be an artist (though in his break-through play *I Love You, Jimmy Spud,* the more abstract conduit of an angel is employed in the same way). Prior to the musical opening in 2005, Hall expanded on the interplay between personal biography and his writing: '*Billy Elliot* is a fantasy version of my childhood, a sort of ugly duckling fairy tale retold in County Durham. I didn't have all of Billy's personal problems but it was the same environment. I grew up roughly at the same time in the Northeast, and my aspiration to be a writer is akin to Billy's to dance, in that nobody I knew was a writer and it wasn't particularly understood what being a writer really meant. If you loved poetry, you were a bit of a poof.'[14]

Jack Common refers to 'the socially-approved poet' as a 'living anomaly' in *Kiddar's Luck,* and if there is a grand unifying theme between his and Hall's writing it is that of class, which, as we know, can be a powerful provoker of Akenside Syndrome disequilibrium.[15] Both had their magnum opus, *Kiddar's Luck* and *Billy Elliot* respectively, initially rejected by people who oddly thought the focus on class somewhat dated. But in terms of their internal dilemma as working-class Geordies who aspired to be writers, a troubled line delivered by the character of Oliver in *Pitmen Painters* encapsulates the poignancy. He restlessly insists that he doesn't have the language, argues that being working class and being an artist are two separate things, and concludes that to be an artist he'd have to become a different person.

Mel Gibson, whose father is a miniaturist and poet who studied at Slade School of Fine Art in London, had an interesting perspective on a related issue: "Something which is very north-eastern is that consciousness of a feeling of having betrayed where you're coming from. How do you become who you need to be without betraying? How do you negotiate that space without letting yourself down? And letting the people you care about down. That's the catch. That's why many people flee, I think, because it's impossible. You can't make that balance. That's why it's heart-breaking."

When Film4 encouraged Sue Clayton to make a film about her growing up/coming of age experience, she chose to adapt Dublin-based novel *The Disappearance of Rory Brophy* rather than be literally autobiographical, as she identified with the protagonist: "The quality that the Rory character can't bear about the Dublin 'village' is that everyone knows everyone's business and you can't change. You can't be different. And he finds that stifling." Considering the dilemma identified by Mel, Sue reflected: "Your community pushes you out and says 'Go on, go on – take the chance, take the chance,' and as soon as you go they're like 'Oh no, so you're too good for us now are you?' I felt sort of double-crossed, like some trick had been played on me. There's this sense you have to achieve something, but you're not told at the time that that means in a weird way you lose your primal thing that you're connected to somehow."

A similar sentiment can be found in *Kiddar's Luck* when the eponymous hero asserts that 'individual success for one of our sort, if contrived and not accidental, incurs a personal severance from the rest.'[16] Keith Armstrong describes how the 'idea of escape is a constant in Common's work', as is a 'sense of oppression of the spirit, the frustration of people who have it in them to be bright sparks of creativity but who usually settle for second best.'[17] Yet despite Common being heralded by Sid Chaplin as 'perhaps the finest chronicler of the English working class to follow Robert Tressel', Armstrong also recognises 'his love-hate relationship with his own city and the proletarians whose cause he adopted'.[18]

Throw the toxic ingredient of class into the historically class-deline-ated arena of the arts then, and deep-rooted Akenside alienation can ensue. Historian Lyall Wilkes, who preceded Ted Short as Labour MP for Newcastle Central, astutely analysed this rupture when discussing Common in *Tyneside Portraits*: 'There is a terrible price that the artist frequently pays for his release from restriction through creative success. Taste, imagination, sensibility and the critical faculty, must often divorce him from his own people; yet he may never feel much or any sympathy with the values and way of life of any other class or group – indeed, he may detest them. This is the limbo world, the no man's land in which some artists live; so that the frustration of a different kind is felt after success is won.'[19]

Brendan Healy has spent over 40 years working in the arts, and with a CV boasting television appearances in Catherine Cookson adaptations, *Spender*, *Byker Grove* and *Auf Wiedersehen, Pet*; theatre gigs including *Andy Capp*; film credits such as *Purely Belter* and *Stormy Monday* (alongside Sting); and musical collaborations with Lindisfarne and his friend Brian Johnson of AC/DC, he seemed like an ideal person to ask whether, historically, creative people may have felt undervalued within the broader working-class culture of Tyneside. "Creative people are undervalued in any working-class culture or any hard industrial culture, because it's out of the norm," he maintained. Although sensing it may be changing, he went on: "It's the *Billy Elliot* story. I can't imagine coming out of the steelworks and saying 'Well yeah Dad, I want to be an actor.' It's going to be much easier to go home to Daddy who's a barrister and Mummy who's a surgeon and say, 'I'd quite like to be an actor, Mummy.'"

Lee Hall has noted how the sphere in which he sought self-expression is defined by class dynamics, claiming 'the "professional theatre" is still statistically a middle class preserve'.[20] And while his Newcastle comprehensive to Oxbridge journey clearly affected his sense of class identity, there also appears to have been class-related mores and expectations gnawing at him from within the working-class culture of Tyneside. 'I thought writing or doing drama … this wasn't proper,' he recollected to Melvyn Bragg, also stating: 'I just came from, I would say, an ordinary working-class background. And my parents were bright, interested, intelligent people, but I think they were rather sceptical about art … They were just very suspicious about it.'[21] Though Hall insists his parents were very supportive, the tension between father and son in *Billy Elliot* is a theme examined more darkly throughout *I Love You, Jimmy Spud*, in which the dying father orders would-be angel Jimmy to turn off Handel's *Messiah* and smashes his celestial trumpet.

Robson Green would perhaps empathise with the characters of Billy Elliot and Jimmy Spud. Following his father's passing in 2009, he reflected on his relationship with Robson Senior, a 'big, powerful' former miner: 'In a way, I knew he loved me but he never said it … I come from a pit village surrounded by five mines. Singing was absolutely acceptable, but acting…'[22] In 2011 Sting similarly spoke of how his father Ernie, a milkman and a fitter, 'never saw [my singing career] as a proper job … Singing for money didn't seem like a man's work to him.'[23] He was talking to Johnnie Walker in New York, where Lee Hall also lived for a while after graduating from Cambridge. Hall enjoyed the social irrelevance of English class distinctions in the US: 'Over there you were just a Brit. And it doesn't matter if you were a working-class Brit, or a Geordie … they haven't got a clue.'[24] He actually started writing *I Love You, Jimmy Spud* in the city, and his class confusion seems to find unconscious expression in Jimmy's odd habit of alternating between calling his mother *Mam* and *Mum*, as Sting does in his autobiography.

The generational misapprehension alluded to by Green and Sting, and depicted in Hall's work, obviously has a universal dimension. Notions of masculinity, the death knell of deindustrialisation, the artist as socially-disapproved outsider, and aspiring artists feeling geographically marginalised and thus compelled to leave their place of upbringing, clearly resonate globally too. James Joyce had a love-hate relationship with Dublin and the same has been said of Philip Roth's ambivalent attitude towards his hometown of Newark. With regard to Akenside Syndrome, an expanded reiteration of Keith Armstrong's earlier point pretty much nails it: 'if your consciousness is raised through learning and experience making you something of an intellectual, an element of alienation can also come into play and sometimes a city like Newcastle can seem too small and too provincial. This can be true of any place away from the centres of political, economic and cultural power.'[25]

The geographical distance between Newcastle and London may be greatly exaggerated in the national and regional consciousness, but in terms of political, economic and cultural power it could hardly be more pronounced. Talking in 2012 about the 'rotting away of the regions', *Guardian* economics editor Larry Elliott insisted that while there are economic regional disparities in other western countries, 'in no other country is the scale of the problem so acute, the commitment in government to do anything about the problem so weak, the outlook so desperate … The real problem is that Britain is the most centralised country in the western world.'[26] Amidst the fall-out from a controversial *Guardian* article in May 2014 that compared the North-East to the US city of Detroit, which filed for bankruptcy in 2013, Peter Hetherington made a similar point: 'Regional cities, rather than capitals, drive national economies. That's the reality in France, Germany, the rest of mainland Europe, much of the USA, China and Asia – but not England. Our nation stands alone as the ultimate centralist state'.[27]

Contributors to *Geordies* who are still with us might nod ruefully at such observations, encapsulating as they do the underlying thesis of their book published over twenty years ago. I took this to be the point underpinning Rob Colls's lament to Melvyn Bragg about why Lee Hall and others feel compelled to leave the North-East. However, while not in *any* sense underplaying the seismic significance of such factors – they are, or should be, self-evident – the main line of investigation pursued here has been alienating factors from within the culture of Tyneside itself. And we must therefore acknowledge that like Shane, Narinder Kaur, Chris Donald and others, Lee Hall was bullied at school, and also examine his relationship with the fourth pillar of Geordie identity – football.

Although not wishing to commit the tedious error of misinterpreting writing imbued with autobiographical feeling as literal autobiography, as Hall himself has said: 'I got into the arts because I hated the competition of sport,' and stated that his early works were about finding a voice for his childhood, it seems reasonable to look for sources of Akenside alienation in *I Love You, Jimmy Spud*.[28] For instance, Jimmy is bullied by a gang of boys, with the leader calling him a *wanker* and – no surprise here – a *puff*, also hitting him on the head with a stone (though it is not made clear whether the gang was spot-checking for Tories). And he elicits scant paternal sympathy after another bullying incident as his father, who we learn ran for the county as a boy, protests that he wouldn't be a target for the bullies if he only tried harder at games.

After engaging him in some reluctant sparring (in *Billy Elliot*, of course, the father wants Billy to pursue boxing, not ballet, as a hobby), Jimmy's dad takes him outside for a football kickabout. Equally uninterested, Jimmy says he doesn't like football, provocatively stating that he likes netball instead, which prompts his dad to express concern about him turning gay. As in *Billy Elliot*, hints of homoeroticism and homophobia hit home, as the father struggles to comprehend his son's artistic inclinations and lack of interest in sport, worries that Jimmy isn't normal because he doesn't play football, and accuses him of becoming a *pervert* and a *deviant* after misjudging his 'cross-dressing' tendencies.

In *Gabriel and Me*, a film adaptation of the play which Hall firmly distances himself from, the Jimmy character actually rejects the gift of a Newcastle United strip and tracksuit from his father. And while in pointing out that Billy Elliott is also the name of a celebrated former Sunderland player we most likely enter the realm of Akenside Syndrome conspiracy theory, on the balance of probability we can safely suppose that Lee Hall would neither describe himself as bleeding black and white blood, nor hopes to have the *Match of the Day* theme tune played at his funeral. So as we extend the *dramatis personae* by progressing from page to stage, from Geordie writer to Geordie actor, let us linger momentarily on a freeze-frame of Jimmy Spud in a goalmouth, described by his father as being disconnected, with the ball whistling past his head as he makes no attempt to save it. Authorial Akenside alienation in a snapshot.

*   *   *

There was an institutionalised problem within the acting profession. Drama schools taught their students to speak 'properly' – a quaint form of English located halfway between Broadcasting House and Buckingham Palace …
any actor from the region knew that his professional future depended on shedding the accent with the speed of light, or faster if possible.
Alan Plater, *The Drama of the North-East* in *Geordies*

When I asked Val McLane why she thought people in the creative industries tend to be more susceptible to Akenside Syndrome, citing Lee Hall as a classic example, she replied: "Well, you're talking about working-class lads. And the expectation is that you're going to stay one of the lads and you're going to go out drinking with them, and you're going to share the same kind of culture. And you're different. And everybody who is slightly different, especially in a teenage environment, is kind of alienated from the rest. So whether it's because you're better educated, you go off to higher education, or you go off to do some art form; whatever it is, you're going to be different from the mass, the norm. And I believe it's inevitable that you're going to feel like that."

In 1973 Val co-founded Live Theatre (Live) based on Newcastle's Quayside, with one of the company's aims being 'to create a venue committed to creating plays with a regional identity for North East audiences and, in particular, for people who didn't usually go to the theatre.'[29] Lee Hall has enjoyed a long association with Live; in 2012 providing additional material for their revival of Alan Plater's 1968 musical play *Close the Coalhouse Door*, based on the mining-themed writing of Sid Chaplin. Like Hall, Sid's son Michael Chaplin went to Cambridge University, telling me at his Jesmond home that whilst there, despite being a 'middle-class' grammar school boy, he "encountered the upper class for the first time and was made to feel like a member of the working class."

Chaplin also enjoys a long-standing relationship with Live, having had a number of his plays staged there including *Tyne*, the Newcastle United-themed *You Couldn't Make It Up* and its sequel *You Really Couldn't Make It Up*. His take on why creative people are more prone to Akenside Syndrome focused on the metro-centric centralisation of the arts. Having previously lived in London for many years, he acknowledged experiencing it on the mild end of the spectrum, but noted that such feelings "kind of come with the territory, in a way. And certainly in the creative industries, which I've always been in, it's almost just the way it is. That economic circumstance and your own ambition drive you to leave this place. But very often that similar impulses or equally powerful impulses force you to come back."

Graeme Danby moved to London as an 18 year old to study at The Royal Academy of Music, and asked whether he had to navigate any barriers as an aspiring singer within the North-East culture he grew up in, said: "I think I've had to navigate barriers by educating people that music is not for cissies." Echoes of Lee Hall's *puff* jibes there, and although his physical prowess meant he personally avoided being bullied at school, he nonetheless reminisced: "I can remember people – and I can see them now in my mind's eye – who were at school with me who played the violin, who played the cello and stuff like that, who were *mercilessly* jumped on. And that is where we're not good." Although qualifying this by saying it's probably the same in other places such as Leeds or Manchester, Danby concluded, "There's that inbuilt thing against the arts which *Billy Elliot* touches on, doesn't it? Big time."

Appropriately enough, in *My North East: By its famous sons and daughters*, published in 2013, Lee Hall actually recalled being bullied and picked on for playing the violin and guitar at school, and actress Jill Halfpenny, an ambassador for anti-bullying charity Kidscape, certainly seems to have experienced something similar whilst attending St Edmund Campion RC Comprehensive School in Gateshead. In the *Daily Mirror* in 2006 she related how the bullying was unrelenting and lasted for years, but in contrast to Narinder Kaur it was primarily at the hands of girls not boys: 'Girls are much more vicious in mental bullying. I've always been a strong person but when you get that kind of abuse constantly you start to think, 'Is there something wrong with me? Do they really hate me? Why don't they like me?' It's hard to be rational when you're so young. No one wants to think they are disliked.'

Starring in *Byker Grove* and appearing in school plays, Halfpenny considered the profession she was pursuing to be a critical factor: 'Most actors have probably had a taste of it because if you have a talent for something and are praised by teachers, the reaction from other kids can be negative.' However, she was able to see the bigger picture, making a comparable observation to that of Simon Donald: 'I think if most people are honest they've had something like that happen. Either they were bullied or they were the ones doing the bullying.'[30] In the same article the actress also spoke of how she'd like to branch out in to more varied roles including comedy and period drama, yet three years later in 2009, speaking to *North East Life* magazine, frustration regarding these ambitions clearly remained, and this leads us on to another potential source of actorly Akenside alienation.

'The problem and the frustrating thing is you rarely get a chance to do all of these different acting ambitions', she bemoaned, saying she'd like to appear in films like *Lost in Translation* and perform classic roles such as Lady Macbeth. 'Actors are always frustrated by the lack of versatility of the casting people who see you for roles. They do pigeonhole you'.[31] It's difficult not to imagine some of the casting people she refers to being mesmerised like Macbeth himself, thinking: *Is this a Geordie, which I see before me ... I have thee not, and yet I see thee still*. In other words they struggle to see (or hear) beyond the fact that Jill is a Geordie. So do actors from Tyneside fear being pigeonholed and typecast as a professional Geordie? Lead on, Brendan Healy: "The fear of being typecast is prevalent, yeah yeah. They hate the idea that they're just cast because they are Geordies."

Val McLane concurred, "Yes it is. And it certainly worried me for a long time. In the first ten years that I was in the business, I think I probably was always cast in that mould. So that was real typecasting." By 2012 the halfpenny had finally dropped for Jill. Publicising a West End production of *Abigail's Party* in which she was playing the lead role, she was quoted in various media outlets protesting that she no longer wished to be pigeonholed as simply a Geordie actress. In *The Sun* an article entitled *Jill's Geord ache* opened with the somewhat misleading line, 'Jill Halfpenny is turning her back on her Geordie roots – claiming she has been pigeon-holed', and quoted her insisting: 'I'm very proud to come from Newcastle. But there is something about the place that makes it stand out, and coming from there does seem to have put me in a bit of a box.'[32] The nationwide pervasiveness of the Geordie stereotype is shown here at its most limiting and restrictive, hindering professional development and appearing to provoke a bout of art-induced Akenside Syndrome in Halfpenny.

Whereas Alan Plater identified historic institutionalised class prejudice within drama schools and the entertainment industry, Halfpenny's experience confirms that though more subtle, such accent prejudice still exists, as her main complaint was only being offered roles with a Geordie accent. Thespian Patrick Stewart exemplifies the traditional route taken by actors with regional accents in the past, pointed out by Plater. Lloyd Evans, interviewing him for *The Spectator*, noted how 'the meticulous and percussive exactitude of his Home Counties accent seems almost too good to be true. And there's the wrinkle. The south of England is alien turf to him. He's a Dewsbury [Yorkshire] lad, from a secondary modern school'.[33] I asked Graeme Danby if, contrary to the popular self-deluding cliché, accent still mattered in this country: "I think that accent does matter because 'You're

Northern' appears in my life quite a lot. Sometimes quite jocular and sometimes *with that little bit of an edge*."

Drama schools often performed the same linguistic function as private schools, and Danby agreed that actors who shed their natural accent in everyday life, rather than learning RP simply to add to their vocal range, could be seen as tacitly endorsing traditional class-based notions of self-improvement. A telling contrast with Halfpenny is Tyneside born and bred Andrea Riseborough, who has starred in recent films such as *Oblivion* (alongside Tom Cruise), *Made in Dagenham* and *Brighton Rock*, and as she-who-must-not-be-named in TV drama *Margaret Thatcher: The Long Road to Finchley*. Discussing the latter role in *The Times* she spoke of her parents being 'working class Thatcherites', and they took their daughter out of state education in Whitley Bay to send her to private school Church High in Jesmond.[34]

Interviewing the actress, Elizabeth Day observed how a 'shift in family circumstance made her more aware of the nuance of class – she softened her northern accent', and Riseborough herself maintained: 'The cultural currency that move afforded me – going from a state school to a private school – made me see a flipside of the coin.'[35] Whether the coin was embossed with a profile of the Church High Head is not made clear, and though no personal criticism of Riseborough is implied here, in my view this Tyneside vignette reveals exactly how class and accent retain a powerful place in modern day society. Little wonder that Riseborough has not been held back in the same way Halfpenny feels she has been for retaining her accent, and is rarely encumbered with the constraining appellation of 'Geordie actress'.

Tim Healy has been described as being 'as much a part of Geordieland as stottie cakes and the Tyne Bridge', and given his iconic role as Dennis in *Auf Wiedersehen, Pet*, he seemed like an appropriate person to explore these themes further with.[36] Speaking to him in the dressing rooms of Live before he was due on stage in the title role of *Looking for Buddy*, Alan Plater's last major stage play, I asked if Plater's observation regarding drama schools and losing a Geordie accent resonated with his experience of the industry. "Well yeah," he assured me. "I came into the business in 1973. Actors, until round about then, all came from middle-class backgrounds. If you wanted to go to drama school, the first question they used to ask you was, 'And what does your father do?' And if you did have any accent at all, it was got shot of. Drama schools were like sausage machines. Everybody came out the same sausage; came out with *no accent at all*."

In some ways the Oz character in *Auf Wiedersehen, Pet* is a coarser descendant of Terry in *The Likely Lads*; both, in my estimation at least, manifestations of Ian La Frenais's genuine affection for – but frustration with – elements of Tyneside culture. Or, put another way, artistic evidence of his personal experience of Akenside Syndrome. In an episode of *Auf Wiedersehen, Pet* called *The Fugitive*, he has Barry (Timothy Spall) say to Neville (Kevin Whately) that Oz's problem is that he has no inclination to educate himself or learn about the world beyond his narrow horizons. Brought up in Whitley Bay and privately educated at Dame Allan's, he once quipped about himself and writing partner Dick Clement: 'We're one sort of people really and we write about another sort. Everything we've done is a complete fraud!'[37]

Healy felt that the actors in *The Likely Lads* "softened their accents a little bit because they were frightened about people in the South not understanding us. Well, when we did *Auf Wiedersehen, Pet*, the director Roger Bamford had the insight to realise that it doesn't matter if some people don't understand an odd phrase or an odd word. What is the most important thing is that this is true. And it's true – like anything it's truth. And totally believable." Clement and La Frenais have talked of *Auf Wiedersehen, Pet* being 'an orchestra for accents', and for Healy it marked a seminal epoch in British television history.[38] "They took a big gamble on casting people like me, who had a big strong Geordie accent," he recalled. "Jimmy Nail in particular – he had a stronger one than I did. And that was the big gamble, casting Oz's character. And it was the best thing they could have done. And what it did, as far as I'm concerned – I'm quite proud of it – I think it changed television. Because I think *Auf Wiedersehen, Pet* was the first time that we got genuine, proper, the real McCoy accents exactly as they were."

The popularity of the original series paved the way for *Byker Grove*, which propelled Ant and Dec to televisual ubiquity – often trotted out in support of 'accent doesn't matter anymore' and 'having a regional accent is an asset' arguments – but I suggested that having a Geordie accent may be more of an asset for presenters and those involved in light entertainment rather than actors. Healy agreed, "Yes, because it's a likeable voice," and pointed out that "a lot of actors do get rid of their accent because they don't want people to think that that's all they can do." Even allowing for this supposed advantage, those susceptible to sophistic statements regarding accent equality on television would do well to consider an observation by Stuart Maconie: 'we'll know that the struggle has been won ... when ... someone who speaks like Ant and Dec is doing *Horizon* or whatever its modern equivalent is. There are certain accents that are not regarded as serious enough for certain jobs on telly ... even the weather.'[39]

Or perhaps remember Kate Fox's insistence that in England a 'reliance on linguistic signals ... reminds us that our culture is not a meritocracy', and further contemplate the following incisive passage, worth reproducing in its entirety:

> We are frequently told that regional accents have become much more acceptable nowadays – even desirable, if you want a career in broadcasting – and that a person with, say, a Yorkshire, Scouse, Geordie or West Country accent is no longer looked down upon as automatically lower class. Yes, well, maybe. I am not convinced. The fact that many presenters of popular television and radio programmes now have regional accents may well indicate that people find these accents attractive, but it does not prove that the class associations of regional accents have somehow disappeared. We may like a regional accent, and even find it delightful, melodious and charming, while still recognising it as clearly working class. If what is really meant is that being working class has become more acceptable in many formerly snobby occupations, then this is what should be said, rather than a lot of mealy-mouthed euphemisms about regional accents.[40]

Melvyn Bragg, who appeared to endorse the 'accent doesn't matter anymore' analysis when concluding his recent documentary series, *Melvyn Bragg on Class and Culture*, should take note.

Perhaps it's partly because of these on-going associations that some Geordies who leave Tyneside still modify their accent beyond a slight but understandable alteration – as Graeme Danby says, "a slight modification is nothing to be disappointed by" – and into the realm of the excruciating. Carole Malone's pantomimic pronouncements on TV (to my ear) for example, and Lynsey Hipgrave's disorientating verbal vicissitudes on Radio 5 Live (again, as I hear it). "A lot of Geordies are frightened, I think," Tim Healy regretted. "It's so sad when you hear people going away and their voices start changing and they get this ridiculous voice that's half and half."

Namesake Brendan agreed: "I won't do one of those hybrid accents that some people seem to have found. Where they say 'you know' [in an affected manner] in the middle of a sentence. I can't see the point – it doesn't make you any bloody posher. Geordies themselves hate hearing it, hate hearing Geordies do it; and there's no reason to do it because people are going to understand 'you know' [in a normal Tyneside accent] as well as 'you know' [the affected version]. And they never get 'you know' quite right!" he laughed, adding, "there's nothing people hate more than a false accent, as you well know. It doesn't matter who you are."

Coincidentally both Tim and Brendan recounted incidents within a school setting similar to Miss Greensill's correction of Freddy's Geordie dialect in *Kiddar's Luck*. Tim recalled having "a horrific woman English teacher at school," who took umbrage at the way he pronounced *eight*, his number in the register. After one exchange, "She took me out the front and thrashed me. Caned me. Because she thought I was taking the piss. She told me that I wasn't saying this word right. And she was a complete horrible posh *Geordie* woman who hated the fact that she had any twang of a Geordie accent in her. It was all about class, I think."

For Brendan, an educational theatre production at a school earlier in his career, in which he played a visitor from another planet in his normal Geordie accent, provoked objections from the staff room afterwards. A female teacher complained, 'I find it ever so odd that they would come down to earth with that accent; they should talk more with a proper accent.' He remembered how "this woman thought she was ever so, ever so – that was a terrible snobbery she had," and revealed that she only desisted when the director, who spoke RP, insisted he couldn't tell any difference between the way she, the children or the actors spoke.

Tim Healy, nominated for an Olivier award for his performances as the inaugural father of Billy in *Billy Elliot – The Musical*, retains a distinct Geordie accent to this day. "I'm an actor and I like to think I've got a good ear for voices and I can do any accent," he said, readily delivering pitch perfect cockney, Australian and 'Shakespearean RP' during the course of our conversation. Acknowledging that despite this vocal versatility 80% of his TV roles have been as Geordie-speaking characters, he reflected: "I'm probably known as a Geordie because most of the stuff I do on TV is Geordie, but I do all sorts of voices. But my voice never changes – I don't know why. It's not something I think about. I don't make an effort at staying as a Geordie, I just always do." Graeme Danby, who has regularly sung in Italian, German, Russian and French throughout his career, made a similar self-diagnosis; "Because I have a strong identity with the North-East, I think subconsciously I keep my accent. I want to retain that whilst not being an arse about it, whilst not ramming it down people's throats."

A quick internet search indicates that one of the North-East's most prolific actors, Robson Green, is perceived by some to have lost or changed his Geordie accent. But as areas of cyberspace can be repositories of spite and malice – Green quit Twitter in 2013, allegedly due to abusive messages – I consulted with some of his fellow industry professionals in an attempt to understand why this might be. The former *Soldier, Soldier* and *Casualty* star secured his Equity card after taking the lead role in Tom Hadaway's *The Long Line* at Live in 1986, aged 21, and Alan Plater eulogised that Hadaway 'became the key writer – arguably the father-figure – in the history of the Live Theatre Company', in an obituary for his fellow playwright.[41]

Max Roberts, Live's long-serving Artistic Director, effectively 'discovered' Green, encouraging him to join what the actor has referred to as a state-funded, working-class drama school after seeing him perform in a school play. Only a few years after *The Long Line* production, Hadaway – who used to attend Newcastle United games with Green – could be found invoking poet Tony Harrison, a long-time Newcastle resident, with regard to actors who lose their natural accent: 'Deploring the actors' 'neutral voice', he reproaches them for 'giving up the quality that first made them actors' … 'How can you kick away the ladder?'[42]

After reading Harrison's quote to Michael Chaplin, I asked to what extent he thought actors from Tyneside felt compelled to tone down or completely neutralise their accents. "The actors that I know or have worked with pretty much haven't done. Tim Healy always just sounds exactly the same ... I've been aware of Robson moderating his accent," he replied. Green starred in Chaplin's TV comedy-drama series *Grafters* in the late 1990s, and contemplating what might have provoked this alteration, the writer mused: "I think it's partly a reflection of where you live and what your life is and who you live it with," pointing out that at the time of our conversation Green had lived outside the region for a number of years (since separating from second wife Vanya he has moved back to Northumberland where he has always retained a home).

Val McLane, who starred alongside Green in *The Long Line*, was also sympathetic, insisting: "I don't think he's completely lost it. I mean it's still there. I don't blame Robson for doing that. He moved out of the area, he married someone who isn't a Geordie – it's understandable that his accent is going to change." Nevertheless, as we discussed the issue in more detail – including how Scottish actors such as Ewan McGregor, James McAvoy and David Tennant seem perfectly capable of performing roles in RP then reverting to their natural accent in everyday life – she reflected: "I must say sometimes I've watched [Green's] programmes – the latest one about fishing – and thought some of the way he was talking was a bit odd."

As my conversation with Brendan Healy progressed it became clear that his observation regarding people who say 'you know' in a perceived affected manner had also been provoked by the *Extreme Fishing* programmes. When I made specific reference to Green's accent, he said: "You've got to watch him on this fishing programme. He says 'you know' [normal Tyneside accent] in one sentence and 'you know' [the perceived affected version] in the next sentence. Either do it or don't do it. I just think he's not very good at it! I mean I don't want to be cruel to Robson, I don't really know him very well ... Robson is very much perceived as having changed his accent. Jimmy [Nail] gets that same perception, about having changed words. Each to their own; where's the problem with that?"

When I asked Tim Healy – who has talked of directing Robson Green in his first show at Live – why he felt some North-East actors' accents appear to undergo a pronounced change, citing Green as an example, he opined: "Well yeah. It's insecurity. It's all it can be. Not happy with who you are. I act as a job – that's all it is. I go home at night and that's it, I'm back to me ... You're dead right about Robson; he's got this ridiculous voice all of a sudden. The vowel sounds are all over the place, almost like Chris Waddle. What's going on there? Robson was like me when he started [accent-wise]. It's become like that. It's become affected sadly. They become affected. It's all to do with insecurity." Well that's one opinion, but nobody will ever know the exact motivation behind Green's vocal evolution; there may well be multiple reasons and because accent change can be subconscious and we're not always honest with ourselves about such things, he may not truly know himself.

It seems plausible that living in rural Surrey for a prolonged period may have had some effect on his speech. The other potential reasons cited by his peers are credible too, as is a desire to evade the sort of typecasting Jill Halfpenny complained of, another factor that occurred to Tim Healy: "That's probably why Robson's going posh. Because he doesn't want everybody to think he's just a Geordie." Perhaps, consciously or otherwise, he wanted to evade the type of 'partial racism' regarding accent that he claims Cheryl Cole has encountered in her career. Speaking to *The Mag* in 2013, he insisted she would not have had to endure such behaviour if she had any accent other than Geordie.[43] Maybe when it comes to his own accent he no longer cares what other people think of it. Maybe he never did.

Robson Green doesn't owe anybody in the North-East anything and has done nothing wrong. Indeed he is living proof of Michael Chaplin's suggestion that while an individual's ambition and drive may take them away, equally powerful impulses can often guide them home again. There's also no obvious reason why actors should be judged more harshly than others with regard to accent change. But control of your voice is the fundamental tool of any actor, and in my opinion the great shame in all this – bearing in mind a perceived need for accent assertion and vocal role models – is that one of the region's most high profile sons, whose pride in the North-East is palpable, cannot be cast in this particular leading role. In *The Mag* interview Green also claimed that whereas he had used his acting career to broaden his horizons, he'd met many actors from the region who viewed theirs as a means of escape, some of whom were bitter, and one thing's for sure – the potential for class and accent-related Akenside alienation amongst actors abounds.

*   *   *

I wanted to stay in Newcastle and it was the dumbest thing I ever did. I thought I was one of the boys and I thought everyone would know that. I'd walk into a club and they were going, "Oh aye, slumming it?" And I'm going, "What d'you mean slumming it? I always come in here." It was awful. But it was my fault for staying there.

Brian Johnson of AC/DC reflecting on how his initial success affected him, *Q magazine* November 2008

Essentially, Sting is as much a lapsed Geordie as he is a lapsed Catholic ... He has never been a local hero in the North-East ... The thing is Sting went away to find success. Then, when The Police broke through in 1979, he bad-mouthed Newcastle. Many took umbrage. "And rightly so," says Sting ... the truth is I'm fiercely proud of coming from Newcastle. All the same I still say it wasn't a great place to grow up. Basically, it's a love-hate relationship I have with Tyneside and because of that it's real. It's not something I take lightly.

Phil Sutcliffe, *Sting: Where the Hell Have You Been?*, *Q magazine* February 1991

The montage on the dust cover of this book, based on John Martin's painting *The Destruction of Sodom and Gomorrah*, is an uncannily accurate artistic depiction of Akenside Syndrome. First used to promote the *Reinventing the City* series of debates in Newcastle in 2009, the apocalyptic portrayal of fire and brimstone consuming Newcastle and Gateshead, and the urge to escape the conurbation represented by Lot and his family, will surely resonate with those who have experienced it regardless of the primary root cause. Those departing Tyneside may have feared that if they looked back, instead of being turned into a pillar of salt like Lot's wife, they would be condemned to seeing out their days defined by the caricatures that coalesce around the *Four Pillars of Geordie Identity*; class, accent, drink and football. *CRASH!* You've ended up like Andy Capp, Sid the Sexist or Oz from *Auf Wiedersehen, Pet*. *BANG!* You've morphed into an over-sized bottle of Brown Ale. *WALLOP!* You're doomed to perpetually play the Geordie, eternally clad in your Toon top and ever-willing to furnish Sky Sports with inane 'Ah'm a propa fuckin' Geordie me like' comments.

Newcastle Royal Grammar School (RGS) has had six different locations in its 450+ year history. The Virgin Mary Hospital site (1607-1844) is where Mark Akenside attended. FROM TOP: Michaelmas Monday outside the school in 1800; entrance to RGS in 1820; the school in the reign of Elizabeth I (1600?).

THIS PILLAR STOOD AT
THE GATEWAY OF THE
ROYAL GRAMMAR SCHOOL
NEWCASTLE-UPON-TYNE
WHICH FROM 1607 UNTIL 1844
OCCUPIED THE CHAPEL OF
THE HOSPITAL OF
St MARY THE VIRGIN
IN THE WEST GATE
FOUNDED NEAR THIS SITE
IN THE 12th CENTURY

ABOVE: A remaining pillar from the entrance
to the Virgin Mary Hospital RGS site. RIGHT:
Dr Bernard Trafford, Head Master of RGS
since 2008.

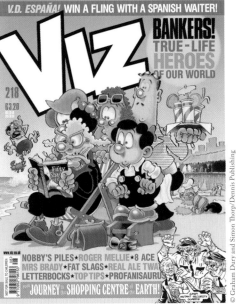

Chris Donald in his bedroom in the family home at Lily Crescent, Jesmond, where *Viz* was first conceived in 1979, and a recent cover of the comic.

OPPOSITE PAGE: Biffa Bacon and Sid the Sexist, created by Chris Donald (top) and Simon Donald (bottom) respectively, are two *Viz* characters that have become synonymous with Geordies. LEFT and BELOW: Bonfire of the Geordie profanities. *The Bus of Fools* event held outside Newcastle Civic Centre on New Year's Eve 2001 involved effigies of *Viz* characters being burnt.

© Simon Donald

© Simon Donald

The Gateshead Millennium Bridge being placed on the River Tyne in 2000. The Baltic Centre for Contemporary Arts in Gateshead opened to the public in 2002.

ABOVE LEFT: Jack Common, author of *Kiddar's Luck*. Keith Armstrong has said that the 'idea of escape is a constant in Common's work'. ABOVE RIGHT: Sid Chaplin, author of *The Day of the Sardine*. LEFT: *Billy Elliot* and *Pitmen Painters* playwright, Lee Hall, has said that growing up in Newcastle: 'If you loved poetry, you were a bit of a poof.'

The Dominion Monarch ready for launch from Swan Hunter Yard in 1938 and HMS York (?) leaving Tyneside. When Willie Kiddar and Arthur Haggerston – the respective protagonists in *Kiddar's Luck* and *The Day of the Sardine* – see ships being launched on the Tyne, they long to be on them.

Man with Potential Selves by Sean Henry, Lower Grainger Street, Newcastle. In *Kiddar's Luck*, Kiddar advises: 'The younger you are the more important it is that you should consort with your unrealized selves. Friends prevent that by their presence.'

Auf Wiedersehen, Pet (top) launched the careers of Tim Healy, Jimmy Nail and Kevin Whately. Healy, pictured above with writers Dick Clement and Ian La Frenais and co-star Whately in 2013, believes the show 'changed television. Because I think *Auf Wiedersehen, Pet* was the first time that we got genuine, proper, real McCoy accents exactly as they were.'

© ncjMedia

Robson Green (above) has claimed that some actors who leave the North-East are bitter and view their profession as a means of escape. Nick Forbes (below left) became embroiled in a debate with the likes of Green and Lee Hall (below right) about proposed cuts to Newcastle's arts budget in 2012/13, hitting out at 'Geordie expats who have made their fortune portraying the North East'.

© ncjMedia

© ncjMedia

© ncjMedia

Sting (above) has talked of being 'brought up in the shadow of the shipyards. I was fascinated and terrified by them at the same time and wondered where I would fit in', also saying: 'The engine that drove me was an important one and it was escape.' TOP: Esso Northumbria at the bottom of a Wallsend street, 1969. RIGHT: In October 2014 Sting's Tyneside-themed musical *The Last Ship* opened on Broadway in New York. His friend Jimmy Nail was in a leading role.

ABOVE: Nineteenth century showman Billy Purvis with and without his costume. Some believe it was his use of the word 'Geordie' as a put down that established it on Tyneside as a way of describing the people.

Spans supported by cables to each shore.
9th February 1928

The changing face of the Quayside in Newcastle and Gateshead. OPPOSITE PAGE: Construction workers on the Tyne Bridge in 1928. FROM TOP: Tyne Bridge under construction, 1928; Quayside scene, 1960; Quayside scene, date unknown. Sir John Hall has said: "The past is holding us back ... If we live in the past, we'll die in the past."

Cities, like individuals, can be a complicated, often contradictory composite of competing factors, forever caught up in restless negotiation between the past, present and future. ABOVE: Plaque dedicated to Richard Grainger on Grainger Street in Newcastle.

Nevertheless, considering the hybrid artistic form of the montage, those in the creative industries will perhaps identify with its implicit themes more readily than others. One of the talks at the debates was actually entitled *We Gotta Get Out of this Place*, focusing on music stars from the area that have left for pastures new, given by TV producer and pop historian Chris Phipps. The song made famous by Tyneside band The Animals in the 1960s was also utilised as a chapter heading by Hilary Fawcett in *Made in Newcastle: Visual Culture*, and referenced by former Director of Northern Arts, Peter Stark: "I left Newcastle in the year of *We Gotta Get Out of this Place*. And it was a generational decision at that time that the city was going nowhere." However, Stark felt the song was symbolic of a generational attitude nationally, not necessarily specific to the North-East. Indeed, when I put it to him that if a group of extreme Akenside Syndrome sufferers were to form a suicide cult, they would probably be found to have topped themselves with *We Gotta Get Out of this Place* on a continuous loop, he actually suggested lyrics from another Animals' cover instead: *Don't let me be misunderstood*.

Although acknowledging a broader generational and national perspective regarding the counter-cultural revolution of the 1960s and 1970s, it seems reasonable to envisage the song's mantra being imbued with added geographical resonance for those on Tyneside, where the band were actually from, and especially for those striving to succeed in the music industry. For instance, in his autobiography Jimmy Nail name-checks the band and paraphrases *We Gotta Get Out of this Place* when reminiscing about his own desire to escape Tyneside; citing Sting, Bryan Ferry and Brian Johnson as examples of Geordies who had escaped by means of their music. Furthermore, in *Northstars* this observation can be found: 'Eric Burdon's autobiography says that he loved Newcastle so much but eventually had to leave, because to know the North-East you have to leave. [Mark] Knopfler concurs: "You do, yeah."[44] It may have been a cover version, but The Animals' song forged a template for music-related Akenside Syndrome – a kind of anthem for the alienated and the ambitious.

A sense of feeling compelled to leave Tyneside recurs amongst Geordie rock stars. For some there seems to be an internal compulsion to escape working alongside a perception of being expelled. To gain a fuller understanding of this we must return to the Law of Jante and its British equivalent – Tall Poppy Syndrome. In his autobiography Jimmy Nail recollects an incident on a bus in Newcastle not long after *Auf Wiedersehen, Pet* was first broadcast, where a curmudgeonly old woman recognised him and had a dig. He also recalls a breakdown in relations with certain friends provoked by his new-found fame, similar to what Brian Johnson described. These can be interpreted as text-book examples of communal Jante Law enforcement. After all, the very act of becoming a nationally recognised television actor, or an internationally celebrated rock star, contravenes several rules of the Law of Jante. As observed earlier, 'the Janters who transgress this unwritten 'law' are regarded with suspicion and some hostility,' and sometimes it seems what's good enough for the Janters is good enough for the Geordies.

In *Bring Home the Revolution* Jonathan Freedland notes how 'Britons are famously afflicted by the tall poppy syndrome, the urge to cut down anyone who gets 'too big for their boots' or 'has ideas above their station' (to name but two English phrases inherently hostile to social mobility).'[45] And there seemed to be a feeling from some contributors that in the North-East, with its historic sense of apartness, a particularly virile variant can be found. Contemplating her own experience of Akenside Syndrome, Val McLane said: "I'm quite honestly quite regularly bemused by people's behaviour towards me. Jealousy, for example, that I've come across quite a lot with – unfortunately – other women who've been jealous of me." Did she feel Tall Poppy Syndrome had played a part in this? "Yeah, I'm sure there's something of it … I don't understand why I've been treated quite regularly with suspicion. I haven't had much *admiration* for my achievements. I've mainly had jealousy and a lot of unpleasantness."

When I read Brian Johnson's quote from *Q* magazine to her, suggesting it sounded like he felt almost compelled to leave Newcastle, she seemed to sigh before asserting: "I suppose I can understand it, but I've got sympathy for anybody in his position. He became a superstar and he was, and he still is to me, a very normal person. But I can understand there is a kind of jealousy." In response to the same line of questioning, Sir John Hall had this to say: "It's always very, very difficult to go back entirely to your roots if you achieve fame as he did. Because in a sense your wealth makes you different. His job and his life made him entirely different. He was travelling the world and that sets him separate from his original pals. And I don't think it was him that actually wanted to change. There's jealousy in a way. There is jealousy in the North-East if people succeed. There is always that jealousy. They're not looked upon basically as 'they're great' – there's a jealousy that goes around the area."

Reinforcing this view, in recent BBC sitcom *Hebburn*, penned by Manchester-based Tynesider Jason Cook, the male protagonist says to his girlfriend: 'Sarah, people round here don't like anyone succeeding at anything.' Hall also recalled going "back to my own places" after establishing himself as an entrepreneur, and remembered how "like [Brian] Johnson, I wasn't accepted at times. There was a gulf." Sue Clayton meanwhile believed that with regard to perceived accent change "any famous person gets judged terribly" on Tyneside, and Mel Gibson recalled her father saying: "There's something about the North-East that even though you love it, it doesn't necessarily love you. It may wish you to stay in a box that's a certain shape, and it isn't always comfortable if you leave that box. Because you can't go back, because it means fitting back into it."

Again talking about the broader North-East region, Mel reflected: "We do have bad Tall Poppy Syndrome here. We're not good with people who succeed; we want to constrain them in some ways, certainly." Similarly, while discussing the influence Newcastle had on *Viz* on *The Culture Show* in 2009, Chris Donald avowed: 'You don't sort of do it to better yourself or make yourself look better. You just do it to bring everyone else down to your level. If you see anyone who you think's getting a bit out of control possibly,' in what sounded to me like a recognition of Geordie Jante Law enforcement.[46]

Whereas Jill Halfpenny felt she had been constrained, put in a box and pigeonholed by people from outside the region, restrictive notions of what it means to be a Geordie from within the area appear to have fortified Bryan Ferry's quest to remake and remodel himself, as David Buckley adroitly analyses in *The Thrill of it All: The Story of Bryan Ferry & Roxy Music*. Ferry has described himself in the past as 'an orchid born on a coal-tip', and claimed that in his formative years: 'I thought, well, I'm not going to just be this, or that, and stay in the north-east all my life. There was this attitude which said you can't do *this* because you're born like *that*. There's a lot of that up there.' The plaque next to All Saints' Church in Newcastle alleges Mark Akenside was 'ashamed of his native place', and the young Ferry could probably have written an empathetic stanza or two, having recollected: 'In the sixth form I was getting into my art – my creative, bohemian phase – and I thought, "Oh no, I'm not of you lot." I was … I can't think of a word other than ashamed, which sounds so awful.'[47]

Lawrie McMenemy, who was brought up in Gateshead but attended the same Newcastle school as Sting, told me: "I do think there's a trait amongst north-easterners where some of them would never ever move away. And so therefore they are the sorts that sometimes poke a bit of fun at you. I don't think it's an element of jealousy, I wouldn't know about that, but I think they like to try and bring you back down, put your feet back on the ground. They assume, especially if they see you on the telly, or they think your accent has changed, they think: 'Aye-aye – bring this bugger back down to earth.'"

Buckley relates how Ferry left the North-East to find fame, fortune and himself, and he may have felt he was fleeing the type of Geordie Jante Law enforcement described by McMenemy, considering this quote: 'I'm so far removed from where I was born that it's ridiculous … And people might say, come on Bryan, bonny lad – back you go. But no, to me, you can become whatever you want to be; do not allow anybody to drag you down.' Buckley also suggests: 'the central theme of the Ferry story [is perhaps] a desire to escape out of his own class whilst simultaneously attempting to "atone" for this by stressing his working-class roots … a lover of the mores of the English gentry, he entered a society that he had not been born into but to which he had always aspired.'[48]

An interview Ferry did with Barbara Ellen in which she asked what had happened to his Geordie accent, complements this: 'When I tell Ferry that it's my favourite accent of all, he looks genuinely astonished. 'Oh really, don't you find it irritating?' For my benefit, Ferry mumbles a few lines of Geordie, announcing at the end: 'I don't think I've lost my accent at all. It's still there, and when I'm animated, it comes out very strong.' I don't have the heart to tell him that he sounds about as Geordie as the Royal Enclosure at Ascot.[49] But while he may be a totem of class-related Akenside Syndrome – previously declaring himself 'the first rock star to join the English aristocracy'

– in more subtle ways, many working-class Tyneside musicians who make it big will be able to identify with 'that sense of discomfort experienced when shedding one class skin only to don another.'[50]

Brian Johnson has recalled a one-upmanship type feud with a neighbour in Jesmond before he moved to Florida in the USA, where rugged individualism is part of the country's creation myth, and where achieving success from humble origins is far more likely to be applauded than abhorred and ridiculed. Johnson certainly can't be accused of losing his Geordie accent en route – it being described as 'industrial-strength Tyneside' in *Q* – but when I paraphrased Sue Clayton's observation about famous people being judged terribly on Tyneside in a general, non-accent specific way, his friend Brendan Healy insisted: "I think they get judged terribly anywhere in England. We're the exact opposite of the Americans. What is it they say about the English? They love to get you up on to a pedestal so they can pull you down. In America they like to get you on a pedestal and try to keep you there. It's the American Dream."[51]

The USA is not being presented as some sort of utopia here, but it is important in terms of understanding Akenside Syndrome (and specifically the strain experienced by rock stars from working-class backgrounds) to have knowledge of this pronounced cultural difference between the UK and America. It is often noted – including by Bill Lancaster in *An Agenda for Regional History* – that the North-East has 'the lowest rate of new business start-ups in Britain', and Sir John Hall tried to address this in recent years by supporting the *Go Wansbeck* initiative in his old neck of the woods.[52] Though music purists would no doubt baulk at such a proposition, forming your own band is in effect a new business start-up, and as Hall has stated in the past, 'I was 36 when I finally set out in private enterprise … It's difficult for a working-class fellow to break the bonds', he seemed a suitable person to test a theory on.[53]

I put it to him that to reach the pinnacle of the business world, to some extent you have to be ruthless, almost obsessively motivated to achieve and determinedly individualistic. And that goes against the recent historical grain of Geordie culture; strongly communal and collectivist, where being down to earth, able to laugh at ourselves and not take ourselves too seriously is applauded, even encouraged. But to reach the level of attainment that

Hall has in business, Robson Green has in television, Sting et al have in the music industry, namesake Lee Hall has in writing or Sarah Millican has in stand-up comedy, an individual has to take him or herself very seriously (ironically so in the case of the latter). And his view on whether the historic culture of the area has militated against such high levels of achievement was unequivocal: "Oh yes. Totally. Because it's not something which is ingrained in us. We're not like the Americans, where we stand with our hand on the heart, and the flag etc., and say 'Come on, you can do it!' It's not part of us."

While discussing how the loud and aggressive aspect of Geordie culture is not conducive to the introverted character with Chris Donald, his mind turned to Newcastle's music scene. "I've often theorised as to why is it that cities like Liverpool and Manchester can come up with decent bands like Oasis and The Beatles, and all these sort of working-class people that can produce good music, whereas in Newcastle all that the working-class could do was make bloody heavy metal and that," he reflected. "And I often wondered why there wasn't that kind of intellectual, more 'thinky' type people doing things in Newcastle. We're more suppressed in Newcastle I think, definitely. You don't really get innovative bands from Newcastle – it's strange."

Writing in *NARC.* – billed as the North-East's premier monthly music magazine – Ewan McIntyre ruminated over the same thing. Having spent half his life in Manchester and half in Newcastle, he bemoaned the disparity between the cities in terms of musical output: 'The sad fact is, the musical impact of Newcastle and the North East grossly under-represents the number of people in the region.' After examining reasons why this musical discrepancy might exist including a historic lack of venues, he concluded: 'overall it's about confidence and attitude ... It's time we kicked against the ridiculous stereotypes of being from the North East. Why? Because if we don't do it, nobody will do it for us.'[54]

Mentioning the region's low business start-up figures to Val McLane, I asked whether on some levels there's a sense of collective low self-esteem. "Yes, I think there is. It's very sad but there definitely is that," she replied. Similarly, while not blaming the victim, and with a full understanding of how the educational, economic and societal structures of the country hold many people back in a way that is beyond their individual control, I asked Chris Donald if too many Geordies know their place, and have low levels of aspiration and expectation of themselves. He continued on a music theme: "I don't know if it's a particularly regional thing but a lot of people do. I get slightly on to the music thing and the fact that there doesn't seem to be many ambitious working-class people [in a music context] – the working-class don't sort of aspire to do anything particularly great, or they didn't when I was a kid.

"And I think in terms of a music culture it's always been a handicap in Newcastle. I'm not sure why. Maybe it's not as bad now. I get the impression that people from housing estates in Manchester regard starting a pop group as being a serious possibility, whereas people on housing estates here would think there was something wrong with you if you did that. It might be a bit of a 'middle class' thing to do and they wouldn't want to do that." Earlier I'd asked whether he believed the constant parodying of Geordies was harmless fun or corrosive cultural stereotyping. Regarding the Paul Whitehouse Geordie caricature in *Harry and Paul* and other representations from outside the region, he asserted: "Paul Whitehouse and others, they're just complete [comedy] mercenaries, so I would be very wary of anything they do as outsiders with that attitude that the Geordies are thick. I would think anything that they're doing along those lines would be corrosive certainly."

However, elaborating on the issue, Donald made an observation which calls on to stage the final act of this chapter, and indeed heralds the conclusion of our exploration into Akenside Syndrome. "It might have helped if Sting had been a little bit more noticeably a Geordie," he pondered, "so that people [from outside the region] could take into account: 'Oh, he's a Geordie as well, so they can't all be thick.'" In 2002, writing in his *Sunday Sun* column, Donald upbraided Sting for what he perceived as the pop star's underwhelming support for Newcastle and Gateshead's European Capital of Culture bid, contrasting it with that of Lindisfarne's Ray Laidlaw. Laidlaw, he pointed out, 'has yet to find his dream mansion in Wiltshire,' and his reasoned and thoughtful comments were, in Donald's opinion, 'a definite improvement on Sting's "Hey! It's a great place, but I wouldn't want to live there" sentiment.'[55]

This brings to mind Nick Forbes talking of 'Geordie expats who have made their fortune portraying the North East' in the heated exchanges concerning Newcastle City Council's proposed arts cuts in 2012/13.[56] Forbes and Donald were tapping into a potent cultural force on Tyneside, whereby famous people who have left and go on about how proud they are of being a Geordie and how much they love the area etc., whilst declining to have a base there, are regarded by some as wanting to have their stottie cake and eat it. At which point we can suggest that although Sting no doubt lives in Wiltshire, and other places including New York, Malibu and Tuscany for manifold reasons, underlying them all may be his profound experience of Akenside Syndrome.

Over the years Sting's ambivalence towards Newcastle has found expression in alleged denigrating comments about his hometown. In *Spirit of Tyneside: Famous sons and daughters*, published in 1990, John Gibson remarked: 'Unlike most Geordies who gained either fame or fortune … he neither clung to his roots nor looked back on Newcastle with great affection. Not for him what he saw as the falseness of those who left the place as fast as they could and then eulogised about it.' Quoting Phil Sutcliffe who wrote an official biography of The Police, the band that propelled Sting to worldwide fame, Gibson related the singer telling his former *Chronicle* colleague: 'Saying Newcastle is a great place, I can't stand that. Newcastle's a **** place. It was a slum from the old industrial revolution and when they knocked down the old slums they built new slums. I don't want to be rooted in Newcastle. I don't want to be a Geordie. I've got none of that awful pride.'[57]

After several years without contact from his schoolmate following his initial rise to fame, Jim Berryman, who wrote *A Sting in the Tale* with the singer's blessing, remembered how he felt Sting's 'public persona of smug superstar making po-faced pronouncements on issues like the Rainforests and drug taking endeared him to very few observers, me included.' The interregnum did not last though, and, keen to defend his lifelong friend, Berryman offered an insider's perspective on another of Sting's Newcastle-related denouncements – one that lodged like a poison-tipped dart in Tyneside's collective consciousness. 'Sting once described Newcastle as 'A good place to bring up your sick', which I know was intended as a joke but offended some locals', he recalled, insisting that 'Sting, whatever has been said before, is, I know, as proud of being a Geordie as any Newcastle United replica-shirt wearing boozer in the Bigg Market on a Friday night.'[58]

So what lies at the heart of the matter? A plausible answer can be found in the concept of Akenside Syndrome, and it seems appropriate to end with an examination of why the man formerly known as Gordon Sumner's experience of it has been so acute. Clearly I don't have access to Sting's consciousness or innermost feelings, and while there is likely to be a multitude of cross-fertilising reasons for his deep ambivalence towards Newcastle which only he is ultimately privy to, our job here – as it has been throughout – is to scratch the surface, and having come so far we can have an educated guess at some of the main contributing factors.

To begin with there is the obvious one, connected with Tyneside's heavy industrial past and what working-class men were, generally speaking, expected to aspire to. Talking to Chrissy Iley in 2012, Sting said: 'I was brought up in the shadow of the shipyards. I was fascinated and terrified by them at the same time and wondered where I would fit in.'[59] It's a quintessential description of incipient Akenside Syndrome. Furthermore, there are perhaps echoes of Lee Hall's experience in his reminiscence to David Whetstone: 'You had to survive in Wallsend and you had to have this front of being tough … But I was also pretty kind of airy-fairy. I was a dreamer, a romantic. So you have that combination of two things: having a very tough front and then, also, being interested in things like music and poetry, landscape. I mean, you had to hide that … you kind of hid what was your artistic bent pretty well.'[60]

Fond of the ship metaphor in relation to his own personal journey – often comparing himself to ships launched on the Tyne venturing into the world and never returning – Sting chose to explore his 'unrealized selves' identified by Jack Common in *Kiddar's Luck*, and heed the advice given to Arthur Haggerston in Sid Chaplin's *The Day of the Sardine*: 'You'll sail the seas … Don't be a sardine. Navigate yourself.' Watching ships leave the Tyne, both Willie Kiddar and Arthur Haggerston yearn to be on them. Sting, metaphorically speaking, built his own super-tanker. Let's call it HMS Gordon.

Another potential source of Sting's ambivalence is more unexpected, and links him with Chris Donald, Jack Common, Jimmy Nail and Bryan

Ferry in a way not immediately obvious. Jim Berryman has recalled how Sting was shy at school, and suggested that the adoption of a rock star persona helps him conquer his introversion. Chris Donald's introversion was touched on in the previous chapter; Keith Armstrong cites more than one source describing Jack Common as an essentially shy man; Jimmy Nail talks of his own shyness in *A Northern Soul*, and in *The Thrill of it All* David Buckley refers to Bryan Ferry's 'fundamental shyness', with Ferry himself quoted saying: 'I'm less shy than I used to be. I used to be really tongue-tied. I guess that's what made me a singer; it's a way of overcoming this verbal insecurity, verbal shyness.'[61]

Susan Cain had a recent publishing success with *Quiet: The Power of Introverts in a World That Can't Stop Talking*, in which she claimed Western society favours extroverts and is loaded against introverts. Discussing the interplay between gender and introversion, she maintained: 'Men are more likely to be introverted than women are, but it's really very slight. But the real difference I think is in how it plays out, how it relates to cultural stereotypes. For men it can be a little more difficult, because there are these cultural demands for men to be very dominant.'[62] The implications for Tyneside, where male-dominated cultural stereotypes and male-focussed notions of Geordie identity have historically prevailed, are obvious. Deep down I suspect Biffa Bacon and Sid the Sexist are introverts too.

Many artists like to think they operate outside the *bien pensant* orthodoxies of society, of course, and the myths and mores of the sphere in which Sting achieved success may have exacerbated his alienation. Take the doctor based on Mark Akenside in *Peregrine Pickle*, who can be found pontificating 'that painters and poets ought to … pay no manner of regard to the impertinent customs of the world.'[63] Michael Chaplin felt part of the reason creative people are more susceptible to Akenside Syndrome is because; "A very common thing in creative people is this feeling of rebellion, of wanting to try new things and do things that your parents might have disapproved of." And speaking of the music industry specifically, NME writer Pat Long notes that 'a lot of rock stars like to imagine themselves as outlaw figures at odds with the strictures of workaday society,' while David Buckley's citation of rock historian Victor Fader is also telling: 'There is a common element in the creation of a star … By keeping details of your genesis shrouded in mist you create mystery. The few facts that do emerge are enlarged upon, deified, become mythic in their import.'

Buckley claims that like 'almost all the great pop icons, [Bryan] Ferry has deliberately sought to mystify his origins,' and it is easy to imagine this being true of the young Gordon Sumner, seeking reinvention and self-definition as Sting after moving away from Newcastle.[64] All of these factors may have fed into his experience of Akenside Syndrome on the extreme end of the scale, but at the core I suspect there is something that has nothing to do with being a rock star and everything to do with being human. The protagonist in Julian Barnes's novel *The Sense of an Ending* articulates it well: 'I certainly believe we all suffer damage, one way or another. How could we not, except in a world of perfect parents, siblings, neighbours, companions? And then there is the question, on which so much depends, of how we react to the damage: whether we admit it or repress it, and how this affects our dealings with others.'[65]

Richard Wilkinson and Kate Pickett cite research published in the *Journal of Personality and Social Psychology*, that concluded: 'conflicts and tensions with other people are by far the most distressing events in daily life in terms of both initial and enduring effects on emotional wellbeing' – more so than the demands of work, money worries or other difficulties.'[66] Likewise, when analysing why unhappiness is much easier to experience than happiness, Sigmund Freud claimed that 'our relations with others' were a primary reason: 'The suffering that arises from this … perhaps causes us more pain than any other'.[67] Freud famously felt that familial relationships and tensions were at the root of many human neuroses, and Sting has recollected a difficult relationship with his father, and occasionally refers to his mother in emotive terms. As HMS Gordon ploughed ever forward it hit an emotional iceberg of arctic proportions, leaving the singer to recall that in 1987, having not attended either of his parents' funerals, he was in an internally shattered emotional state.

In *Broken Music* he reflects on how, as a young man, he believed he could escape these emotional embroilments by maintaining a constant sense of forward momentum, something he elaborated on in discussion with David Whetsone in 2013: 'The engine that drove me was an important one and it was escape. I wanted to escape my family. I wanted to escape the environment that I didn't feel had any future for me. And that engine drove me for a very long time. I just drove myself to escape. Luckily, I did.'[68] He has also talked of how the unhappiness of his parental relations remained lodged in his unconscious, and all things considered it seems likely that Sting's experience of Akenside Syndrome has been heavily underscored by this – a classic example of emotional trauma becoming associated with and difficult to distinguish from the place where it occurred. Rock star affirmation of Dolores Claiborne's insight that running doesn't resolve your emotional problems if the scars run deep enough. The self is inescapable, after all.

No man is an island or even a one direction of travel super-tanker and in recent years HMS Gordon has been frequently sighted docked on the Tyne again. Not permanently berthed but proudly bedecked in its Geordie insignia once more. In 2008 Sting attended the unveiling of a painting he'd commissioned by landscape artist Stephen Hannock at the Laing Art Gallery, where John Martin's *The Destruction of Sodom and Gomorrah* hangs. Entitled *Northern City Renaissance*, Hannock's painting depicts an aerial view of the Tyne in the present day, while also paying homage to Tyneside's industrial past. 'It is very touching,' purred Sting. 'I think he has captured the spirit of the place I have very strong roots with and still consider to be my home.'[69] *The Journal* reported him telling guests: 'I'm proud to be here. I've always carried a sense of belonging. I'm still a Geordie.'[70]

In 2009 Sting fired the starting gun for the Great North Run. During the visit he agreed to feature in an advert promoting Newcastle, appearing 'in the shadows of a city street, as the voice over says: "Get into my city, get into Newcastle."'[71] Later that year the rock star performed songs from his album *If on a Winter's Night...* in a special televised event at Durham Cathedral. In the resulting television programme, *Sting's Winter Songbook*, he asserted: 'Being a Geordie ... it matters to us ... It's a fierce regional identity which I don't see very often ... I don't feel anything but a Geordie.'[72] Aptly, he was filmed near the bottom of Dean Street with the word *AKENSIDE* hovering above his head; it being part of the Akenside Traders' pub signage.

In 2010 Sting could be found singing at The Central pub near the Gateshead end of the Tyne Bridge, with a playwright in attendance. The playwright's presence was explained in 2011 when it was announced that

Sting was overseeing a musical theatre project partly set in the Tyneside of his youth. Called *The Last Ship*, the star attended two read-throughs of the production at Live in February 2012. Playing a central role was Jimmy Nail, joined by his sister Val McLane for the read-throughs. According to the *Evening Chronicle*, '*The Last Ship* tells of a group of North East shipyard workers who are inspired by a local priest to build their own ship and sail it round the world after their yard is sold.'[73]

In 2013 the Wallsend-born singer said the ship in the musical is 'a kind of symbol … It's from there but its job is elsewhere. The ship gets too big to come back.'[74] Due to open on Broadway in September 2014, at time of writing there had been no confirmation as to whether the ship is named HMS Gordon, but the protagonist's name consists of six letters, beginning with *G* and ending with *on* – that's right, *Gideon*. One thing of which we can be fairly certain though, is that as with *The Poet: A Rhapsody, Kiddar's Luck, The Day of the Sardine, Spender* and *Billy Elliot*, somewhere in the narrative will reside the anguish of the artist as a young Geordie.

The closing sentence of F. Scott Fitzgerald's *The Great Gatsby* reads, 'So we beat on, boats against the current, borne back ceaselessly into the past', and some of Henrik Ibsen's plays are informed by an old sailors' term: 'There is a corpse in the cargo.'[75] It's been said that the corpse symbolises 'a willingness to be dominated by one's past; in Ibsen's plays the past is both oppressive and potentially liberating if acknowledged.'[76] Elaborating on why he felt people in the arts are more prone to Akenside Syndrome, Michael Chaplin mentioned, "the old cliché about you spend the first forty years of your life trying to get away from what you were and what you've been and all the rest of it. And then you spend the next forty years trying to get back to it. And, you know, that is a very archetypal thing." It suitably summarises Sting's attempts to alter his Akenside Syndrome arc; to reset the navigational and narrative trajectory of HMS Gordon from unflinchingly linear to satisfyingly circular, as Chrissy Iley has inferred.

Talking about *The Last Ship* with her, he said of Newcastle: 'There's a spiritual connection with this place. It's not dewy-eyed, sentimental nostalgia. This town is genuinely loveable, with its own river and football team. I don't know another region of England that has this feeling. So coming back, having been away so long, I think I see it more clearly.'[77] In another interview with his fellow Tynesider, Sting insisted: 'There's always a gravitational pull towards your roots. It's like a homing instinct ... Going back to your roots, realising what gifts you've been given from your environment and from your culture is important at this stage in my life.' He further explained: 'I'm not running away from anything at the moment. I'm tying up the loose ends everywhere, and that's why I'm here.' All of which led Iley to conclude that 'Sting seems comfortable now in his own skin, at ease with his Geordie self.'[78]

Someone from Newcastle wrote in the comment book that accompanied *Northern City Renaissance* in the Laing Art Gallery: 'Beautiful painting, shame the a** Sting commissioned it (Thought he hated Tyneside!)'. And while I understood the back story that prompted such a message, having experienced ambivalence towards Tyneside myself – to the extent of feeling compelled to write this book at a heavy personal cost – I opted to leave a note welcoming Sting home after a prolonged bout of Akenside Syndrome. I'm sure he was delighted.

AKENSIDE AFTERTHOUGHTS

I T IS WELL DOCUMENTED THAT NOBODY TRULY KNOWS THE ORIGIN OF the name Geordie. A factsheet produced by Newcastle Libraries puts forward three possibilities: **a.** derived from Newcastle's support for King George during the Jacobite Rebellion of 1745, **b.** born out of the Northumberland and Durham coalfield, **c.** named after George Stephenson and his miners' lamp. But it also cites Frank Graham, who suggested 'that the name originally was a term of abuse meaning "fool". It was first used in this way in 1823, when a local showman Billy Purvis, used it to put down a rival. He is quoted as saying "Noo yor a fair doon feul, not an artificial feul like Billy Purvis! Thous a real Geordie!"'[1] Likewise, in a recent letter to *The Times*, Professor J. Neville Fawcett of Northumberland proposed that in the same year Purvis said his Town Moor audience was as mad as King George III, hence Geordies.

And so it goes on. Keith Armstrong references work by James Gregory: 'The idea of mental aberration was connected with the original 'Geordie' which possibly originates in a term of abuse suggesting 'idiocy".[2] It really isn't difficult to discern a historic continuity with the present-day thick, daft Geordie stereotype so beloved by comedians and the national media, and still sometimes propagated from within the area itself, in what Mike Summersby called the "introspective celebration of perhaps the less savoury aspects of our culture."

When I asked Sue Clayton whether she thought the constant cultural parodying of Geordies casts us into the role of the nation's village idiot, she agreed, saying: "I don't like the stereotyping. And I especially don't like it because I think people collude with it, sometimes out of embarrassment. They play on it because they lack the confidence to transcend it. You feel you have to send yourself up to be funny, take the piss out of yourself, which we really shouldn't. Whenever anybody says to me 'Oh go on, say it in Geordie' or 'Do it in a Geordie accent', I absolutely refuse and just think…" At which point we both said "Fuck off!" in unison.

What we've learnt from our investigation into Akenside Syndrome is that being identified as a Geordie can be something of a mixed blessing; can take away as much as it gives, sometimes more. Asked if too many Geordies know their place, Sir John Hall responded: "Oh yes, we've done that for years," and his assertion that "we look too much inward on ourselves and sometimes I think maybe in a sense the word Geordie draws us in and is a hindrance," strikes a chord. The Detroit comparison spat between *The Guardian* and local luminaries epitomised what I referred to in the introduction as 'defensive dislocation from within, and misplaced misapprehension from without'. In an incisive overview of the melee, former *Guardian* journalist Peter Hetherington, writing in *The Journal*, avowed that 'the endemic defensive mechanism in the North East … does us no favours.'[3] When it comes to the application of Newcastle's city motto there's been too much defence over the years and not enough attack, not enough triumphing on our own terms.

And certainly it could be argued that in the not too distant past, and residually to this day, the word Geordie became too rigidly defined, narrowly describing one type of person – the mythical *proper* Geordie – to the exclusion of others. Lacking malleability to absorb and embrace on-going extension of the term, it didn't seem to take too kindly to prefixes or suffixes. The recent promotional campaign by Newcastle NE1 that Sting contributed to had the slogan: *Everyone can have their own Newcastle. Original. Modern. Unique. Eclectic. There is only one you. This city fits you perfectly.* There seemed to me a tacit, perhaps unconscious acknowledgement that this has not always been the case.

The *Whatever Happened to the Likely Lads?* theme tune co-penned by Ian La Frenais warned that all Tynesiders might have to look forward to is the past, and this dovetails neatly with what Bill Williamson has called, 'the prevailing sense of the past which is such a central component of regional culture', and Paul Younger described as 'the great Geordie pastime of looking back'.[4] The despair of deindustrialisation, the fear of what may or may not come in industry's place, and the inevitable yearning for and celebration of past glories is poignantly portrayed in the lyrics. Speaking of the necrophilic national tendency toward nostalgia in cultural output, Alexander Chancellor noted: 'A people that is no longer making history looks to the past for reasons to feel proud', and though perfectly understandable in historical terms, there is a sense that Tyneside's past has hung on its frame like Jacob Marley's chain in *A Christmas Carol*.[5] The area destined to be designated as some sort of Greater Beamish.

Learning from your past is always preferable to living in it and there has been a backlash against this retrograde mind-set recently. In *Made in Newcastle* Paul Barlow talked of 'the now slightly-embarrassing lost utopia, represented by the solidarities of mining and shipbuilding industries'.[6] Discussing North-East regeneration in *The Journal*, Kevan Carrick quoted Mark Twain: 'if you always do what you always did then you'll always get what you always got', and in the same paper Mark Robinson asserted: 'I think nostalgia is an acceptable indulgence when looking through photo albums or meeting old friends. As a way of life, it's not to be recommended.'[7] Referring to former Newcastle City Council leader John Shipley advocating progress, Stuart Jeffries said for people like him, 'this nostalgic lament for Geordie culture past is an intolerable luxury.'[8] Meanwhile Sir John Hall insisted: "The past is holding us back. I think it is a malaise of the North-East that we're still rooted in that image of [ourselves as] working class and feeling very proud of it. If we live in the past, we'll die in the past."

Though frustrated by what he sees as the slow pace of change and lack of strong political leadership in the region, Hall was not advocating a Year Zero approach. "We can't live in the past, but we've got to take from it the very good things. The willingness to think of other people has never left us

… we've got to be extrovert but not lose that kindness," he reasoned. Neither was the man who coined the phrase Geordie Nation in favour of a complete break with the past in terms of what it means to be a Geordie, insisting, "We should never lose totally that identity. It is a bonding tool for the area," but also reckoning: "We don't really know what our new *raison d'être* is. What's our place in the world?" In a similar vein, although the blurb for *Newcastle upon Tyne: A Modern History* proclaimed that Newcastle 'seeks a new identity', in the preface Colls and Lancaster talked of how 'a city in the throes of redefining itself needs its history most.'[9]

Almost a decade earlier, in *Geordies*, Lancaster said, 'Retaining a sense of the past does not necessarily involve a rejection of the modern. Contemporary Newcastle's acknowledged vitality owes much to this combination of past and present', whilst Colls averred: 'No regional identity which lives on hearsay can have a future. Nor does it deserve to.'[10] All of which demonstrates that cities, like individuals, can be a complicated, often contradictory composite of competing factors, forever caught up in restless negotiation between the past, present and future.

Renowned architect Sir Terry Farrell (another product of St Cuthbert's), who has played a key role in the recent urban renewal of Newcastle, says that cities 'can never remain static if they are going to remain relevant to today's society,' and John Shipley makes a similar point: 'We can't just rely on cultural regeneration and being a party city. We have to diversify as much as possible.'[11] For some this drive to diversify is disorientating, indicative of how the desire to be different is dissipating on Tyneside. But anyone who doubts its necessity may be in need of a Billy Purvis-style tongue-lashing. Because thous a real Geordie.

It's been said that 'a nation isn't great if its citizens can't take a critical look at who they are', and this applies to the Geordie Nation too.[12] Come with me on one final walk. Let's start at Live Theatre on Broad Chare, where the productions 'celebrate, probe and affirm the power of regional cultural identity.'[13] That's exactly what this book has endeavoured to achieve, albeit in an abstract way. Stroll past Trinity House then climb up to All Saints' Church and read the plaque which describes Mark Akenside being ashamed of his native place. Let's resolve to try and build a society where present and future Geordies never have to feel that way. Amble down Akenside Hill. Nip into

Akenside Traders for a drink if you fancy; not too many though – remember what we've discussed. Now let's head for the Tyne Bridge; absorbing the majesty of Tyneside's past, the vigour of the present, and embracing possibilities for the future. Pass under the Tyne Bridge and approach Fenwick's Entry. Once there you'll see a plaque on the wall dedicated to 18th century radical Thomas Spence. At the bottom of the plaque are these words:

"Dare to be free"

This is my story about being a Geordie. Tell me yours.

ENDNOTES

PREFACE

1. (i) K.V. Thomas '*History & Anthropology*', Past & Present no 24 (1963), p18 – cited in David Cannadine *Class in Britain* (2000). London: Penguin, px.
   (ii) Alistair Moffat and George Rosie *Tyneside: A History of Newcastle and Gateshead from Earliest Times* (2005). Edinburgh: Mainstream, p9.

INTRODUCTION

1. Michael Collins *The Likes of Us: A Biography of the White Working Class* (2004). London: Granta Books, p131.
2. (i) Germaine Greer *Essex girls? We're the best*, *The Observer* 5ᵗʰ February 2006, p26.
   (ii) Stuart Maconie *Pies and Prejudice: In Search of the North* (2007). London: Ebury Press, p221.
3. Robert Colls and Bill Lancaster (Eds.) *Geordies: Roots of Regionalism* (1992). Edinburgh: Edinburgh University Press, pxi.
4. Tom Gutteridge *No paradise in these shore lines*, *The Journal* 30ᵗʰ May 2011, p11.
5. Jeremy Paxman *The English: A Portrait of a People* (1998). London: Penguin, p183.
6. Charles Jennings *Up North: Travels Beyond the Watford Gap* (1995). London: Abacus, p109.
7. http://britcoun.org.pl.i_regide.htm. (no longer available online)
8. Kate Fox *Watching the English: The Hidden Rules of English Behaviour* (2004). London: Hodder, p22.

9. Kate Fox *Watching the English*, p9.
10. Diana Treffry (Ed.) *Collins Dictionary & Thesaurus* (2004). Glasgow: HarperCollins, p1168.
11. Kate Fox *Watching the English*, pp14, 21.
12. Moffat and Rosie *Tyneside*, p402.
13. Stuart Maconie *Pies and Prejudice*, pxii.
14. Harry Pearson *The Far Corner: A Mazy Dribble through North-East Football* (1997). London: Abacus, pp136-137.
15. (i) Colls and Lancaster *Geordies*, pxii.
    (ii) Peter J. Taylor '*The English and their Englishness*' in *Scottish Geographical Magazine* vol.107, no.3, p159 (1991) – cited by Colls and Lancaster in *Geordies*, pxvi.
16. Barry Carr *Black Geordies*, in Colls and Lancaster *Geordies*, p143.
17. (i) Peter Hetherington *Northern exposure: Does the north-east want self-rule?*, in *SocietyGuardian*, *The Guardian* 27th October 2004, p2.
18. Moffat and Rosie *Tyneside*, p157.
19. Bill Lancaster *The North East, England's most distinctive region?*, in Bill Lancaster, Diana Newton and Natasha Vall (Eds.) *An Agenda for Regional History* (2007). Newcastle: Northumbria University Press, p38.
20. Jane Austen *Pride and Prejudice* (first published 1813 – this edition 2003). London: Penguin, p318.
21. Stuart Maconie *Pies and Prejudice*, p290.
22. A.A. Gill *The Angry Island: Hunting the English* (2006). London: Phoenix, p10.
23. Judith Holder *It's Not Grim Up North: The real truth about the North-South divide* (2005). London: BBC Books, pp45, 46.
24. Liz Edwards *Northumberland, Waitrose Food Illustrated* August 2009, p88.
25. Simon Walters *An MP is paid less than a Commons sous chef*, *The Mail on Sunday* 3rd February 2008, p8.
26. Tim Adams *Newcastle, 5am: the tired and weary take the bus south to fight the cuts*, *The Observer* 27th March 2011, p5.

PILLAR ONE
Class

1. Bill Lancaster *Newcastle - Capital of What?*, in Colls and Lancaster *Geordies*, pp64, 65.
2. Stuart Maconie *Pies and Prejudice* (citing Steve Gibson from a Martin Samuel column in *The Times*), p322.
3. Stuart Maconie *Pies and Prejudice*, p292.
4. Ferdinand Mount *Mind the Gap: The New Class Divide in Britain* (2005). London: Short Books, p11.
5. Tom Hampson and Jemima Olchawski *Ban the word 'chav'*, 15th July 2008 – accessed at www.guardian.co.uk.
6. David Cannadine *Class in Britain*, p18.

7. (i) E.P. Thompson *The Making of the English Working Class* (1963 Victor Gollancz Ltd: London), cited by Ferdinand Mount in *Mind the Gap*, p120.
    (ii) A.A. Gill *The Angry Island*, p89.
8. Barbara Ellen *You stay working class all your life. So be proud of it*, The Observer 26th February 2012, p17.
9. Owen Jones *CHAVS: The Demonization of the Working Class* (2011). London: Verso, p250.
10. (i) Jonathan Freedland *Bring Home the Revolution: The Case for a British Republic* (1999). London: Fourth Estate, p120.
    (ii) Kate Fox *Watching the English*, pp82, 192.
11. Richard Wilkinson and Kate Pickett *The Spirit Level: Why Equality is Better for Everyone* (2010). London: Penguin, p28.
12. Ferdinand Mount *Mind the Gap*, p102.
13. Roger Scruton *England: An Elegy* (2006). London: Continuum pp159, 25, 139.
14. Tony Blair *A Journey* (2010). London: Hutchinson, p135.
15. David Cannadine *Class in Britain*, p145.
16. Roger Scruton *England: An Elegy*, p236.
17. Bill Lancaster *Newcastle - Capital of What?*, in Colls and Lancaster *Geordies*, p66.
18. Ferdinand Mount *Mind the Gap*, p21.
19. Keith Gregson and Mike Huggins *The Media, Regional Culture and the Great North Run: 'Big Bren's Human Race'*, in *Culture, Sport, Society, Vol. 4, No. 1* (Spring 2001). London: Frank Cass, p43.
20. Owen Jones *CHAVS*, p138.
21. David Cannadine *Class in Britain*, p185.
22. Bill Lancaster *Newcastle - Capital of What?*, in Colls and Lancaster *Geordies*, pp59, 65, 66.
23. Ferdinand Mount *Mind the Gap*, p33.
24. A.J.P. Taylor cited by Charles Jennings in *Up North*, p48.
25. Diana Treffry (Ed.) *Collins Dictionary & Thesaurus*, p1126.
26. C. Rossiter *Seedtime of the Republic* (New York, 1953), cited by David Cannadine in *Class in Britain*, p38.
27. Robin Fox *The Red Lamp of Incest* (1980 Penguin: New York), cited by Kate Fox in *Watching the English*, p11.
28. (i) Kate Fox *Watching the English*, p323.
    (ii) Jonathan Freedland *Bring Home the Revolution*, p130.
29. David Cannadine *Class in Britain*, p150.
30. (i) Owen Jones *CHAVS*, p33.
    (ii) Ferdinand Mount *Mind the Gap*, p102.
31. David Cannadine *Class in Britain*, p9.
32. David Byrne *What Sort of Future?*, in Colls and Lancaster *Geordies*, p35.
33. Kate Fox *Watching the English*, p44.
34. Michael Collins *The Likes of Us*, p254.
35. Jack Common *Kiddar's Luck* (first published 1951 – this edition 1990). Northumberland: Bloodaxe, p63.

36. Richard Barber *Ever Green, e-motion magazine* (2004) Issue 4, p18.

37. Harry Pearson *The Far Corner*, p46.

38. Danuta Kean *Martyn Waites: Why the Geordie crime writer is choosing to keep it real*, 13th January 2008 – accessed at www.independent.co.uk.

39. Viktor E. Frankl *Man's Search for Meaning* (first published in German 1946 – this edition 2004). London: Rider Books, p61.

40. Ferdinand Mount *Mind the Gap*, pp202, 273.

41. Owen Jones *CHAVS*, pp5, 72.

42. Michael Collins *The Likes of Us*, pp209, 225.

43. (i) Michael Collins *The Likes of Us*, (review of the book in *Sunday Telegraph* quoted on first page).
    (ii) Charles Jennings *Up North*, pp58, 7.
    (iii) Richard Wilkinson and Kate Pickett *The Spirit Level*, p164.

44. Harvey Taylor *Sporting Heroes*, in Colls and Lancaster *Geordies*, p113.

45. (i) David Cannadine *Class in Britain*, p179.
    (ii) Michael Collins *The Likes of Us*, p237.

46. Bill Lancaster *The North East, England's most distinctive region?*, in *An Agenda for Regional History*, p33.

47. Nick McGrath *Endnotes: My family values: Kevin Keegan* in *FamilyGuardian, The Guardian* 16th April 2011, p8.

48. Stephen Milton *Robson Green on escaping a life in the pits and why he thinks Simon Cowell is a genius*, 11th September 2012 – accessed at www.northeastlifemag.co.uk.

49. Keith Armstrong *Common Words and the Wandering Star: A biographical study of culture and social change in the life and work of writer Jack Common* (2009). Durham: University of Sunderland Press, p6.

50. A.C. Grayling (*Guardian Review*, 13th July 2002), cited by Ferdinand Mount *Mind the Gap*, p232.

51. (i) *Movie Connections: Lee Hall*, BBC1 – broadcast 24th September 2007.
    (ii) Alfred Hickling *Oils to Newcastle*, *The Guardian G2* 25th September 2007, p26.

52. *Perspectives: Robson Green and the Pitmen Painters*, ITV1 – broadcast 8th May 2011.

53. Richard Wilkinson and Kate Pickett *The Spirit Level*, p115.

54. Tom Hadaway *Comic Dialect*, in Colls and Lancaster *Geordies*, pp87, 86.

55. Jack Common *Kiddar's Luck*, pp84, 100, 127.

56. (i) Gordon Burn *Living memories*, *Guardian Review* 11th June 2005, p6.
    (ii) Alfred Hickling *Oils to Newcastle*, *The Guardian G2* 25th September 2007, p26.

57. Alan Plater *The Drama of the North-East*, in Colls and Lancaster *Geordies*, p72.

58. David Cannadine *Class in Britain*, p69.

59. *A Picture of Tyneside* presented by Chris Donald, BBC3 – broadcast 27th June 2005.

60. Chris Donald *Rude Kids: The Unfeasible Story of Viz* (2005). London: HarperCollins Entertainment, pp36, 44.

61. *A Picture of Tyneside*, BBC3 – broadcast 27th June 2005.

62. David Byrne *The Reconstruction of Newcastle: Planning since 1945*, in Robert Colls and Bill

Lancaster (Eds.) *Newcastle upon Tyne: A Modern History* (2001). Chichester: Phillimore, pp358, 360.

63. Chris Donald *Rude Kids*, p231.
64. Bill Lancaster *Sociability and the City*, in Colls and Lancaster *Newcastle upon Tyne: A Modern History*, pp339, 340.
65. A.A. Gill *The Angry Island*, p85.
66. Richard Wilkinson and Kate Pickett *The Spirit Level*, p165.
67. (i) Jonathan Freedland *Bring Home the Revolution*, p129.
    (ii) Ferdinand Mount *Mind the Gap*, pp114, 316.
68. (i) David Cannadine *Class in Britain*, px.
    (ii) Kate Fox *Watching the English*, p60.

PILLAR TWO
Accent

1. Ferdinand Mount *Mind the Gap*, pp40, 283.
2. Kate Fox *Watching the English*, pp73, 82.
3. Kate Fox *Watching the English*, p265.
4. A.A. Gill *The Angry Island*, pp56, 57, 46, 47, 53.
5. Tracey Emin interviewed by Sean O'Hagan, *The Observer Review* 22nd May 2005, p3.
6. Ben Dowell *"Too common for telly" BBC presenter lashes out at Corporation*, 15th July 2013 – accessed at www.radiotimes.com.
7. (i) Kate Fox *Watching the English*, p82.
    (ii) Cristina Odone's Diary *Our obsession with regional accents is class warfare by another name*, *The Observer* 1st January 2006, p21.
    (iii) William Goldman *Which Lie Did I Tell? More Adventures in the Screen Trade* (2001). London: Bloomsbury, p96.
8. Lynsey Hanley *In the ear of the stupid*, *The Guardian* 18th July 2013, p28.
9. Harry Pearson *The Far Corner*, p24.
10. Moffat and Rosie *Tyneside*, pp153, 310.
11. Andrew Taylor *A Plum in Your Mouth: Why the Way We Talk Speaks Volumes About Us* (2006). London: Harpercollins*publishers*, pp128, 236.
12. Simon Elmes *Talking for Britain: A Journey through the Nation's Dialects* (2005). London: Penguin Books, ppxi, xiii.
13. Raymond Williams *Keywords* (1983 Fontana Paperbacks: London), cited by Andrew Taylor in *A Plum in Your Mouth*, p20.
14. Andrew Taylor *A Plum in Your Mouth*, p46.
15. Harvey Taylor *Sporting Heroes*, in Colls and Lancaster *Geordies*, p125.
16. Sam Wonfor *Woman who 'fell on sword' joins The Sage*, *The Journal* 1st November 2008, p5.
17. Simon Elmes *Talking for Britain*, pviii.
18. Judith Holder *It's Not Grim Up North*, pp215, 216.
19. (i) Andrew Taylor *A Plum in Your Mouth*, p73.

(ii) Stuart Husband *Up Front: This Much I Know: John Humphrys, The Observer Magazine* 21st November 2004, p10.

20. James Robinson *The Observer Profile: Huw Edwards, The Observer* 19th December 2010, p32.

21. Simon Elmes *Talking for Britain*, ppvii, xiv.

22. Harry Pearson *The Far Corner*, p37.

23. (i) Chris Donald *Rude Kids*, p67.
    (ii) A.A. Gill *The Angry Island*, p57.

24. Charles Jennings *Up North*, p124.

25. Andrew Taylor *A Plum in Your Mouth*, pp19, 20, 22.

26. Simon Elmes *Talking for Britain*, pp251, 252.

27. Andrew Taylor *A Plum in Your Mouth*, p58.

28. Simon Elmes *Talking for Britain*, p257.

29. Andrew Taylor *A Plum in Your Mouth*, pp6, 244.

30. Simon Elmes *Talking for Britain*, p261.

31. Andrew Taylor *A Plum in Your Mouth*, p244.

32. Andrew Taylor *A Plum in Your Mouth*, p69.

33. Simon Elmes *Talking for Britain*, p251.

34. Tom Hadaway *Comic Dialect*, in Colls and Lancaster *Geordies*, p89.

35. Val McDermid *The Wire in the Blood* (1997). London: HarperCollins*publishers*, p154.

36. Charles Jennings *Up North*, pp4, 5, 117, 118, 119.

37. Stuart Maconie *Pies and Prejudice*, pp289, 290, 291.

38. Paul Gascoigne with Hunter Davies *Gazza: My Story* (2005). Headline: London, pp38, 116, 99.

39. Harry Pearson *The Far Corner*, p57.

40. Bill Lancaster *Newcastle – Capital of What?*, in Colls and Lancaster *Geordies*, p53.

41. Andrew Taylor *A Plum in Your Mouth*, p47.

42. Barbara Ellen *Cheryl, you should take that Simon Cowell to a tribunal, The Observer* 29th May 2011, p15.

43. Tom Hadaway *Comic Dialect*, in Colls and Lancaster *Geordies*, p88.

44. Andrew Taylor *A Plum in Your Mouth*, p12.

45. Andrew Taylor *A Plum in Your Mouth*, p28.

46. Lee Ryder *Word-perfect Santon's embraced our culture and desire to win, Evening Chronicle* 24th July 2013, p60.

47. Emma Brockes *This Time it's Serious, The Guardian Weekend* 18th August 2007, p24.

48. Robert Rowell *Back Lanes and Muddy Pitches* (2004). Newcastle upon Tyne: Zymurgy, p138.

49. Cristina Odone's Diary *'Our obsession with regional accents is class warfare by another name', The Observer* 1st January 2006, p21.

50. Andrew Taylor *A Plum in Your Mouth*, pp34, 67, 98.

51. Robert Colls *Born-again Geordies*, in Colls and Lancaster *Geordies*, pp22, 23.

52. Diana Treffry (Ed.) *Collins Dictionary & Thesaurus*, p37.

53. Jack Common *Kiddar's Luck*, p89.

54. Andrew Taylor *A Plum in Your Mouth*, p3.

PILLAR THREE
Drink

1. Stuart Maconie *Pies and Prejudice*, p309.

2. Brian Bennison *Drink in Newcastle*, in Colls and Lancaster *Newcastle upon Tyne: A Modern History*, p167.

3. (i) Jeremy Paxman *The English*, p245.

   (ii) A.A. Gill *The Angry Island*, p148.

4. (i) *Binge drinking 'worst in north'*, 4th August 2006 – accessed at http://news.bbc.co.uk/1/hi/health/5243402.stm.

   (ii) Zoe Hughes *Dying to live in the North*, *The Journal* 11th October 2006 – accessed at www.journallive.co.uk.

   (iii) *New drive to tackle binge-drinking*, *The Journal* 12th February 2009, p5.

5. Sigmund Freud *Civilisation and its Discontents* (first published in German 1930 – this edition 2002). London: Penguin, pp13, 16.

6. (i) Bill Lancaster *Newcastle - Capital of What?*, in Colls and Lancaster *Geordies*, p59.

   (ii) Bill Lancaster *Sociability and the City*, in Colls and Lancaster *Newcastle upon Tyne: A Modern History*, p320.

7. Brian Bennison *Drink in Newcastle*, in Colls and Lancaster *Newcastle upon Tyne: A Modern History*, p186.

8. Kate Fox *Watching the English*, pp101, 254.

9. Ruth Sunderland *My name is Ruth. I have a drink problem. I never touch it*, *The Observer* 3rd February 2008, p31.

10. Dennis Campbell *Women: the hidden risks of drinking*, *The Observer* 24th February 2008, p8.

11. Stuart Maconie *Pies and Prejudice*, p312.

12. Chris Donald *Rude Kids*, p130.

13. Bill Lancaster *Newcastle – Capital of What?*, in Colls and Lancaster *Geordies*, p61.

14. Simon Donald in *Comics Britannia: Anarchy in the UK*, BBC2 – broadcast 9th August 2008.

15. Jeremy Paxman *The English*, p245.

16. Brian Bennison *Drink in Newcastle*, in Colls and Lancaster *Newcastle upon Tyne: A Modern History*, p191.

17. Helen Rae *Shock figures show alcohol incidents cost North East millions*, *The Journal* 24th July 2012 – accessed at www.journallive.co.uk.

18. Brian Bennison *Drink in Newcastle*, in Colls and Lancaster *Newcastle upon Tyne: A Modern History*, p192.

19. (i) *Evening Chronicle* 20th December 2007, cover story/editorial comment, p6.

    (ii) Rob Pattinson *It's why they call it Black Eye Friday*, *Evening Chronicle* 22nd December 2007, p7.

20. David Old *Arrivederci Roma*, *Evening Chronicle* 16th October 2008, p3.
21. *Summer revellers named and shamed*, 26th May 2005 – accessed at http://news.bbc.co.uk/1/hi/england/4581959.stm.
22. Michael Collins *The Likes of Us*, p244.
23. Colls and Lancaster *Geordies*, pxi.
24. Kate Fox *Watching the English*, p347.
25. Paul Gascoigne *Gazza: My Story*, pp4, 5.
26. James Corbett *Observer Profile – Paul Gascoigne: Likely lad of too many own goals*, *The Observer* 24th February 2008, p49.
27. Simon Callow *'Wake the people and make them think big'*, 19th October 2005 – accessed at www.guardian.co.uk.
28. Ruth Sunderland *My name is Ruth. I have a drink problem. I never touch it*, *The Observer* 3rd February 2008, p31.
29. Kate Fox *Watching the English*, p262.
30. Ferdinand Mount *Mind the Gap*, p310.
31. Richard Wilkinson and Kate Pickett *The Spirit Level*, p36.
32. Nick Danziger *Danziger's Britain: A Journey to the Edge* (1997). London: Flamingo, p84.
33. Gemma Calvert *Miserablebrough*, *News of the World* 2nd December 2007, p32.
34. (i) Haroon Siddique *Use of antidepressants exploded after financial crisis, study finds*, *The Guardian* 28th May 2014, p4.
    (ii) James Ball and Sarah Boseley *Northern GPs much more likely to give antidepressants*, *The Guardian* 5th March 2011, p14.
35. Jane Picken *Suicide Action*, *Evening Chronicle* 19th December 2007, p12.
36. Erich Fromm *The Fear of Freedom* (first published in UK in 1942 – this edition 2001). London: Routlede Classics, p168.

PILLAR FOUR
Football

1. Adam Jupp *History will judge him more harshly than anyone who has strode the corridors of power at United. Ashley is the ultimate wrecker of Geordie dreams*, *Evening Chronicle* 29th July 2009, p7.
2. Rob Shepherd *Tyne for Reality*, *News of the World* 13th January 2008, p79.
3. A.A. Gill *The Angry Island*, p165.
4. Gabriele Marcotti *The Times, the game*, 10th June 2009.
5. Gordon Burn *Living memories*, in *Guardian Review* 11th June 2005, p6.
6. Quote attributed to Bill Lancaster in David Whetstone *Respected North East writer dies aged 61*, *The Journal* 27th July 2009 – accessed at www.journallive.co.uk.
7. Gordon Burn *Living memories*, in *Guardian Review* 11th June 2005, p6.
8. John Carey *The Intellectuals and the Masses: Pride and Prejudice among the Literary Intelligentsia, 1880-1939* (1992). London: Faber and Faber, p39.
9. Gordon Burn *No More Local Heroes*, *Observer Sport Monthly* January 2006, p12.

10. Kate Fox *Watching the English*, p249.
11. Richard Holt & Ray Physick *Sport on Tyneside*, in Colls and Lancaster *Newcastle upon Tyne: A Modern History*, p212.
12. Sid Waddell interviewed by Nick Greenslade *First & Last*, *Observer Sport Monthly* February 2006, p69.
13. Chris Oakley *Small doses of madness essential for a sane life*, *The Observer Sport* 29th October 2006, p10.
14. Gabriele Marcotti *The Times, the game*, 10th June 2009.
15. Neil Farrington *Champagne football at Gallowgate?*, *Sunday Sun* 30th December 2007, p51.
16. Michael Calvin *Planet Toon no place for unbelievers*, *Sunday Mirror* 20th January 2008, p71.
17. (i) Erich Fromm *The Fear of Freedom*, p181.
(ii) Tony Henderson *Professor who philosophises about football*, *The Journal* 13th January 2010, p14.
18. Stuart Maconie *Pies and Prejudice*, p295.
19. Kate Fox *Watching the English*, pp270, 272, 273, 293.
20. Stuart Maconie *Pies and Prejudice*, p294.
21. *Newcastle v Portsmouth live text commentary* by John Ashdown at www.guardian.co.uk, 27th April 2009.
22. (i) Paul Wilson *Ashley's odd cast at theatre of the absurd*, *The Observer Sport* 3rd February 2008, p13.
(ii) Paul Wilson *Thank heavens for devil-may-care Ashley and the St James' Park rollercoaster*, *The Observer Sport* 20th January 2008, p9.
(iii) Paul Wilson *Newcastle v Fulham* match review, *The Observer Sport* 23rd March 2008, p3.
(iv) Paul Wilson *No names mentioned in the race to sign bad-boy Barton*, *The Observer Sport* 3rd August 2008 – accessed at www.guardian.co.uk.
23. Paul Hayward *Carr has the last laugh in great Geordie rejig*, *The Observer Sport* 9th October 2011, p13.
24. www.bbc.co.uk/606 - quoted in *The Times* 17th January 2008, p82.
25. (i) *The Observer Sport – Letters*, 20th January 2008, p22.
(ii) *The Observer Sport – Letters*, 27th January 2008, p22.
26. *Newcastle v Portsmouth live text commentary* by John Ashdown at www.guardian.co.uk, 27th April 2009.
27. (i) A.A. Gill *The Angry Island*, p113.
(ii) Louise Taylor *Arca gives Boro spark to silence bigoted Geordie fans*, *The Guardian Sport* 27th August 2007, p5.
(iii) Steve Brenner *SHUT IT! Mido in a fury over bomb slur*, *The Sun Super Goals* 27th August 2007, p1.
28. Harry Pearson *The Far Corner*, pp29, 31.
29. www.nufc.com.
30. *United Fans Praised* – accessed at www.nufc.co.uk.
31. *Premier League Special*, *The Observer* August 2007, p24.

32. *Anti-racism taskforce must tackle 'nastiness' – Lord Ouseley*, 6th May 2013 – accessed at www.bbc.co.uk.

33. Harvey Taylor *Sporting Heroes*, in Colls and Lancaster *Geordies*, p126.

34. (i) Ian Jack *Not so much a religion, more a way of life*, *Guardian Review* 31st May 2003, p7.
    (ii) Derek Hatton quoted in Tim Adams *A Tale of Two Cities*, *The Observer Review* 22nd May 2005, p1.

35. Phil Thomas *Shearer's Champion night on the Toon*, *The Sun* 24th April 2002, p52.

36. David Cannadine *Class in Britain*, p81.

37. (i) Jamie Carragher interviewed by Jonathan Northcroft, *The Sunday Times Sport* 12th October 2008, p7.
    (ii) Phil Redmond interviewed by Stuart Jeffries *Question Time*, *The Guardian G2* 17th January 2008, p21.

38. (i) Jeremy Paxman *The English*, p245.
    (ii) A.A. Gill *The Angry Island*, p59.

39. Robert Rowell *Back Lanes and Muddy Pitches*, pp134, 72, 35.

40. Michael Collins *The Likes of Us*, p55.

41. *Pages for pleasure*, *Guardian Review* 28th June 2003, p4.

42. Kate Kellaway *Up Front: This Much I Know: John Carey*, *Observer Magazine* 19th June 2005, p11.

43. David Whetstone *Pomp and Pageantry*, *The Journal* 6th October 2008, p31.

44. Brendan O'Neill *An acceptable hatred: The last politically correct form of prejudice is against football's working-class supporters*, *The Spectator* 4th February 2012, p18.

45. Simon Kuper *Football is not about corporations. It's about clubs and communities*, *The Observer* 28th February 2010, p37.

46. Daniel Finkelstein *Rooney's foot? Our World Cup may be ruined by class war and GCSEs*, *The Times* 7th June 2006, p19.

47. (i) Michael Henderson *It's England, my England – but not at this World Cup*, *The Observer* 4th June 2006, p25.
    (ii) Michael Henderson *The Spectator* 25th January 2003, cited in Paul Gascoigne *Gazza: My Story*, p419.

48. Letter featured in *Prize Post*, *Sunday Sun* 12th October 2008, p77.

49. Harry Pearson *The Far Corner*, p15.

50. Robert Rowell *Back Lanes and Muddy Pitches*, p36.

51. Ross Brewster *From the terraces to catwalk for unwanted Toon shirts*, 1st October 2008 – accessed at www.newsandstar.co.uk.

WOMEN
Y'alreet, Pet?

1. Stuart Maconie *Pies and Prejudice*, p291.

2. Elaine Knox *'Keep Your Feet Still, Geordie Hinnie' – Women and Work on Tyneside*, in Colls and Lancaster *Geordies*, p95.

3. Colls and Lancaster *Geordies*, pxiv.
4. Bill Lancaster *The North East, England's most distinctive region?*, in *An Agenda for Regional History*, p33.
5. Robert Colls *Born-again Geordies*, in Colls and Lancaster *Geordies*, pp19, 25.
6. Elaine Knox *'Keep Your Feet Still, Geordie Hinnie' – Women and Work on Tyneside*, in Colls and Lancaster *Geordies*, p111.
7. Harvey Taylor *Sporting Heroes*, in Colls and Lancaster *Geordies*, p130.
8. Steve Black *Blackie: The Steve Black Story* (2005). Edinburgh: Mainstream Publishing, p50.
9. Peter Hitchens *The Cameron Delusion* (2010). London: Continuum, p111.
10. Jack Common *Kiddar's Luck*, p74.
11. Jo now reports that in the intervening time since making her contribution the second man has given up alcohol, is something of a reformed character, and is focussing his energies on forming a band.
12. Hilary Fawcett *"We Gotta Get Out of This Place": Fashion, Gender and Identity in the North East in the 1960s*, in Hilary Fawcett (Ed.) *Made in Newcastle: Visual Culture* (2007). Newcastle: Northumbria University Press, p31.
13. *"She can drink, she's a Geordie"*, 4th February 2010 – accessed at www.bbc.co.uk/tyne.
14. Charles Jennings *Up North*, p109.
15. Ruth Sunderland *My name is Ruth. I have a drink problem. I never touch it, The Observer* 3rd February 2008, p31.
16. Helen Rae *A drinker dies every 18 hours in the North East*, 27th January 2012 – accessed at www.chroniclelive.co.uk.
17. Dennis Campbell *Women: the hidden risks of drinking, The Observer* 24th February 2008, p8.
18. Tanya Gold *For more and more women, booze offers the only escape, The Guardian* 29th January 2008, p30.
19. *Comics Britannia: Anarchy in the UK*, BBC2 – broadcast 9th August 2008.
20. Peter Hetherington *Northern exposure: Does the north-east want self-rule?*, in *SocietyGuardian, The Guardian* 27th October 2004, p2.
21. Theodore Dalrymple *Young Turks: Put in an international perspective, British youth looks even nastier, The Spectator* 2nd July 2011, p22.
22. Simon Elmes *Talking for Britain*, ppvii, xiv.
23. Jack Common *Kiddar's Luck*, pp19, 26, 31, 32, 36.
24. Andrew Taylor *A Plum in Your Mouth*, p27.
25. Sid Waddell interviewed by Donald McRae *'The thing about darts is that you've got to shout', The Guardian Sport* 28th August 2007, p7.
26. Sue Clayton interviewed by Melanie McFadyean *This woman has made a super cool film… Well, it is set in the Arctic, Guardian Review* 14th October 1998 – accessed at www.sueclaytonfilm.com.
27. Harry Pearson *The Far Corner*, p37.
28. Kate Fox *Watching the English*, p343.
29. Robert Colls *Born-again Geordies*, in Colls and Lancaster *Geordies*, p30.
30. Sue Wilkinson *Chris Donald Q&A*, 23rd June 2005 – accessed at www.bbc.co.uk/tyne.

31. (i) Elaine Knox *'Keep Your Feet Still, Geordie Hinnie' – Women and Work on Tyneside*, in Colls and Lancaster *Geordies*, p95.

(ii) Bill Williamson *Living the Past Differently: Historical Memory in the North-East*, in Colls and Lancaster *Geordies*, p165.

32. Peter Hetherington *Northern exposure: Does the north-east want self-rule?*, in *SocietyGuardian*, *The Guardian* 27th October 2004, p2.

GAY
Black and White and... Pink?

1. Hannah Davies *Political lesson in a school of bullies*, *The Journal* 15th March 2008, p39.
2. *region's first openly gay council leader* in *out! northeast* Issue 26 June/July 2011 – accessed at www.outnortheast.com.
3. Lucy Tobin *The kissing game*, *EducationGuardian* 4th January 2011, p9.
4. Paul Flynn *Pride and Prejudice*, *The Observer Magazine* 20th February 2011, p33.
5. Hannah Davies *Political lesson in a school of bullies*, *The Journal* 15th March 2008, p38.
6. Eric Anderson quoted in Lucy Tobin *The kissing game*, in *EducationGuardian* 4th January 2011, p9.
7. Peter Tatchell *Kick homophobia out of football*, 28th September 2006 – accessed at www.guardian.co.uk.
8. Cris McCurley *Opinion*, *out! northeast* Issue 15 April/May 2009, p16.
9. The short-lived chant about 'Jenas' was based on unfounded rumours that former Newcastle United player Jermaine Jenas was gay. He is married with children.
10. Simon Garfield *Is anyone out there?*, *Observer Sport Monthly* May 2003, p36.
11. Cris McCurley *Opinion*, *out! northeast* Issue 15 April/May 2009, p16.
12. Philip Oltermann *In a league of their own*, *The Guardian Weekend* 25th August 2007, pp28, 31.
13. (i) *5 reasons to stay in the closet: Why gay athletes still choose to keep their sexuality hidden*, *Observer Sport Monthly* February 2008, p31.

(ii) Jamie Doward *Most British fans 'would give their backing' to openly gay footballers*, *The Observer* 8th August 2010, p17.
14. Hannah Davies *Political lesson in a school of bullies*, *The Journal* 15th March 2008, p38.
15. (i) Daniel Boffey *Drug death 'capital' Brighton to put treatment ahead of punishment*, *The Observer* 26th June 2011, p16.

(ii) Tracy McVeigh *Homophobia is vanishing in schools, study claims*, *The Observer* 4th March 2012, p18.

RACE
Toon, Toon... Black and White are we?

1. Sophie Doughty *Naz to return home: Racism fears won't stop star*, *Sunday Sun* 15th March 2009, p19.

2. Dave Renton *Colour Blind? Race and Migration in North East England Since 1945* (2007). Durham: University of Sunderland Press, pp4, 215.

3. (i) Dave Renton *Colour Blind? Race and Migration in North East England Since 1945*, p7.
    (ii) Anna Kessel *Racism alive and kicking in England, say UEFA, Observer Sport* 5th February 2006, p7.

4. Michael Collins *The Likes of Us*, pp8, 223.

5. Dave Renton *Colour Blind? Race and Migration in North East England Since 1945*, p7.

6. *Racist Incidents Report 2010: Report for Asylum Seekers Unit; Report prepared by Your Homes Newcastle, Research Services – August 2010*, p2.

7. (i) Helen Rae *Our health is improving, Evening Chronicle* 20th July 2009, p8.
    (ii) Seumas Milne *Either Labour represents its core voters – or others will, The Guardian* 13th March 2008, p25.

8. Michael Collins *The Likes of Us*, pp225, 247.

9. Dave Renton *Colour Blind? Race and Migration in North East England Since 1945*, p217.

10. Peter Hetherington *Northern exposure: Does the north-east want self-rule?*, in *SocietyGuardian, The Guardian* 27th October 2004, p2.

11. Michael Collins *The Likes of Us*, pp188, 189.

12. Jason Solomons *This much I know: John Waters, Observer Magazine* 30th September 2007, p12.

13. Dave Renton *Colour Blind? Race and Migration in North East England Since 1945*, p219.

14. Cited in D. Clark, *We do not want the earth: the history of South Shields Labour Party* (Whitley Bay: Bewick Press, 1992), p2, cited in Dave Renton *Colour Blind? Race and Migration in North East England Since 1945*, p84.

15. (i) Jane Hall *Naz's Silver Lining, The Journal* 12th October 2004.
    (ii) *I hope Shilpa wins, but this is what I endured at school, Evening Chronicle* 18th January 2007 – accessed at www.thefreelibrary.com.

16. Dave Renton *Colour Blind? Race and Migration in North East England Since 1945*, p156.

17. Sam Wonfor *North film-makers backed by Sir Ben, The Journal* 16th May 2009, p14.

18. Richard Wilkinson and Kate Pickett *The Spirit Level*, p168.

19. Elizabeth Day *Mugabe's thugs exact their toll on Tatchell, the great protestor, The Observer* 20th December 2009, p26.

20. Jeremy Paxman *The English*, p74.

21. Stuart Maconie *Pies and Prejudice*, p308.

22. Chi Onwurah *Why all identity begins at home*, first published at www.labour list.org; republished in *The Ofi Press* Issue 30, June 2013 – accessed at www.theofipress.webs.com.

23. Alastair Craig *We all need to tackle racists says Shola, Evening Chronicle* 27th November 2010 – accessed at www.chroniclelive.co.uk.

24. (i) David Morton *Pardew to be patron of charity battling racism, Evening Chronicle* 12th February 2011 – accessed at www.chroniclelive.co.uk.
    (ii) Alastair Craig *We all need to tackle racists says Shola, Evening Chronicle* 27th November 2010.

25. (i) Lee Ryder *Pitch invasion brings shame to Newcastle United*, Evening Chronicle 16th

July 2011 – accessed at www.chroniclelive.co.uk.

(ii) *Club Statement by Newcastle Manager Alan Pardew*, 16th July 2011 – posted on www. nufc.co.uk.

26. Louise Taylor *'Shola keeps me on the right track'*, *Guardian Sport* 21st May 2011, p7.

27. Dave Renton *Colour Blind? Race and Migration in North East England Since 1945*, p4.

28. (i) *Appeal over racist attack*, *Evening Chronicle* 28th May 2011, p19.

(ii) *Racist thug locked up for 12 months after attack*, *The Journal* 28th May 2011, p4.

(iii) Paul Clifford *Six charged with racist abuse on Metro*, 12th July 2011 – accessed at www. shieldsgazette.com.

29. (i) *Police deal with hundreds of racial attacks on Tyneside*, 2nd February 2011 – accessed at www.bbc.co.uk/tyne.

(ii) *Killingworth hunt for dog walker over racist attack*, 11th July 2011 – accessed at www. bbc.co.uk/tyne.

30. *Racist Incidents Report 2010: Report for Asylum Seekers Unit; Report prepared by Your Homes Newcastle, Research Services – August 2010*, p10.

31. Dave Renton *Colour Blind? Race and Migration in North East England Since 1945*, pp220, 221.

32. Adrian Pearson *Wannabe MP is returning home*, *Sunday Sun* 27th September 2009, p23.

33. Dave Renton *Colour Blind? Race and Migration in North East England Since 1945*, p221.

34. Anushka Asthana *Why did multiculturalism become a dirty word? It made me who I am*, *The Observer* 19th December 2010, p33.

35. Adrian Pearson *Wannabe MP is returning home*, *Sunday Sun* 27th September 2009, p23.

36. Contribution by 'Alex' to *Inside Out – North East* message board, 2nd February 2007 – accessed at www.bbc.co.uk/insideout/northeast.

37. Ed Vulliamy *Toxteth revisited, 30 years after the riots*, *The Observer – The New Review* 3rd July 2011, p11.

38. Keith Armstrong *Common Words and the Wandering Star*, pp64, 65.

POLITICS
Black and White and Red all over?

1. Jasper Gerard *Even as Brown ails, the Tyne runneth over with cash*, *The Observer* 2nd December 2007, p11.

2. Dave Renton *Colour Blind? Race and Migration in North East England Since 1945*, p43.

3. *Geordie Finishing School for Girls*, BBC3 – broadcast 26th July 2011.

4. Jeremy Paxman *The English*, p164.

5. Roger Scruton *England: An Elegy*, p154.

6. Tom Bower *The new Thatcher?*, *The Guardian G2* 11th July 2005, p7.

7. Stuart Jeffries *The Saturday interview: John Bercow*, *The Guardian* 23rd July 2011, p39.

8. Peregrine Worsthorne *If you will mix with the wrong types…*, *The Independent* 25th October 2008, p41.

9. David Cannadine *Class in Britain*, p125.

10. (i) Rachel Wearmouth *New poll shows changing social attitudes in the North East*, *The Chronicle* 10th September 2013 – accessed at www.chroniclelive.co.uk.

(ii) David Byrne *What Sort of Future?*, in Colls and Lancaster *Geordies*, p35.

11. David Byrne *Labour combines farce and tragedy*, *The Journal* 13th January 2010, p11.

12. David Byrne *What Sort of Future?*, in Colls and Lancaster *Geordies*, p41.

13. David Cannadine *Class in Britain*, pxi.

14. Grace McCombie *Pevsner Architectural Guides: Newcastle and Gateshead* (2009). New Haven and London: Yale University Press, p195.

15. Dave Renton *Colour Blind? Race and Migration in North East England Since 1945*, p44.

16. Moffat and Rosie *Tyneside*, p332.

17. David Cannadine *Class in Britain*, p135.

18. Moffat and Rosie *Tyneside*, p332.

19. Extract from *Sunday Express* 20th July 1975, cited in John Campbell *Margaret Thatcher Volume One: The Grocer's Daughter* (2001). London: Pimlico, p17.

20. Natasha Vall *The Emergence of the Post-Industrial Economy in Newcastle 1914-2000*, in Colls and Lancaster *Newcastle upon Tyne: A Modern History*, pp60, 61.

21. John Campbell *Margaret Thatcher Volume Two: The Iron Lady* (2003). London: Jonathan Cape, p247.

22. Charles Jennings *Up North*, p123.

23. (i) David Cannadine *Class in Britain*, p173.

(ii) John Campbell *Margaret Thatcher Volume One: The Grocer's Daughter*, p30.

(iii) John Campbell *Margaret Thatcher Volume Two: The Iron Lady*, p352.

24. Beverley Addy *Playing in a big game*, *The Journal* 23rd March 1998 – accessed at www.wiki-north-east.co.uk.

25. (i) *Sir John brands derelict town centre 'a disgrace'*, *The Northern Echo* 13th July 2007 – accessed at www.thenorthernecho.co.uk.

(ii) Mary Braid *Analysis: The moment Sir John met his match*, *The Independent* 3rd March 1999 – accessed at www.independent.co.uk.

(iii) Polly Mackenzie *Sir John's back in Toon*, 17th October 2003 – accessed at www.propertyweek.com.

26. Stephen Warrick *Thatcher comments in appalling taste* – lead letter in *Voice of the North*, *The Journal* 9th June 2010, p10.

27. *Vent your spleen*, *Evening Chronicle* 8th November 2007, p51.

28. David Cannadine *Class in Britain*, pp2, 13, 14.

29. Owen Jones *CHAVS*, p48.

30. Hunter Davies *Being John Prescott*, *New Statesman* 2nd June 2008, p28.

31. Craig Hope *Accent claim provokes scorn*, *Evening Chronicle* 29th December 2005 – accessed at www.thefreelibrary.com.

32. Jonathan Freedland *Bring Home the Revolution*, p119.

33. Kate Fox *Watching the English*, p82.

34. (i) John Campbell *Margaret Thatcher Volume One: The Grocer's Daughter*, p98.

(ii) Judith Holder *It's Not Grim Up North*, p99.

35. Geoffrey Wheatcroft *The Strange Death of Tory England* (2005). London: Penguin Books, p114.

36. *In the house, Evening Chronicle* 1st June 2005 – accessed at www.chroniclelive.co.uk.

37. *Famous People: The North-East (Lord Eldon 1751-1838)* at www.myersnorth.co.uk.

38. Moffat and Rosie *Tyneside*, p208.

39. Joan Hugman *Print and Preach: The Entrepreneurial Spirit of Nineteenth-Century Newcastle*, in Colls and Lancaster *Newcastle upon Tyne: A Modern History*, pp113, 130.

40. (i) Steve Newman and Graeme Peacock *Newcastle upon Tyne* (2005). Northumberland: Sanderson Books Limited, pp152, 153.

41. (i) Grace McCombie *Pevsner Architectural Guides: Newcastle and Gateshead*, pp78, 76.
    (ii) Steve Newman and Graeme Peacock *Newcastle upon Tyne*, pp152, 153.

42. *Law of Jante* as described at www.wikipedia.org, 14th May 2013 (article may have been edited since).

RGS

Class dismissed?

1. Anushka Asthana, Nicky Woolf, Cal Flyn *Can these new faces at Westminster break the mould of old politics?*, *The Observer* 9th May 2010, p28.

2. *The Educational Backgrounds of Government Ministers in 2010*, report by The Sutton Trust published in May 2010 – accessed at www.suttontrust.com.

3. Margaret Wilkinson *The Impact of Central Government 1888-1922*, in Brian Mains and Anthony Tuck (Eds.) *Royal Grammar School, Newcastle upon Tyne: A History of the School in its Community* (1986). Stocksfield: Oriel, p146.

4. (i) Fiona Millar *This elitism has to stop*, *The Guardian* 2nd April 2012, p33.
   (ii) Anthony Tuck *Some impressions of the school in the twentieth century; The School in the 1950s*, in Mains and Tuck *Royal Grammar School, Newcastle upon Tyne*, p293.
   (iii) Alister Cox *Debts to the Past and Prospects for the Future*, in Mains and Tuck *Royal Grammar School, Newcastle upon Tyne*, p318.

5. Alister Cox *Debts to the Past and Prospects for the Future*, in Mains and Tuck *Royal Grammar School, Newcastle upon Tyne*, pp322, 320.

6. (i) David Byrne '*That Lot Stood for it: The Demise of Northern Labourism*', *Northern Review*, Vol. 6, pp85-94, cited in Keith Armstrong *Common Words and the Wandering Star*, p252.
   (ii) David Byrne *What Sort of Future?*, in Colls and Lancaster *Geordies*, p35.

7. Tony Blair *A Journey*, p57.

8. (i) Joan Hugman *Print and Preach: The Entrepreneurial Spirit of Nineteenth-Century Newcastle*, in Colls and Lancaster *Newcastle upon Tyne: A Modern History*, p131.
   (ii) Keith Armstrong *Common Words and the Wandering Star*, pp245, 246.

9. Anthony Seldon *Public schools can't go on in splendid isolation*, *The Observer* 1st July 2012, p32.

10. Brian Mains *Uncertain Progress 1820-1888*, in Mains and Tuck *Royal Grammar School, Newcastle upon Tyne*, p92.

11. *Bidisha's thought for the day: Public school*, *The Guardian* 16th April 2011, p29.

12. A.A. Gill *The Angry Island*, p199.

13. David Cannadine *Class in Britain*, p187.

14. (i) Andrew Adonis and Stephen Pollard *'A Class Act, The Myth of Britain's Classless Society'* (1998). London: Penguin – cited in Keith Armstrong *Common Words and the Wandering Star*, pp28, 29.
    (ii) 5 Live Breakfast show, BBC Radio 5 – broadcast on 13th January 2009.

15. (i) Anthony Seldon *'Enough of this educational apartheid'*, *The Independent* 15th January 2008 – accessed at www.independent.co.uk.
    (ii) Elizabeth Day *What happened when the pupils at £9,000-a-term Wellington met underprivileged teenagers from Burnley?*, *The Observer Magazine* 4th January 2009, p35.
    (iii) Anthony Seldon *Public schools can't go on in splendid isolation*, *The Observer* 1st July 2012, p32.

16. Bernard Trafford *We're not all toffs*, *The Guardian* 19th June 2008, p34.

17. (i) Stephen Glover *My worry is that Mr Cameron simply doesn't understand ordinary people*, *Daily Mail* 13th September 2007, p14.
    (ii) Owen Jones *Private school parents are wasting their money*, *The Independent* 13th October 2011 – accessed at www.independent.co.uk.

18. RGS first admitted girls to its Sixth Form in 2001 and became fully co-educational in 2008.

19. James Meikle *Children aware of difference between chavs and chav-nots*, *The Guardian* 7th September 2007, p18.

20. Mark Akenside *The Poet: A Rhapsody, The poetical works of Mark Akenside: Edited with a life, by Rev. Alexander Dyce* (1834) – this edition University of Michigan University Library, p431.

21. Gordon Hogg *Achievement amidst Decay 1700-1820*, in Mains and Tuck *Royal Grammar School, Newcastle upon Tyne*, pp54, 69.

22. 19th century poet and critic Rev. George Gilfillan reflecting on a contemporary and colleague of Akenside's (Dr Lettsom) opinion of him in *The Poetical Works of Mark Akenside* (preface to the 2006 edition: BiblioBazaar).

23. William Munk *Munk's Roll* Volume II (1701-1800), p195 – *Lives of the fellows* – accessed at www.munksroll.rcplondon.ac.uk.

24. Margaret Wilkinson *The Impact of Central Government 1888-1922*, in Mains and Tuck *Royal Grammar School, Newcastle upon Tyne*, pp164, 165, 157.

25. Andrew Taylor *A Plum in Your Mouth*, pp20, 22.

26. (i) Kate Fox *Watching the English*, p342.
    (ii) Roger Scruton *England: An Elegy*, p153.

27. Brian Mains *Uncertain Progress 1820-1888*, in Mains and Tuck *Royal Grammar School, Newcastle upon Tyne*, p92.

28. Margaret Wilkinson *The Impact of Central Government 1888-1922*, in Mains and Tuck *Royal Grammar School, Newcastle upon Tyne*, p125.

29. Alister Cox *Debts to the Past and Prospects for the Future*, in Mains and Tuck *Royal*

Grammar School, Newcastle upon Tyne, p316.

30. Alister Cox *Debts to the Past and Prospects for the Future*, in Mains and Tuck *Royal Grammar School, Newcastle upon Tyne*, p311.

THE BIG HARD *VIZ* ONE
Donalds Ducked?

1. Stuart Maconie *Pies and Prejudice*, p312.
2. *Viz Annual: The Last Turkey in the Shop* (2008). United Kingdom: Dennis, p45.
3. (i) Charles Jennings *Up North*, p117.
   (ii) Stuart Maconie *Pies and Prejudice*, p311.
4. William Cook *25 Years of Viz: Silver Plated Jubilee* (2005). Coventry: Index, p8.
5. William Cook *25 Years of Viz*, p75.
6. Bill Lancaster *Newcastle – Capital of What?*, in Colls and Lancaster *Geordies*, pp66, 65.
7. Simon Donald *Him off the Viz* (2010). Newcastle: Tonto Books, pp3, 125.
8. (i) Kate Fox *Watching the English*, p72.
   (ii) William Cook *25 Years of Viz*, pp25, 12.
9. (i) *Melvyn Bragg on Class and Culture: Episode 3*, BBC2 – broadcast 9th March 2012.
   (ii) William Cook *25 Years of Viz*, p12.
10. Jack Common *Kiddar's Luck*, p83.
11. Margaret Wilkinson *The Impact of Central Government 1888-1922*, in Mains and Tuck *Royal Grammar School, Newcastle upon Tyne*, p144.
12. John Collings, acting executive director of children's services at Newcastle City Council quoted in Dan Warburton *North East has lessons to learn*, *Evening Chronicle* 13th January 2010, p8.
13. Chris Donald *Stardust Memories*, *Sunday Sun* 7th July 2002, p23.
14. Chris Donald *Rude Kids*, pp11, 12.
15. (i) Chris Donald *Rude Kids*, p9.
   (ii) William Cook *25 Years of Viz*, p13.
16. Simon Donald *Him off the Viz*, pp27, 35, 28, 29.
17. Simon Donald *Him off the Viz*, p29.
18. (i) Kate Fox *Watching the English*, p135.
   (ii) Simon Donald *Him off the Viz*, p74.
19. Andrew Taylor *A Plum in Your Mouth*, p31.
20. Tom Hadaway *Comic Dialect*, in Colls and Lancaster *Geordies*, pp88, 89.
21. William Cook *25 Years of Viz*, pp27, 26.
22. *Stamping out school bullies*, *Evening Chronicle* 27th April 2009, p9.
23. William Cook *25 Years of Viz*, p29.
24. Simon Donald *Him off the Viz*, pp23, 24, 168.
25. Simon Donald *Him off the Viz*, p2.
26. Simon Donald *Him off the Viz*, p164.
27. Simon Donald *Him off the Viz*, p303.

28. Stephen King *Dolores Claiborne* (1993). London: Hodder and Stoughton/New English Library, p105.

29. Paul Gascoigne *GAZZA: My Story*, p397.

30. Colls and Lancaster *Newcastle upon Tyne: A Modern History* – inner dust jacket blurb.

31. Although the Fat Slags are actually from Mansfield, Nottinghamshire, in the author's experience at least they are overwhelmingly identified with Newcastle.

32. Vanessa Thorpe *Now true Geordies mock the Tyne's 'art revolution'*, *The Observer* 26th June 2005, p14.

A PORTRAIT OF THE ARTIST
AS A YOUNG GEORDIE
Should I stay or should I go?

1. Tobias Smollett *Peregrine Pickle* (first published 1751 – this edition 1956). London: J.M. Dent & Sons, p208.

2. (i) Keith Armstrong *Common Words and the Wandering Star*, p12.
   (ii) Sid Chaplin *The Guardian* 1960 © Estate of Sid Chaplin.

3. Keith Armstrong *Common Words and the Wandering Star*, p218.

4. Mark Akenside *The Poet: a Rhapsody*, p431.

5. Sid Chaplin *The Day of the Sardine* (first published 1961 – this edition 1983). Leeds: The Amethyst Press, pp286, 203, 267, 286.

6. Sid Chaplin *The Day of the Sardine*, p76.

7. Jack Common *Kiddar's Luck*, pp127, 141.

8. (i) Mark Akenside *The Poet: A Rhapsody*, p429.
   (ii) Sid Chaplin *The Day of the Sardine*, p191.

9. Jack Common *Kiddar's Luck*, pp73, 127.

10. Jack Common *Kiddar's Luck*, p128.

11. *The South Bank Show: Lee Hall*, ITV1 – broadcast 18th October 2009.

12. Richard Wilkinson and Kate Pickett *The Spirit Level*, p116.

13. Nicola Juncar *Screenwriter steps into the limelight: Author goes back to school*, *Evening Chronicle* 4th June 2009, p20.

14. Terri Paddock *20 Questions With... Lee Hall*, 11th April 2005 – accessed at www.whatsonstage.com.

15. Jack Common *Kiddar's Luck*, p143.

16. Jack Common *Kiddar's Luck*, p143.

17. Keith Armstrong *Common Words and the Wandering Star*, p224.

18. (i) Sid Chaplin *A Wry Smile from Tyneside: A Farewell to Jack Common*, *Sunday Times* obituary 12th May 1968 – cited in Keith Armstrong *Common Words and the Wandering Star*, p192.
    (ii) Keith Armstrong *Common Words and the Wandering Star*, p65.

19. Lyall Wilkes *Tyneside Portaits* (1971 Frank Graham: Newcastle), cited by Keith Armstrong in *Common Words and the Wandering Star*, pp174, 175.

20. Terri Paddock *20 Questions With... Lee Hall*, 11th April 2005 – accessed at www.whatsonstage.com.

21. *The South Bank Show: Lee Hall*, ITV1 – broadcast 18th October 2009.

22. *Robson rides the wild waters on voyage of self-discovery*, *The Journal* 5th December 2009, p33.

23. *Johnnie Walker Meets Sting: Two Englishmen in New York (Episode 2)*, BBC Radio 2 – broadcast 21st November 2011.

24. *The South Bank Show: Lee Hall*, ITV1 – broadcast 18th October 2009.

25. Keith Armstrong *Common Words and the Wandering Star*, pp64, 65.

26. Larry Elliott *Why Galloway's win in Bradford West owes more to a failed war on poverty than the war on terror*, *The Guardian* 2nd April 2012, p30.

27. Peter Hetherington and Mark Dolder *Time to give our cities some air*, 22nd May 2014 – accessed at www.thejournal.co.uk.

28. Terri Paddock *20 Questions With... Lee Hall*, 11th April 2005 – accessed at www.whatsonstage.com.

29. Description taken from www.live.org.uk *History* section – this has since been updated and changed.

30. Jane Oddy *Vicious bullies made my life hell for being in Byker Grove*, *Daily Mirror* 17th March 2006, p21.

31. Michael Hamilton *Dancing queen dreams of the silver screen*, *North East Life* May 2009, p17.

32. Stewart Williams *Jill's Geord ache*, 5th May 2012 – accessed at www.thesun.co.uk.

33. Lloyd Evans *From Dewsbury to the stars*, *The Spectator* 4th February 2010, p22.

34. Lesley White *Andrea Riseborough plays the young Margaret Thatcher*, *The Times* 1st June 2008.

35. Elizabeth Day *Rise and shine*, *The Observer Magazine* 8th January 2012, p17.

36. *When Tim Healy 'died' on stage in Jarrow*, 4th December 2007 – accessed at www.shieldsgazette.com.

37. Andrew Martin *'Everything we've done is a fraud'*, *Daily Telegraph* 26th April 2002 – accessed at www.telegraph.co.uk.

38. Andrew Martin *'Everything we've done is a fraud'*, *Daily Telegraph* 26th April 2002.

39. Judith Holder *It's Not Grim Up North*, p96.

40. Kate Fox *Watching the English*, pp82, 75.

41. Alan Plater *Obituary: Tom Hadaway*, 11th March 2005 – accessed at www.guardian.co.uk.

42. Tom Hadaway *Comic Dialect*, in Colls and Lancaster *Geordies*, p88.

43. Mark Jensen *Robson Green Interviewed*, *The Mag Issue 281* 10th August 2013, p24.

44. Chris Phipps, John Tobler, Sid Smith *Northstars* (2005). Newcastle: Zymurgy Publishing, p92.

45. Jonathan Freedland *Bring Home the Revolution*, p131.

46. *The Culture Show*, BBC2 – broadcast 6th March 2009.

47. David Buckley *The Thrill of it All: The Story of Bryan Ferry & Roxy Music* (2004). London: André Deutsch, pp4, 15, 22.

48. David Buckley *The Thrill of it All*, pp16, 12, 13.

49. Barbara Ellen *The Life of Bryan*, *The Observer Magazine* 13th May 2001, p14.

50. David Buckley *The Thrill of it All*, pp16, 186.

51. *The Q Interview: AC/DC*, *Q Magazine* November 2008, p62.

52. Bill Lancaster *The North East, England's most distinctive region?*, in *An Agenda for Regional History*, p33.

53. Beverley Addy *Playing in a big game*, *The Journal* 23rd March 1998 – accessed at www. wiki-north-east.co.uk.

54. Ewan McIntyre *Opinion*, *NARC*. April 2009, p38.

55. Chris Donald column, *Sunday Sun* 10th March 2002, p23.

56. Charlotte Higgins *Culture clash as threat of 100% cut in arts funding divides Newcastle*, *The Guardian* 30th January 2013, p1.

57. John Gibson *Spirit of Tyneside: Famous sons and daughters* (1990). Edinburgh: John Donald Publishers Ltd, pp19, 20.

58. James Berryman *A Sting in the Tale* (2000). Gateshead: Mirage Publishing, pp160, 161, 165.

59. Chrissy Iley *'I've never been an ideal father because of my job and because of the way I was parented'*, *The Times Magazine* 10th March 2012, p23.

60. David Whetstone *The young dreamer who had to escape*, *The Journal* 21st September 2013, p53.

61. David Buckley *The Thrill of it All*, pp313, 130.

62. Susan Cain interviewed by Ian Tucker *My bright idea: Society is biased toward extroverts*, *The Observer: The New Review* 1st April 2012, p26.

63. Tobias Smollett *Peregrine Pickle*, p304.

64. (i) Pat Long *Why are there so few right-wing rock stars?*, *New Statesman* 8th March 2012 – accessed at www.newstatesman.com.
    (ii) Victor Fader cited in David Buckley *The Thrill of it All*, px.
    (iii) David Buckley *The Thrill of it All*, px.

65. Julian Barnes *The Sense of an Ending* (first published by Jonathan Cape 2011 – this edition 2012). London: Vintage, p44.

66. J.B. Lassner, K.A. Matthews and C.M. Stoney *'Are cardiovascular reactors to asocial stress also reactors to social stress?'*, *Journal of Personality and Social Psychology* (1994) 66 (I) pp69-77 – cited in Richard Wilkinson and Kate Pickett *The Spirit Level*, p205.

67. Sigmund Freud *Civilisation and its Discontents*, p15.

68. David Whetstone *The young dreamer who had to escape*, *The Journal* 21st September 2013, p53.

69. Laura Caroe *Geordie Pride: Rock star Sting unveils artwork of his Tyne roots*, *Evening Chronicle* 31st October 2008, p16.

70. *Singer reveals love for Tyneside at painting's unveiling*, *The Journal* 31st October 2008, p7.

71. *Sting does a little magic for adverts*, *Evening Chronicle* 26th September 2009, p6.

72. *Sting's Winter Songbook*, BBC1 – broadcast 29th December 2009.

73. *Review: Sting, Sage Gateshead*, *Evening Chronicle* 6th February 2012 – accessed at www. chroniclelive.co.uk.

74. David Whetstone *The young dreamer who had to escape*, *The Journal* 21st September 2013, p52.

75. F. Scott Fitzgerald *The Great Gatsby* (first published 1926 – this edition 2000). London: Penguin Classics, p172.

76. Simon Callow *'Wake the people and make them think big'*, 19th October 2005 – accessed at www.guardian.co.uk.

77. Chrissy Iley *'I've never been an ideal father because of my job and because of the way I was parented'*, *The Times Magazine* 10th March 2012, p23.

78. Chrissy Iley *"I'm just Gordon from Wallsend"*, *Traveller* August 2010, pp80, 81, 82, 83.

AKENSIDE AFTERTHOUGHTS

1. *Origins of the name Geordie* Local Studies Factsheet No.5, Newcastle Libraries.

2. James Gregory *'The North East in the Nineteenth Century'*, *Northern History* Vol. 42, No. 1, March 2005, pp164-187 – cited in Keith Armstrong *Common Words and the Wandering Star*, p63.

3. Peter Hetherington and Mark Dolder *Time to give our cities some air*, 22nd May 2014 – accessed at www.thejournal.co.uk.

4. (i) Bill Williamson *Living the Past Differently: Historical Memory in the North-East*, in Colls and Lancaster *Geordies*, p153.

   (ii) Paul L. Younger *Coda*, in Colls and Lancaster *Geordies*, p169.

5. Alexander Chancellor column, *The Guardian G2* 10th September 2009, p5.

6. Paul Barlow *Tyneside's Modern Rome: the North East's Image of its Roman Past and its Lost Englishness*, in Hilary Fawcett (Ed.) *Made in Newcastle: Visual Culture*, p149.

7. (i) Kevan Carrick *We should be ready to fight our corner*, *The Journal* 10th March 2010, p37.

   (ii) Mark Robinson *This is no time to wallow in nostalgia*, *The Journal* 7th February 2009, p11.

8. Stuart Jeffries *Spirit of the north*, *The Guardian G2* 14th February 2008 – accessed at www.guardian.co.uk.

9. Colls and Lancaster *Newcastle upon Tyne: A Modern History* – inner dust jacket blurb, pvii.

10. (i) Bill Lancaster *Newcastle - Capital of What?*, in Colls and Lancaster *Geordies*, p59.

    (ii) Robert Colls *Born-again Geordies*, in Colls and Lancaster *Geordies*, p25.

11. (i) Tony Henderson *Why a 19th Century treasure will not be a 21st Century relic*, *The Journal* 23rd May 2009, p8.

    (ii) Stuart Jeffries *Spirit of the north*, *The Guardian G2* 14th February 2008.

12. Victoria Markham cited in Catherine Elsworth *300m: America hits a population landmark and is warned it must change its ways*, *Daily Telegraph* 18th October 2006, p20.

13. Bill Lancaster *Newcastle - Capital of What?*, in Colls and Lancaster *Geordies*, p64.

BIBLIOGRAPHY

Adonis, Andrew and Pollard, Stephen, *A Class Act, The Myth of Britain's Classless Society'* (Penguin, 1998)

Akenside, Mark, *The poetical works of Mark Akenside: Edited with a life, by Rev. Alexander Dyce* (University of Michigan University Press Library, [1834] 2013)

Akenside, Mark, *The Poetical Works of Mark Akenside* (BiblioBazaar, 2006)

Armstrong, Keith, *Common Words and the Wandering Star: A biographical study of culture and social change in the life and work of writer Jack Common* (University of Sunderland Press, 2009)

Austen, Jane, *Pride and Prejudice* (Penguin, [1813] 2003)

Barnes, Julian, *The Sense of an Ending* (Vintage, [2011] 2012)

Berryman, Jim, *A Sting in the Tale* (Mirage Publishing, 2000)

Black, Steve, *Blackie: The Steve Black Story* (Mainstream Publishing, 2005)

Blair, Tony, *A Journey* (Hutchinson, 2010)

Buckley, David, *The Thrill of it All: The Story of Bryan Ferry & Roxy Music* (André Deutsch, 2004)

Campbell, John, *Margaret Thatcher Volume One: The Grocer's Daughter* (Pimlico, 2001)

Campbell, John, *Margaret Thatcher Volume Two: The Iron Lady* (Jonathan Cape, 2003)

Cannadine, David, *Class in Britain* (Penguin, 2000)

Carey, John, *The Intellectuals and the Masses: Pride and Prejudice among the Literary Intelligentsia, 1880-1939* (Faber and Faber, 1992)

Chaplin, Sid, *The Day of the Sardine* (The Amethyst Press, [1961] 1983)

Clark, D, *We do not want the earth: the history of South Shields Labour Party* (Bewick Press, 1992)

Collins, Michael, *The Likes of Us: A Biography of the White Working Class* (Granta Books, 2004)
Colls, Robert and Lancaster, Bill (Eds.), *Geordies: Roots of Regionalism* (Edinburgh University Press, 1992)

Colls, Robert and Lancaster, Bill (Eds.), *Newcastle upon Tyne: A Modern History* (Phillimore, 2001)

Common, Jack, *Kiddar's Luck* (Bloodaxe, [1951] 1990)

Cook, William, *25 Years of Viz: Silver Plated Jubilee* (Index, 2005)

Danziger, Nick, *Danziger's Britain: A Journey to the Edge* (Flamingo, 1997)

Donald, Chris, *Rude Kids: The Unfeasible Story of Viz* (HarperCollins *Entertainment*, 2005)

Donald, Simon, *Him off the Viz* (Tonto Books, 2010)

Dury, Graham and Gamble, Wayne and Glover, Stevie and Jones, Davey and Thorp, Simon (Production Team), *Viz Annual: The Last Turkey in the Shop* (Dennis, 2008)

Elmes, Simon, *Talking for Britain: A Journey through the Nation's Dialects* (Penguin Books, 2005)

Fawcett, Hilary (Ed.), *Made in Newcastle: Visual Culture* (Northumbria University Press, 2007)

Fitzgerald, F. Scott, *The Great Gatsby* (Penguin Classics [1926] 2000)

Fox, Kate, *Watching the English: The Hidden Rules of English Behaviour* (Hodder, 2004)

Fox, Robin, *The Red Lamp of Incest* (Penguin, 1980)

Frankl, Viktor E., *Man's Search for Meaning* (Rider Books, [1946] 2004)

Freedland, Jonathan, *Bring Home the Revolution: The Case for a British Republic* (Fourth Estate, 1999)

Freud, Sigmund, *Civilisation and its Discontents* (Penguin, [1930] 2002)

Fromm, Erich, *The Fear of Freedom* (Routledge Classics, [1942] 2001)

Gascoigne, Paul with Davies, Hunter, *Gazza: My Story* (Headline, 2005)

Gibson, John, *Spirit of Tyneside: Famous sons and daughters* (John Donald Publishers Ltd, 1990)

Gill, A.A., *The Angry Island: Hunting the English* (Phoenix, 2006)

Goldman, William, *Which Lie Did I Tell? More Adventures in the Screen Trade* (Bloomsbury, 2001)

Hitchens, Peter, *The Cameron Delusion* (Continuum, 2010)

Holder, Judith, *It's Not Grim Up North: The real truth about the North-South divide* (BBC Books, 2005)

Jennings, Charles, *Up North: Travels Beyond the Watford Gap* (Abacus, 1995)

Jones, Owen, *CHAVS: The Demonization of the Working Class* (Verso, 2011)

King, Stephen, *Dolores Claiborne* (Hodder and Stoughton/New English Library, 1993)

Lancaster, Bill and Newton, Diana and Vall, Natasha (Eds.), *An Agenda for Regional History* (Northumbria University Press, 2007)

Maconie, Stuart, *Pies and Prejudice: In Search of the North* (Ebury Press, 2007)

Mains, Brian and Tuck, Anthony (Eds.), *Royal Grammar School, Newcastle upon Tyne: A History of the School in its Community* (Oriel, 1986)

McCombie, Grace, *Pevsner Architectural Guides: Newcastle and Gateshead* (Yale University Press, 2009)

McDermid, Val, *The Wire in the Blood* (HarperCollins*publishers*, 1997)

Moffat, Alistair and Rosie, George, *Tyneside: A History of Newcastle and Gateshead from Earliest Times* (Mainstream, 2005)

Mount, Ferdinand, *Mind the Gap: The New Class Divide in Britain* (Short Books, 2005)

Newman, Steve and Peacock, Graeme, *Newcastle upon Tyne* (Sanderson Books Limited, 2005)

Paxman, Jeremy, *The English: A Portrait of a People* (Penguin, 1998)

Pearson, Harry, *The Far Corner: A Mazy Dribble through North-East Football* (Abacus, 1997)

Phipps, Chris and Tobler, John and Smith, Sid, *Northstars* (Zymurgy, 2005)

Pickett, Kate and Wilkinson, Richard, *The Spirit Level: Why Equality is Better for Everyone* (Penguin, 2010)

Renton, Dave, *Colour Blind? Race and Migration in North East England Since 1945* (University of Sunderland Press, 2007)

Rowell, Robert, *Back Lanes and Muddy Pitches* (Zymurgy, 2004)

Scruton, Roger, *England: An Elegy* (Continuum, 2006)

Smollett, Tobias, *Peregrine Pickle* (J.M. Dent & Sons, [1751] 1956)

Taylor, Andrew, *A Plum in Your Mouth: Why the Way We Talk Speaks Volumes About Us* (Harpercollins*publishers*, 2006)

Thompson, E.P., *The Making of the English Working Class* (Victor Gollancz Ltd, 1963)

Treffry, Diana (Ed.), *Collins Dictionary & Thesaurus* (HarperCollins, 2004)

Wheatcroft, Geoffrey, *The Strange Death of Tory England* (Penguin Books, 2005)

Wilkes, Lyall, *Tyneside Portaits* (Frank Graham, 1971)

Williams, Raymond, *Keywords* (Fontana Paperbacks, 1983)

COPYRIGHT NOTICES

INDEX

cultural identity 12

D

Dalglish, Kenny 80
Dame Allan's School 183, 190, 236
Danby, Graeme 92–3, 97, 124, 232–3, 234–5, 239
Daniels, Anthony 115
Danziger, Nick 78
Davis, David 164
dialect, Geordie *see also* accent, Geordie
  as distinct from accent 57–8
  evolution of 52–4
  and Standard English 47–8
  in *Viz* 212
  women and 116–17
Djalili, Omid 60
domestic violence 111
Donald, Chris *see also Viz*
  on accent 51, 212–13
  class and drinking culture 71
  on class and identity 36–7, 205–7, 208
  Geordie aggression 11
  influence of Newcastle on *Viz* 245
  on Newcastle United supporters 91–2
  on regional identity 121, 216, 249
  school bullying and Akenside Syndrome 210–11
  Viz and Akenside Syndrome 209, 216–18
Donald, Simon *see also Viz*
  accent and bullying 212
  aggression and drinking culture 72
  on city culture 216
  on class and identity 164, 207–9
  escape from Newcastle 219–20
  on his accent 214–15
Donald, Steve 208, 210–11, 212
Douglass, David John 40
drink (alcohol)
  aggression and 72–3, 111, 135, 216–17
  binge-drinking culture 68, 113

and class 70–1, 77–8
drinking culture and 'proper' Geordie identity 68–9, 70, 71–2, 74–7, 78, 111
health problems and 68, 78–9, 112–14
middle classes and 71
Paul Gascoigne and 66, 75–6
in popular culture 202
teetotalism 76–7
women and cultural expectations 106, 109–10, 111, 112–13, 114, 115

E

education, mistrust of 34–5, 226
Edwards, Huw 51
Eldon, Lord (John Scott) 176
Ellen, Barbara 23, 58, 246
Elmes, Simon 51, 52, 53, 54, 116, 202
Emin, Tracey 44
Enfield, Harry 59
Errington, Bob 162, 163, 166

F

Family Guy 57
Farrell, Sir Terry 260
Farrington, Neil 85
Farrow, Pete 134
the Fat Slags 71, 106, 109, 110, 114–15, 204, 218, 220
Fawcett, Hilary 106, 111
Fenton, Stephen 134
Ferry, Bryan 25, 245–7, 253
55° North 15–16
Finkelstein, Daniel 98, 197
Fitzgerald, F. Scott 255
football *see also* Newcastle United Football Club
  aggression and 93–4
  cultural snobbery and 96–8
  fans' bigoted behaviour 90–1
  gay-friendly teams 132–4
  homophobia and 130–4
  introduction of, RGS 197–8

middle classes and 96, 98

overwhelming importance of 94–6

racism and 90–1, 132, 133, 152–5

working classes and 94–5, 97–8, 230–1

Forbes, Nick 66, 124, 126, 127, 250

Forster, John 218

Fox, Kate

  on class 24, 29, 38, 120

  on class and accent 43, 45, 173, 193, 237

  on class and humour 207, 211

  on drinking cultures 70, 75

  on English stereotypes 12–13

  on football 83

Fox, Robin 28

Frankl, Viktor E. 31

Freedland, Jonathan 24, 26, 38, 173, 244

Freud, Sigmund 68–9, 253

friendliness, as Geordie stereotype 11

Friends 75

Fromm, Erich 86

Frostrup, Mariella 106, 116

Fulgenzi, Pascal 73

The Full Monty 169

G

Gascoigne, Paul

  Akenside Syndrome and 5

  battles with alcohol 69

  on drinking culture/battles with alcohol 66, 75–6

  on escaping the self 220

Geordie accent 48–9, 56

Gateshead Metro Centre 170

gay culture

  acceptance in the region/homophobia 126–9, 137–8

  and Akenside Syndrome 138–41

  homophobic bullying in schools 124, 126–9

  homophobic football chants 130–1

  indifference to football 131–2, 134

isolation from Geordie identity 127, 135–6

separate social areas, Newcastle city centre 136–7

and the term *puff* 125, 129–30, 138, 230

Gay Men Tyneside (GMT) 126

gender

  Akenside Syndrome and 112, 121–2

  cultural expectations of women 112–13

  differences and accent 117–20

  gender roles and class norms 111–12, 115–16

Geordie identity as masculine 107–8, 111–12, 128, 150

  introversion and 252

  Ladette culture 110, 114–15

  misogynistic Geordie culture 108–9, 110–11, 112

  racism and 150

  women and binge-drinking 109–10, 112–14

  women's equality, partial achievement of 109–10

Geordie, name 257

Geordie Nation 14, 147

Geordie Shore 8, 11

'Geordie Warrior' 2

George, Rosie 46

Gerrie, Malcom 49

Gibson, Dr Melanie 114–15, 122, 227, 245

Gibson, John 250

Gibson, Steve 21

Gill, A.A.

  on accent 43–4, 51

  on class 38

  on drinking culture 68

  on football 82, 90, 96

  on the North-East 16

  on private schooling 178, 182, 184

Glenamara, Lord 1